DUMBARTON OAKS
MEDIEVAL LIBRARY

Daniel Donoghue, General Editor

THE LABYRINTH OF FORTUNE

JUAN DE MENA

DOML 88

DUMBARTON OAKS MEDIEVAL LIBRARY

Daniel Donoghue, General Editor
Josiah Blackmore, Medieval Iberian Editor

Jan M. Ziolkowski, Founding Editor

Medieval Iberian Editorial Board
David Arbesú
Marina Brownlee
E. Michael Gerli
Luis Manuel Girón-Negrón
Dorothy Severin
Ryan Szpiech

The Labyrinth of Fortune

Juan de Mena

Edited and Translated by

FRANK A. DOMÍNGUEZ

RYAN D. GILES

DUMBARTON OAKS
MEDIEVAL LIBRARY

HARVARD UNIVERSITY PRESS
CAMBRIDGE, MASSACHUSETTS
LONDON, ENGLAND
2025

Copyright © 2025 by the President and Fellows of Harvard College
ALL RIGHTS RESERVED
Printed in the United States of America

First Printing

Library of Congress Cataloging-in-Publication Data

Names: Mena, Juan de, 1411–1456, author. | Domínguez, Frank, 1945– editor, translator. | Giles, Ryan D. (Ryan Dennis), editor, translator.

Title: The labyrinth of fortune / Juan de Mena ; edited and translated by Frank A. Domínguez, Ryan D. Giles.

Other titles: Trescientas. English

Description: Cambridge, Massachusetts : Harvard University Press, 2025. | Series: Dumbarton Oaks medieval library ; 88 | Includes bibliographical references and index.

Identifiers: LCCN 2024038693 | ISBN 9780674290914 (cloth)

Subjects: LCSH: Mena, Juan de, 1411–1456 —Translations into English. | LCGFT: Poetry.

Classification: LCC PQ6413.M2 T713 2025 | DDC 861/.2—dc23/eng/20240826

LC record available at https://lccn.loc.gov/2024038693

Contents

Introduction   *vii*

THE LABYRINTH OF FORTUNE   2

Note on the Text   *221*
Notes to the Text   *223*
Notes to the Translation   *229*
Bibliography   *287*
Index   *289*

Introduction

The most translated Castilian compositions of the fifteenth century into English deal with love, death, or consolation, themes that are easily understood because we have all experienced them. These poems also tend to be shorter and written in simple lines of eight syllables or less. This is not the case with Juan de Mena's *The Labyrinth of Fortune* (*El Laberinto de Fortuna*, 1444). Its length, complexity, and form are the probable reasons it has not been translated until now, even though it is undeniably the most important work of the fifteenth century and has long been considered a classic.

The Labyrinth is an epic vision poem that is rooted in what has been called the allegorical-dantesque school of poetry.[1] Its 2,400-lines are grouped into three hundred stanzas composed (almost always) of eight 12-syllable verses separated into two equal hemistiches by a caesura. Each hemistich has two stresses, and their repetition gives the poem a strange staccato sonority that is now out-of-fashion. In addition, the poem challenges the understanding of the reader at every step, because its interpretation requires a discerning knowledge of classical and medieval texts and cultures.

The title of the work points out one of the difficulties it presents. The best-known labyrinth appears in the Greek myth of Theseus, who enters the Cretan labyrinth, kills the Minotaur, and escapes with the help of Ariadne's thread. This is the story that the word "labyrinth" most frequently evokes, except that it is not relevant to Mena's title.[2]

Unlike Theseus, who emerges triumphant from his labyrinth after killing the Minotaur rather than being killed himself, Mena's *The Labyrinth of Fortune* is not about the avoidance of physical death. By the fourth century, the pavements of many churches and cathedrals depicted a labyrinth to represent the difficulties faced by worshippers in their journey to Christ; that is, they alluded to a process that was mediated by a priest whose function was (and still is) to help Christians reunite with God at the end of life and attain immortality. The allegory of *The Labyrinth* has much more in common with the purpose of these pavements than with the Greek myth; however, it is a poem with a more specific objective.

After the dedicatory stanzas of *The Labyrinth*, Mena (who is one of the two main characters) laments over the calamities of history: Why, he asks, do the misfortunes and injustices of the past still affect the world of Juan II of Castile (1405–1454)? He is then transported to heaven in a vision by the goddess Belona and meets Divine Providence, who answers his concerns by first describing the geography of the world below their feet and then explaining the meaning of three great wheels of the past, present, and future that they see in the House of Fortune. The exemplary characters that hang on these wheels, Divine Providence says, demonstrate the influence of the stars and constellations on everyone and at the same time show that the misfortunes that afflict Castile are a common occurrence in a fallen world.

INTRODUCTION

The calamities of Juan II's epoch are caused by the disobedience of arrogant nobles and clergy, who subvert the social order for their own benefit; the duplicity of vassals, who change lords as frequently as chameleons change color when it is to their advantage, and who fail to take root like trees that are too often transplanted; as well as the perfidy of those who dabble in the forbidden arts to their own detriment. Mena, who seems to portray men who die in battle as brave, also shows their arrogance, carelessness, and foolhardiness, and he comments that commoners have more sense than them. The most praiseworthy exemplars are those devoted to contemplation, study, or music, even though they also often fail to control their own fates.

Toward the end, however, the poem underscores that in spite of all the uncertainties, the goal of every Castilian should be the recovery of the territories they lost to the Moors—an objective that was yearned for, but not yet attained in the middle of the fifteenth century—and predicts that this state of affairs will be remedied by the divinely appointed Juan II, who, with the help of his political favorite, Álvaro de Luna, will render equitable justice to all, keep the vicious at bay, and bring the Reconquest to an end.

The paralysis of the Reconquest during the reign of Juan II was largely due to the king's cousins, the Infantes (Princes) of Aragon, who often intervened in the politics of the kingdom, made war against it, and even imprisoned the king at one point. The fractious nobles who supported the Infantes were known to wreak violence on anyone who opposed them. This may be one of the reasons why the message of *The Labyrinth* is couched in a style that Mena had used before but that here serves an added purpose: the poem's un-

INTRODUCTION

usual syntax, Latinisms, and neologisms shift the attention of its readers away from what is said to how it is said, thereby veiling its meaning and diffusing the virulence of Mena's censure.

This difficulty served as a barrier to a largely unlearned nobility, but it also quickly won Mena praise from the more literate. Hernán Núñez, one of the poem's earliest and most accomplished editors, for example, went so far as to say that there would never be another poet as good as Mena,[3] and Juan de Lucena called him the prince of poets and one of the three Petrarchs that graced Spanish letters.[4] Others, however, found him to be a flawed poet.

Already in the sixteenth century, readers criticized Mena's excessive Latinate diction, hyperbata (changes in word order), frequent allusions to classical or medieval figures, and stresses that often conflicted with the normal accentuation of a word.[5] Juan de Valdés, for example, said that "of those who have written in poetry, all commonly give first place to Juan de Mena," but added, "he used certain words that because of their impropriety should be expunged, and others so Latinate that they cannot be understood by all . . . which I think is more like writing in poor Latin than in good Castilian."[6]

When medieval texts began to regain a readership in the eighteenth century, Tomás Antonio Sánchez still referred to Mena as "a man of talent" who "started a new age for Castilian poetry . . . but made it ugly with improper metaphors, violent dislocations, Latinate or invented words, and finally with a verbose and pompous style."[7]

A true appreciation of Mena's contributions to the development of the language had to wait until recent times, when the study of Luis de Góngora, one of the greatest poets of Golden Age Spain, cast a new light on *The Labyrinth*. However, in its time, the poem continued to be the vehicle through which subsequent generations learned knightly conduct, in spite of the ironic fact that its readers were well aware that it was Isabel I and not her father, Juan II, who wrested the remaining Spanish territories from the Moors. Also, no text is more important to highlight the shifts in culture and warfare that took place with the adoption of new armaments and the emergence of a standing army. Both clashed with traditional knightly conduct and account for the behavior of the (anti)heroes in the underappreciated parody of *The Labyrinth* called *Carajicomedia* (1517) and in Cervantes's *Don Quijote*.[8]

Nevertheless, Mena is one of the first Castilian humanist poets to embrace the new spirit of the Renaissance, find inspiration in the classical past, and propose a civic role for poets along the lines of his Florentine counterparts. He belongs to a line of writers that, as with the works of Alfonso X of Castile, approach language as more than a mere vehicle for meaning. We are not as conscious of Mena's surprising inventiveness as we should be, because aspects of his syntax, his borrowings from Latin, and his neologisms have been adopted by Spanish and appear in modern dictionaries; however, their sheer number makes *The Labyrinth* crucial to our understanding of how the early Spanish humanists created a literary culture in the vernacular by transforming late medieval Castilian into a more learned language worthy of being studied and taught.[9]

INTRODUCTION

Life and Works

Most of what we know about Juan de Mena (1411–1456) comes from the prologue to Hernán Núñez's edition of *Las Trezientas,* which claims that he was the son of a citizen of Cordoba "named . . . Pedrarias, a man of middling station, and a sister of Rui Fernández de Peñaloza, alderman in said city and lord of Almenara."[10] Further research has revealed that some of Núñez's statements are baseless, but the fact that Fernández de Peñaloza and Mena were both councilmen of Cordoba indicates that the writer was indeed of "middling station"—that is, he belonged to a class of *hidalgos* that permeated cities of the Iberian Peninsula.[11]

Support for this view can be found in one of the works attributed to Mena, which claims that his family was originally from the valley of Mena in the mountains and settled in Baeza at the time of Fernando el Santo.[12] Genealogical works like this, however, are always suspect. We are on firmer grounds when we turn to some comments in Mena's other works and a few surviving documents related to him that can flesh out Núñez's brief *vita*. Mena refers to himself as a second son in another of his works, and we surmise that this was why he pursued a career as a priest in Salamanca between 1423 and 1429, where he earned a master's degree and took minor orders. He obtained his first benefices around 1431. Documents published by Vicente Beltrán de Heredia have also revealed that Mena traveled to Rome and Florence at least twice, possibly under the auspices of Cardinals Juan de Cervantes and Juan de Torquemada, but we do not know much else about these trips other than that he returned around August of 1443, a year before *The Labyrinth* was dedicated to Juan II.[13] Soon after, the king appointed him royal chronicler (ca. 1445), secretary of Latin letters, and alderman of Cordoba.[14] Around 1450, Mena renounced his church benefices and married a fellow Cordoban, Marina Méndez. There is no evidence that he worried about the loss of church income implied by this decision, because it was more than compensated for by her dowry, his salary at court, and by his future allotment in the redistribution of Álvaro de Luna's revenue after the favorite was beheaded in Cordoba in 1453.[15] The fact that he approved of his wife's renunciation of her inheritance without remuneration in 1456 suggests that he considered himself well-off.

Mena died suddenly that very same year, perhaps as a result of a fall from a mule, and was buried in Torrelaguna, a small town north of Madrid.[16] According to Núñez, the marquis of Santillana (Iñigo López de Mendoza), another important humanist poet of the era, paid for his burial and was possibly the author of his epitaph, which reads: "Joyous Homeland, Known for its Worth / Cranny where Death Lodges / Here Chance Decreed a Spot / for the Poet Juan de Mena." The earliest citation of the epitaph appears on the last page of a 1493 incunable of the *Orationes* of Isocrates, in a gloss written in the hand of Hernán Núñez, who died in 1553. It is kept at the University of Salamanca (BG/I.333, folio 208b) and is available in its digital library.[17]

Mena's other works consist of the allegorical poem titled *Coronación o Calamicleos del marqués de Santillana* (1438); a Spanish translation of the medieval Latin abridgment of the *Iliad* known as *Sumas de la Ylíada de Omero* (ca. 1442; also known as *Ilíada en romance, Omero romançado,* and *Destrucción de Troya*); a *Tratado sobre el título de duque* (1445); the *Coplas de los pecados mortales* (1456; also known as *Debate de la Razón contra la Voluntad* and *Disputación de vicios*); and a prologue to Álvaro de Luna's *Libro de las virtuosas e claras mugeres* (1446). Attributed to him are the *Tratado de amor* (ca. 1444) and *Memorias de algunos linages* (1448; alternate title, *Memorias genealógicas*). He was also a very good lyric poet, whose compositions appear in about fifty-eight *cancioneros* (poetic anthologies).

Plot

After a dedication to the king (stanza 1), a character called Mena invokes Apollo, Calliope (the muse of epic poetry), and her sisters (2–3). He then contrasts the orderliness of the universe to the arbitrariness of Fortune, compares her changeable nature to storms at sea, and asks her to show him her wheel and its effects on the lives of people (4–12). At that point, the goddess Bellona appears in a vision and transports him to heaven, where he meets a maiden called Divine Providence, who offers to explain the workings of fate as far as it is possible for the human mind to understand (13–19).

Divine Providence leads him to the House of Fortune (20–33). As he enters, Mena sees and describes the known world as it appears below the clouds (34–55), but once they arrive, he notices that the house contains not one but three great wheels that represent the workings of fate in the past, the present, and the future. Each wheel is made up of seven circles, or "orders," that are associated with one of the seven planets of the Ptolomaic cosmos, and on each circle are literary, mythological, and historical figures that exemplify the presence or absence of one of the seven theological or cardinal virtues influenced by that planet.

The circle of the moon is associated with chastity (63–84); Mercury, with avarice (85–99); Venus, with good and bad love (100–115); the sun, with prudence (116–37); Mars, with fortitude (138–213); Jupiter, with just rule (214–31); and Saturn, with measured justice (232–91). The remaining stanzas conclude the conversation between the poet and Divine Providence (292–97) with an added finale (298–300).

The exemplars in the circles of the moon, Venus, Mercury, and sun are predominantly derived from the ancient past, while those on the circles of Mars, Saturn, and Jupiter are mostly drawn from the Castilian recent past or contemporary events. The work splits into two parts almost at the beginning of the section that corresponds to Mars. Its first two stanzas concern the Romans: the Metelluses, the Camilluses, Petreius, Afranius, and Caesar (stanza 139), and Crassus and Mucius (stanza 140). But they just serve to introduce a new invocation (stanza 141):

¡Belígero Mares, tú sufre que cante
las guerras que vimos de nuestra Castilla,
los muertos en ellas, la mucha mancilla
que el tiempo presente nos muestra delante!

Belligerent Mars, allow me to sing
about the wars that we witnessed in our Castile,
those who died in them, the great disgrace
that the present time forecasts for us!

What follows is an extended ekphrastic passage that describes the carvings and paintings of a throne on which Juan II sits (142), which depict the famous battles that the king's ancestors had waged (Navas de Tolosa, 1212; and the two battles of Algeciras, 1278 and 1344; stanzas 143–47) and the clashes with the Infantes of Aragon while fighting the Moors. However, *The Labyrinth* does not adhere to chronology. It divides the battles according to whether they are against Moors (Vega de Granada, 148–53; Higueruela, 151–53) or between Christians (Real de Ariza and Velamazán, 154; Medina del Campo, 155–58). In other words, it notes whether or not they advance the Christian "Reconquest" of the Peninsula from Muslims.[18]

Next is a description of Castilian knights who lost their lives between 1434 and 1443, and treated in order of their social standing, beginning with a lengthy account of the death of the count of Niebla, who drowned while trying to conquer Gibraltar (159–86); followed by the count of Mayorga, Diego de Rivera, who is compared to Scaeva, the warrior from antiquity (190–92); heroes like Rodrigo de Perea and Pedro de Narbáez, who are compared to the classic figures of Curio (194–95) and Pallas (196–97), respectively; the exploits of Juan de Merlo (198–99); and the untimely death of Lorenzo Dávalos (or de Avalos) (201–2), which elicits a lament from his grieving mother (203–7). The section ends with a definition of the virtue of fortitude, after which it praises the king and states that his vassals should display exemplary fortitude, loyalty, and self-sacrifice (211–13).

The Labyrinth's review of the past is above all concerned with influencing the future actions of Juan II.[19] This is most clearly seen in the sections that follow: the circles of Jupiter (214–31) and Saturn (232–91). The circle of Jupiter praises justice and observes how its correct application or misapplication leads to virtuous or vicious governance. Its past exemplars are Octavian, Marcus Manlius, Codrus, Deciuses, Torquatus, the Brutuses, the Catos, and Fabricius (215–19),

INTRODUCTION

but they precede a treatment of the present glory of Juan II (221–22). The poet then enumerates negative examples of tyranny from antiquity, in particular the Dionysiuses of Syracuse (228–29), before returning to Juan II and the true meaning of justice (230–31). The section reflects on the virtue of poverty, embodied by the fisherman Amyclas (227), who, while living simply, was righteously spared from the whims of Fortune, and on how covetousness and envy can bring down the rich and powerful from their lofty stations (223–26).

The circle of Saturn is to a certain degree a continuation as it also deals with good government. It portrays Álvaro de Luna, Juan II's constable, triumphing over Fortune (235–36), in spite of the efforts of enemies, led by the Infantes of Aragon (237–39, 257–63), who sought to undo him through the divinations of a witch (240–56), but found that, although they could destroy a statue of the favorite, the constable was destined to hold onto his power (264–67).

When the narrator asks Providence about the future of Juan II (269–70), she predicts that his greatness will outshine that of his predecessors, cataloging the deeds of peninsular rulers from the time of the Visigoths (271–73) to the Asturian, Leonese, and Castilian kings, and closing with the current Trastámara dynasty (274–91). Mena then expresses the hope that the great prosperity of Juan II's reign will come to pass as prophesized (292–93); however, when he attempts to learn more about what the future holds, Providence disappears. The allegory ends with a plea for the king to triumph over the Moors through the efforts of his loyal subjects (294–97).

In all, thirty-one of *The Labyrinth*'s stanzas are devoted to the dedication and to the start of the vision; nineteen to the description of the Earth's geography, its inhabitants, and the cosmos; and seven to a general description of the three wheels of Fortune. The remainder describe the circles, or orders, of the planets, but have an uneven number of stanzas: moon (63–84), Mercury (85–99), Venus (100–115), sun (116–37), Mars (138–213), Jupiter (214–31), and Saturn (232–91). As can be easily seen, the poem gives clear preference to the last three circles (Mars, Jupiter, and Saturn), which describe the virtues of fortitude, just rule, and measured justice, respectively, which the author would have judged as more appropriate for a king.

The remaining stanzas conclude the conversation between the poet and Divine Providence (292–97), before the final three stanzas (298–300) tell us that the poet, exhausted by his labors, hears a divine voice that urges him to continue writing. These stanzas were probably not written by Mena, but became part of the poem in early manuscripts and printed editions.

THE SPANISH TEXT OF *THE LABYRINTH OF FORTUNE*

The Spanish text of this edition is based on Bibliothèque nationale de France, Espagnol MS 229 (also known as manuscript PN7), with occasional emendations taken from Núñez's *Las Trezientas*. It consists of three hundred stanzas of eight mostly twelve-syllable verses that generally rhyme ABABBCCB. Each twelve-syllable line is divided by a caesura into two hemistiches of six syllables each, and there are two accents per hemistich, the second of which always falls on the next to last syllable. Its language has been modernized, with these exceptions:

- Unusual words that are essential to the rhyme are kept. For example, *Lopia* rhymes with *Etiopia, copia,* and *inopia,* whereas *Leptis* does not; *elegïanos* rhymes with *manos, romanos,* and *humanos,* whereas *elegíacos* does not; *ocorra* rimes with *engorra* whereas *ocurra* does not.
- Unusual words that shorten or lengthen a line (most of the time by one syllable) to fit metric requirements are kept. For example, *britano* for *británico; criminoso* for *criminal; Sila* for *Escila; Pleyas* for *Pleyades; humil* for *humilde; linceo* for *lince,* etc.
- Antiquated words that affect the syllable count of a line are kept. For example, *ca* instead of *porque, desque* instead of *desde que, vido* instead of *vió, veyéndome* instead of *viéndome,* etc.

All significant departures from the text of manuscript PN7 are recorded in the Notes to the Text. Allusions to classical, mythological, and historical figures or works are explained in the Notes to the Translation (although they do not necessarily refer to any specific text from which Mena might have derived his information).

Finally, we have consulted the early sixteenth-century gloss of Hernán Núñez to *Las Trezientas* and the later commentary of Francisco Sánchez de las Brozas (ca. 1582, also known as el Brocense), as well as the marginal notes found in the PN7 manuscript itself. Among the several modern editions that are available, we have profited most from those of Maxim P. A. M. Kerkhof (Madrid, 1995), and of John G. Cummins (Salamanca, 1968); both of those editors also took as their base PN7 because of its clarity. Other scholarly, well-annotated editions have also informed our reading, including those of Louise Vasvari Fainberg (Madrid,

INTRODUCTION

1976) and Carla de Nigris (Barcelona, 1994), along with the extensive lexicon that was compiled by María del Carmen Gordillo Vázquez, *El léxico de "El laberinto de Fortuna"* (Cordoba, 1992).

The Translation of *The Labyrinth of Fortune*

The style and meter of *The Labyrinth* are impossible to reproduce.[20] We have opted instead to create a prose translation that closely approximates the meaning of the stanzas but disregards Mena's meter and the hyperbata. We also do not attempt to replicate his rhyme scheme, line length, accentual pattern, or caesura, although we graphically distribute the translation over eight lines that, for the most part, correspond to the sequence of verses in the Spanish text. These changes are made to render the substance of Mena's masterpiece more intelligible to English readers. Otherwise, it would be as impenetrable to them as it was for early readers without the aid of extensive glosses.

The poem's first stanza can be used as an example of what the translation does and what it does not do:

¡Al muy prepotente   don Juan el Segundo,
aquel con quien   Júpiter tuvo tal celo
que tanta de parte   le hizo del mundo
cuanta a si mismo   se hizo del cielo!
¡Al gran rey d'España,   al César novelo,
al que con Fortuna   es bien fortunado,
aquel en quien caben   virtud y reinado,
a él la rodilla   hincada por suelo!

INTRODUCTION

> To the very prepotent Don Juan the Second,
> to him to whom Jupiter showed such great love
> that he gave as large a share of the world
> as he gave to himself in the heavens!
> To the great king of Spain, to the new Caesar,
> to him who is greatly favored by Fortune,
> to him in whom both virtue and power abide,
> to him, knee bent to the ground!

This highly rhetorical stanza consists of one sentence broken into a series of encomiastic allusions to heaven and to Juan II that are introduced by deictics *(al, a él, aquel)* that appear on the left hemistiches of lines 1 to 8, while the verbs appear on the right hemistiches *(tuvo, hizo, es)* of lines 2, 3, 4, and 6. However, the word that controls the sentence appears in the last hemistich of line 8 (or 8b)—but it is not the singular form *hinco* (I bend), because he needs the extra syllable for the hemistich. Thus, he uses the singular participial adjective *hincada* (bent). This form, instead of the three-syllable *hincamos* (we bend), has the advantage of referring to himself and, at the same time, alluding to the fact that all the world's knees should be compelled to bend to the ground before the majesty of the king. The resulting repetition and patterning give the stanza a grandiloquent staccato resonance that we attempt to emulate, but cannot precisely replicate.

Hyperbata and Language

One of the most recurring features of *The Labyrinth* is its frequent use of hyperbata (changes in word order), which is illustrated by the following verses taken from stanza 2 (lines 14–15):

> de hechos pasados codicia mi pluma
> y de los presentes hacer breve suma,
>
> my pen is eager to write about the deeds of the past
> and tersely describe those now transpiring,

The hyperbaton places *hechos pasados* (deeds of the past) and *los presentes* (those now transpiring) in the first half lines of the two verses, and again makes them dependent on verbs that appear in the second hemistiches. This allows Mena not only to accommodate his accentual pattern and rhyme scheme but also to achieve a certain symmetry that we sometimes approximate. However, it is impossible to reproduce this stylistic game in comprehensible English prose with consistency; therefore, the translation often rearranges Mena's words to make the meaning clearer by doing away with the hyperbata; suppressing, adding, or relocating words whose purpose is often to just fill the length of a line (of which there are many). We avoid English cognates when those words exist but have acquired a different meaning or stress a secondary use and change obscure or obsolete words in favor of more idiomatic expressions. For example, a word like *falaces* is not translated as "fallacious" (wrong) but as "doleful" (or "dire"); *disponedora* is not "dispenser" but "determiner" (or "arranger"), because Fate does not dispense social roles but rather determines the place of everyone in society; *relegado* is not "relegated" but "exiled." The poem also contains many Spanish proper names and toponyms that are not translated (Juan II, not John II), with the exception of those that have common English forms (Seville for Sevilla).

INTRODUCTION

Classical and Christian Citations

The numerous classical and Christian citations of *The Labyrinth* presented as much of an obstacle for its original audience as they do now. Editors solve this problem by providing notes to explain them and to point out the possible texts from which they derive. The greatest effort in this direction was made by its early editor, Hernán Núñez, who was tutor of the children of the second count of Tendilla in the late fifteenth century. His notes explain the myths and stories that Mena only alludes to and the texts from which they might have been derived. In other words, they contain information that would today be found in dictionaries of mythology, classical texts, philosophical tracts, and religious, geographical, cosmological, and astrological works, but that hardly existed in the vernacular when Hernán Núñez was writing his notes. His glosses therefore served as a crutch for readers, especially when a citation was indirectly suggested by an attribute, an epithet, or an event, and not by a name. Our Notes to the Translation explain who or what such oblique allusions refer to in a briefer fashion, and are designed to help those who may be unfamiliar with the erudite peculiarities of the poem's references, style, and language. With their inclusion, our hope is that readers will find this bilingual edition to be a more approachable entryway to the study of Juan de Mena's classic, yet underappreciated, political allegory.

We would like to extend our gratitude to the editors of this series, who worked with us over the years it took to produce this book. In particular, we are indebted to Josiah

INTRODUCTION

Blackmore for encouraging us to pursue a translation of Mena's poem, and to Nicole Eddy for her close attention to every aspect of the project. We additionally benefited from the valuable feedback provided by Ryan Szpiech, Dorothy Severin, and Marina Brownlee. Thanks are also due to Giada Mirelli, a graduate research assistant whose help lessened our initial workload. Finally, we are grateful to our families for supporting our efforts to complete this book

Notes

1 Critics have always wondered to what extent Mena's poem was influenced by Dante's *Commedia,* although it does not appear to have had a direct impact on the Spanish writer. Miguel Ángel Pérez Priego, "De Dante a Juan de Mena: Sobre el género literario de *Comedia,*" *1616: Anuario de la Sociedad Española de Literatura General y Comparada* 1 (1978): 151–58, at 152, best summarizes this opinion: "Se suele admitir un conocimiento efectivo y hasta cierta presencia de la *Divina Commedia* en Juan de Mena, particularmente en la *Coronación* y el *Laberinto,* aunque sólo se han podido detectar unos cuantos versos que guardan una discutible semejanza y apenas si se encuentran en toda la obra un par de citas directas de Dante." (A working knowledge and even a certain presence of the *Divine Comedy* in Juan de Mena's work is often acknowledged, particularly in the *Coronación* and *Labyrinth,* although only a few verses with a disputable resemblance have been detectable, and in all of his work only a couple of direct quotes from Dante are to be found.) All translations are by the authors unless otherwise noted. Recently, Daniel Harnett, "Biographical Emulation of Dante in Mena's *Laberinto de Fortuna* and *Coplas de los siete pecados mortals,*" *Hispanic Review* 79, no. 3 (2011): 351–73, at 367, has modulated this perception by concluding that Mena's poem owes its persuasive weight to Dante's reputation.

2 There are two exemplars in *The Labyrinth* that are associated with the myth: Theseus's son, Hypolitus (stanza 63), and Pasiphae, the Minotaur's mother (104). There is also an etiological reference to the flight of Daedalus's son Icarus (52) as the origin of the name of the Icarian Sea, and a com-

INTRODUCTION

parison of Juan II's throne to something that Daedalus might have made (142).

3 Hernán Núñez, *Las Trezientas* (Seville, 1499), ed. Julian Weiss and Antonio Cortijo Ocaña, *Glosa sobre las "Trezientas" del famoso poeta Juan de Mena* (Madrid, 2015), 8. References to *Las Trezientas* are always to Weiss and Cortijo's edition.

4 Juan de Lucena, *Tractado de vita beata* (Medina del Campo, 1543), folio 1.

5 On the texts that Mena might have known, see Juan Casas-Rigall, *Humanismo, gramática y poesía: Juan de Mena y los auctores en el canon de Nebrija* (Santiago de Compostela, 2010). These criticisms were even more frequent from his first monolingual readers, because at the time Spanish was primarily used to express the concerns of everyday life. The lexical poverty of the spoken language had not prepared them to deal with such texts.

6 Juan de Valdés, *Diálogo de la lengua,* ed. J. Moreno Villa (Madrid, 1919), 227–28.

7 Tomás Antonio Sánchez, *Colección de poesías castellanas anteriores al siglo XV* (Madrid, 1779), 15: "Hombre de talento, sin duda, para la poesía, fijó nueva época a la castellana y levantó el estilo mas que cuantos le habían precedido; pero la afeó con metáforas improprias, con colaciones violentas, con palabras latinas o inventadas, y finalmente con un estilo hinchado y pomposo." We have modernized the orthography of this citation.

8 *Carajicomedia* was the erotic, highly politicized multiple-author parody of the first section of *The Labyrinth* and the gloss of Hernán Núñez. Its publication and circulation in the early sixteenth century is evidence of *The Labyrinth*'s influence in certain circles; see Frank A. Domínguez, *Carajicomedia: Parody and Satire in Early Modern Spain* (Woodbridge, 2015).

9 See María del Carmen Gordillo Vázquez, *El léxico de "El laberinto de Fortuna"* (Cordoba, 1992).

10 Núñez, *Las Trezientas,* ed. Weiss and Cortijo, *Glosa,* 8.

11 On the theory that Mena was a *converso* (the Christian descendant of Iberian Jews), see María Rosa Lida de Malkiel, "Notas para la biografia de Juan de Mena," *Revista de filología hispánica* 3 (1941): 150–54, and Américo Castro, *España en su historia, cristianos, moros y judíos* (Buenos Aires, 1948), 82.

12 *Memoria de algunos linajes,* ed. Alfredo Carballo Picazo, "Juan de Mena: Documento inédito y una obra atribuida," *Revista de Literatura* 1 (1952): 293.

INTRODUCTION

13 Vicente Beltrán de Heredia, "Nuevos documentos inéditos sobre el poeta Juan de Mena," *Salmanticensis* 3 (1956): 502–8.
14 Mena's appointment as chronicler must have happened on or after 1445 according to M. A. Belmonte Ortí, "Aportaciones a la vida y obra de Juan de Mena," *Boletín de la Real Academia de Córdoba* 28 (1957): 72. Because no historiographical work from his pen survives, the charge is more likely to have been an honorific one attached to an income; José Luis Bermejo Cabrero, "Orígenes del oficio de cronista real," *Hispania* 40 (1980): 399, and Francisco Bautista Pérez, "Historiografía y poder al final de la edad media: En torno al oficio de cronista," *Studia histórica; Historia medieval* 33 (2015): 101.
15 The reallocation of confiscated lands, goods, and revenues was a frequent practice, done to secure loyalty to the court.
16 Núñez, *Las Trezientas,* ed. Weiss and Cortijo, *Glosa,* 9.
17 Much has been written about the epitaph. The latest and best summary of it can be found in Juan Casas-Rigall, "El epitafio de Juan de Mena: Enigmas y vicisitudes," in *"Et amicitia et magisterio": Estudios en honor de José Manuel González Herrán,* ed. Santiago Díaz Lage, Raquel Gutiérrez Sebastián, Javier López Quintáns, and Borja Rodríguez Gutiérrez (Alicante, 2021), 165–80. He believes the first citation about the existence of the epitaph dates from 1582. The Salamanca version, however, is earlier, since Núñez died in 1553. The gloss reads: "En el sepulcro de Juan de Mena está este petafio. Tierra foenjx dicha buena / escondrijo de la muerte / a vos os cupo por suerte / el poeta Juan de Mena" (One can find this epitaph in the sepulcher of Juan de Mena. Land of the phoenix, called good, hideout of death, where chance decreed that the poet Juan de Mena be buried); for the transcription, see Charles Faulhaber, "Adivinanza y Epitafio de Juan de Mena (BU Salamanca BG/I.333)," Berkeley Library Update, February 4, 2018, https://update.lib.berkeley.edu/2018/02/04/adivinanza-y-epitafio-de-juan-de-mena-bu-salamanca-bg-i-333/.
18 Chronologically, in 1429, the forces of the Castilian king entered Aragon and laid siege to Ariza, but Alfonso V of Aragon did not give battle, so they withdrew. The following year, they sortied against the Aragonese towns Almazan and Berlanga, and again Alfonso V refused to engage. The turn toward Granada came in 1431, when the Castilians inflicted great losses on the Moors and achieved a great victory but did not conquer the

city. Finally, in 1441, the Infantes of Aragon besieged Juan II in Medina del Campo. The siege ended with a seeming reconciliation of both parties. The final defeat of the Infantes, at the Battle of Olmedo in 1445, falls outside the scope of *The Labyrinth*.

19 See Philip O. Gericke, "The Narrative Structure of the *Laberinto de Fortuna*," *Romance Philology* 21, no. 4 (1968): 512–22, and Galen B. Yorba-Gray, "The Future as Eschatological Presence in Juan de Mena's *Laberinto de Fortuna*," *Journal of Christianity and Foreign Languages* 5 (2004): 23–39.

20 Monique de Lope-Rivière and France Autesserre recently published a French translation in decasyllables as an eSpania Book, *Labyrinthe de Fortune* (Paris, 2019).

THE LABYRINTH
OF FORTUNE

LAS TREZIENTAS
DE JUAN DE MENA LLAMADAS
EL LABERINTO DE FORTUNA

1 *Suprainscripción*

¡Al muy prepotente don Juan el Segundo,
aquel con quien Júpiter tuvo tal celo
que tanta de parte le hizo del mundo
cuanta a si mismo se hizo del cielo!
5 ¡Al gran rey d'España, al César novelo,
al que con Fortuna es bien fortunado,
aquel en quien caben virtud y reinado,
a él la rodilla hincada por suelo!

2 *Argumenta contra la Fortuna*

Tus casos falaces, Fortuna, cantamos,
10 estados de gentes que giras y trocas,
tus grandes discordias, tus firmezas pocas,
y los qu'en tu rueda quejosos hallamos
hasta que al tiempo de ahora vengamos;
de hechos pasados codicia mi pluma
15 y de los presentes hacer breve suma,
y dé fin Apolo pues nos comenzamos.

THE THREE HUNDRED
OF JUAN DE MENA CALLED
THE LABYRINTH OF FORTUNE

1 *Dedication*

To the very prepotent Don Juan the Second,
to him to whom Jupiter showed such great love
that he gave as large a share of the world
as he gave to himself in the heavens!
To the great king of Spain, to the new Caesar, 5
to him who is greatly favored by Fortune,
to him in whom both virtue and power abide,
to him, knee bent to the ground!

2 *He Argues against Fortune*

Of your ruinous cases, Fortune, we sing,
of the ranks of people you spin around and whose fate you 10
  alter,
your boundless discords, your lack of permanence,
and of those who we find muttering upon your wheel
until we come to present times;
my pen is eager to write about the deeds of the past
and tersely describe those now transpiring, 15
so let Apollo conclude, for we are about to begin.

3 *Invocación*

Tú, Calíope, me sey favorable
dándome alas de don virtuoso
y por que discurra por donde no oso;
convida mi lengua con algo que hable,
levante la Fama su voz inefable
porque los hechos que son al presente
vayan de gente sabidos en gente:
¡Olvido no prive lo que es memorable!

4 *Enarra*

Como que creo que no fuesen menores
que los d'Africano los hechos del Cid,
ni que feroces menos en la lid
entrasen los nuestros que los agenores,
las grandes hazañas de nuestros señores,
la mucha constancia de quien los más ama,
yace en tinieblas dormida su fama,
dañada d'olvido por falta de autores.

5 *Pone en ejemplo*

La gran Babilonia, que hubo cercado
la madre de Nino de tierra cocida,
si ya por el suelo nos es destruida,
¡cuánto más presto lo mal fabricado!
Y si los muros que Febo a trabado
argólica fuerza pudo subverter,
¿que fábrica pueden mis manos hacer
que no hagan curso según lo pasado?

3 Invocation

You, Calliope, be favorable to me,
giving me wings of a marvelous nature
and with which I am able to talk about things I dare not;
fill my tongue with words that are certain, 20
let Fame lift its ineffable voice
so that the deeds of the present
spread from person to person:
Let oblivion not shroud what is memorable!

4 He Narrates

Because I believe that the deeds 25
of the Cid were not less important than those of Africanus,
and that our people did not enter the field of battle
with any less ferocity than the Agenores,
then the great deeds of our nobility,
the wonderful constancy of those who cherish them most, 30
lie in darkness, their fame asleep,
doomed to oblivion for lack of authors.

5 He Gives an Example

Great Babylon, which the mother of Ninyas
circled with baked bricks—
if it already lies leveled to the ground, 35
how much quicker will fall what is poorly created!
And if the walls that Phoebus erected
Argolic might was able to destroy,
what work can my hands fashion
that will not follow a similar fate? 40

6 *Otra vez invoca*

E ya pues derrama de tus nuevas fuentes
en mi tu subsidio, inmortal Apolo;
aspira en mi boca por que pueda sólo
virtudes y vicios narrar de potentes.
45 A estos mis dichos mostraos presentes —
¡o hijas de Tetis!— con vuestro tesoro
y con armonía de aquel dulce coro
suplid cobijando mis inconvenientes.

7 *Disputa con la Fortuna*

Pues dame licencia, mudable Fortuna,
50 por tal que yo blasme de ti como debo.
Lo que a los sabios no debe ser nuevo
ignoto a persona podrá ser alguna;
y pues que tu hecho así contrapugna,
haz a tus casos como se concorden,
55 ca todas las cosas regidas por orden
son amigables de forma más una.

8 *Ejemplifica*

La orden del cielo ejemplo te sea:
Guarda la mucha constancia del Norte;
mira el Trión, que ha por deporte
60 ser inconstante, que siempre rodea;
y las siete Pleyas que Atlas otea,
que juntas parecen en muy chica suma,
siempre s'esconden venida la bruma.
¡Cada cual guarda cualquier ley que sea!

6 *He Again Invokes*

And so, from your new springs spill
onto me your bounty, immortal Apollo;
breathe into my mouth so that I can only
speak about the virtues and vices of the powerful.
To these my utterances show yourselves present,   45
oh daughters of Thespis! With your treasure
and with the harmony of that sweet chorus
remedy them by covering up for my shortcomings!

7 *He Disputes with Fortune*

Therefore, give me license, mutable Fortune,
so that I can speak as ill of you as I should.   50
What to the wise must not be surprising
should not be unknown to anyone else;
and, since your nature is to always be contentious,
make your cases harmonize with each other,
for all things ruled by order   55
are friendlier the closer they are to each other.

8 *He Offers Examples*

Let the order of the sky be your guide:
Consider the great constancy of the North Star;
look at the Trion, whose sport is to be habitually
inconstant, for it always circles around;   60
and the seven Pleiades that Atlas sees from its heights,
how they appear close together to each other,
but always hide at the coming of winter.
Each one keeps to whatever principle it follows!

9 *Concluye contra la Fortuna*

65 ¿Pues cómo, Fortuna, regir todas cosas
con ley absoluta, sin orden, te place?
¿Tú no harías lo que'l cielo hace,
y hacen los tiempos, las plantas y rosas?
O muestra tus obras ser siempre dañosas
70 o prósperas, buenas, durables, eternas:
¡No nos fatigues con veces alternas,
alegres ahora y ahora enojosas!

10 *Propiedades de la Fortuna*

Mas, bien acatada tu varia mudanza,
por ley te gobiernas, aunque discrepante,
75 ca tu firmeza es no ser constante,
tu temperamento es destemperanza,
tu más cierta orden es desordenanza.
Es la tu regla ser muy enorme,
tu conformidad es no ser conforme,
80 ¡tú desesperas a toda esperanza!

11 *Comparación*

Como los nautas que van en poniente
hallan en Cádiz la mar sin repunta,
Europa por pocas con Libia que junta,
cuando Boreas se muestra valiente,
85 pero si el Austro conmueve al tridente,
corren en contra de como vinieron

9 *He Concludes His Argument against Fortune*

So how can you, Fortune, take pleasure 65
in ruling all things with an absolute law, without order?
Would you not imitate what heaven does
and what the seasons, plants, and roses do?
Either show how your actions are always destructive
or prosperous, good, durable, eternal. 70
Do not confuse us by alternating your deeds,
now full of joy and now irritating!

10 *The Properties of Fortune*

However, when your incessant spinning is more closely examined,
we see that you do abide by a law, although inconsistent,
because your steadfastness consists in not being constant, 75
your temperament is distemper,
your most certain order is disorder!
Your norm is to be very unmeasurable,
your conformity is to be unconforming,
you turn all hope into despair! 80

11 *Comparison*

Like sailors who sail toward the west
find in Cadiz a sea without obstructions,
where Europe and Libya nearly meet,
when Boreas blows strongly,
but when the Australis churns the sea, 85
the waters run in the opposite direction,

las aguas, que nunca tendrán ni tuvieron
allí, donde digo, reposo patente.

12 *Aplicación*

Así fluctuosa, Fortuna aborrida,
90 tus casos inciertos semejan a tales,
que corren por ondas de bienes y males,
haciendo no cierta ninguna corrida.
¡Pues ya porque vea la tu sin medida,
la casa me muestra do anda tu rueda,
95 porque de vista decir cierto pueda
el modo en que tratas a la nuestra vida!

13 *Ficción*

No bien formadas mis voces serían
cuando robada sentí mi persona,
y llena de furia la madre Belona
100 me toma en su carro que dragos traían;
y cuando las alas no bien remecían
heríalos esta con duro flagelo,
tanto que hizo hacerles tal vuelo
que presto me dejan adónde querían.

14 *Comparación*

105 Así me soltaron en medio d'un llano
Des'que hubieron dado conmigo una vuelta,
como a las veces el águila suelta

then they will never have nor ever had
absolute repose there where I mention.

12 *Application*

As unpredictable, despicable Fortune,
the uncertainty of your cases seem to be similar to theirs,   90
for they sail over currents of good and evil,
making uncertain the outcome of any journey.
In order for me to judge your immeasurable size,
show me the house where your wheel turns,
so that I can better bear witness by sight   95
to the way that you deal with our life!

13 *Fiction*

No sooner were my words uttered
than I felt myself seized,
and Mother Bellona, full of fury,
bears me away in her dragon-drawn chariot;   100
and, when their wings beat too slowly,
she flogged them with a harsh scourge,
so much so that she forced them to make such quick flight
that they soon left me where they wished.

14 *Comparison*

Without warning, they released me in the middle of a plain   105
after they had once circled around with me,
like sometimes an eagle lets go

la presa que bien no le finche la mano.
Yo de tal caso mirable, inhumano,
110 halléme'spantado en un gran desierto,
do vi multitud, no número cierto,
en son religioso y modo profano.

15 *Enarra el número de la casa de la Fortuna*

Y toda la otra vecina llanura
estaba cercada de nítido muro,
115 así trasparente, clarífico, puro,
que mármol de Paro parece en albura;
tanto que el viso de la criatura,
por la diáfana claror de los cantos,
pudiera traer objetos a tantos
120 cuantos celaba so sí la clausura.

16 *Engaño que hace la vista viendo por medio diáfano o especular*

Mas ya porque en otros algunos lugares
mi vista, bien antes que yo lo demande,
me hace gran cuerpo de cuerpo no grande
cuando los medios son especulares,
125 dije: "Si formas tan mucho dispares
bien no reguardo, jamás seré ledo
si de más cerca mirar ya no puedo
sus grandes misterios y muy singulares."

of prey that does not quite fill its talons.
I, by such a miraculous inhuman event,
found myself terrified in a vast desert, 110
where I saw a multitude, uncertain in number,
religious in appearance and secular in behavior.

15 *He Narrates the Number of the House of Fortune*

And all the rest of the neighboring plain
was surrounded by a resplendent wall,
so transparent, clear, and pure 115
that it rivaled Parian marble in whiteness;
so much so, that its face,
reflected in the diaphanous clarity of its stones,
could attract as many things as possible to itself
as the enclosure already contained within it. 120

16 *Deceit Caused by the Eyes When We Look by Transparent or Speculative Means*

But already because in some other circumstances,
my sight, well before I bade it,
made a shape seem larger to me than the shape is in reality,
when looking through ocular instruments,
I said: "If forms so much unlike to each other 125
I do not carefully examine, I will never be happy
if I cannot at once more closely observe
their great and very singular mysteries."

17 *Comparación*

    Como el que tiene el espejo delante,
130 aunque se mire de derecho en derecho,
se parte pagado, mas no satisfecho
como si viese su mismo semblante,
tal me sentí ya por el semejante,
que nunca así pude hallarme contento
135 que no desease mirar más atento,
mi vista culpando por no ser bastante.

18 *Prosigue y compara con ficción*

    Estando yo allí con este deseo,
abaja una nube muy grande, oscura,
el aire fuscando con mucha presura,
140 me ciega y me ciñe que nada no veo;
y ya me temía, hallándome reo,
no me aconteciese como a Polifemo,
que desque ciego venido en extremo
hubo lugar el engaño uliseo.

19

145 Mas como tenga miseria licencia
de dar más aguda la contemplación,
y más y más en aquellos que son
privados de toda visiva potencia,
comencé ya cuanto con más elocuencia
150 en esta mi cuita, de dialogar,
al pro y a la contra, y a cada lugar
siempre divina llamando clemencia.

17 *Comparison*

Like one with a mirror before him,
even though he might look at himself from all angles, 130
leaves pleased, but not totally satisfied
that he was seeing his own likeness,
so I felt in comparison,
for I never could find myself so content
as to not desire to more closely examine, 135
blaming my sight for its failings.

18 *He Continues and Compares with Fiction*

While I stood there mulling over this wish,
a large dark cloud descends,
hastily darkening the air;
it blinds and confines me, so that I can hardly see anything; 140
and I feared right away, finding myself imprisoned,
that the fate of Polyphemus lay in wait for me,
who, after being completely blinded,
was duped by Ulysses's deception.

19

But since misery is licensed 145
to sharpen one's perspicuity,
and all the more so in those who are
bereft of all their power of vision,
I at once started to ponder more eloquently
over my concerns, 150
the pros and the cons, and at every point
constantly calling on divine mercy.

20 *Prosigue como le apareció la Providencia*

  Luego resurgen tamaños clarores
que hieren la nube, dejándola enjuta,
155 en partes pequeñas así resoluta
que toda la hacen volar en vapores;
y resta en el medio, cubierta de flores,
una doncella tan mucho hermosa
que ante su gesto es loco quien osa
160 otras beldades loar de mayores.

21 *Del remedio que le trae*

  Luego del todo ya restituida
hubieron mis ojos su virtud primera,
ca por la venida de tal mensajera
se cobró la parte que'staba perdida;
165 y puesto que fuese así descogida,
más provocaba a bueno y honesto
la gravedad del su claro gesto
que no por amores a ser requerida.

22 *Proposición del autor y como pregunta a la Providencia de Dios que le aparece.*

  Desque sentida la su proporción
170 de humana forma no ser discrepante,
el miedo pospuesto, prosigo adelante
en humil estilo tal breve oración:
"¡O más que seráfica, clara visión!:

20 *He Continues by Saying How Providence Appeared to Him*

Suddenly, a great radiance surges forth
that pierces the cloud, leaving it drawn,
and in this manner dissolved into small fragments 155
that quickly melted away in the mist;
and, in its middle, covered in flowers, remained
a maiden so incredibly beautiful
that, when exposed to her countenance, only a madman
would dare judge other beauties superior! 160

21 *Of the Remedy She Brings to Him*

Without delay my eyes were completely restored
to their former condition,
for, with the arrival of such a messenger,
the faculty that was lost was recovered;
and, although she was shown in this fashion, 165
she predisposed one more toward goodness and truth
by the solemnity of her resplendent face
than to the demands of love's service.

22 *The Author's Purpose and How He Questions the Providence of God When She Appears before Him*

From the moment I realized that her proportions
were not unlike those of a human form, 170
my fear allayed, I continued
to make this brief request in a self-effacing manner:
"Oh, more than seraphic, pure vision!:

suplico me digas de cómo viniste
175 ¿y cuál es el arte que tú más seguiste,
o cómo se llama la tu discreción?"

23 *Respuesta*

Respondió: "No vengo a la tu presencia
de nuevo, mas antes soy en todas partes;
segundo, te digo que sigo tres artes
180 de dónde depende muy grande excelencia:
las cosas presentes ordeno en esencia
y las por venir dispongo a mi guisa,
las hechas revelo; si esto te avisa
Divina me puedes llamar Providencia."

24 *Admiración del autor*

185 "¡O principesa y disponedora
de jerarquías y todos estados,
de paces y guerras, y suertes y hados,
sobre señores muy grande señora!
¡Así que tú eres la gobernadora
190 y la medianera de aqueste gran mundo!"
(¿Y cómo bastó mi seso infacundo
fruir de coloquio tan alto a deshora?)

25 *Suplicale el autor que lo guíe*

"Ya que tamaño placer se le ofrece
a esta mi vida no merecedora,

I beg you to tell me why you came forth,
and what is the art you most keenly followed, 175
or what is the name of Your Wisdom?"

23 *Answer*

She responded: "I do not come before you
anew, but rather I am in all places;
second, I will tell you that I follow three arts
from which stem very great excellence: 180
In essence, I rule over things that belong to the present
and dispose of those yet to come as I want,
those done, I reveal; if this makes things clearer to you,
you may call me Divine Providence."

24 *The Author's Wonder*

"Oh, princess and determiner 185
of hierarchies and all worldly states,
of peacetimes and wartimes, of chances and fates,
over lords a very great mistress!
So, you are the ruler
and mediatrix of this great world!" 190
(And how could my modest intellect be suddenly sufficient
to benefit from this lofty discussion?)

25 *The Author Pleads for Her Guidance*

"Since such a great joy is bestowed
on this my unworthy life,

195 suplico tú seas la mi guiadora
en esta gran casa que aquí nos parece,
la cual toda creo que más obedece
a ti, cuyo santo nombre convoco,
que no a Fortuna, que tiene allí poco,
200 usando de nombre que no le pertenece."

26 *Respuesta*

Respondió: "Mancebo, por trámite recto
sigue mi vía, tú ven y sucede.
Mostrarte he yo algo de aquello que puede
ser apalpado de humano intelecto.
205 Sabrás a lo menos cuál es el efecto,
vicio y estado de cualquier persona,
y con lo que vieres contento perdona,
y más no demandes al más que perfecto."

27 *Prosigue la historia*

Y contra do vido mostrarse la puerta
210 se iba, llevándome ya de la mano.
Notar el entrada me manda temprano,
de cómo era grande y a todos abierta.
"Mas una cautela yace encubierta,"
dijo, "que quema muy más que la brasa,
215 que todos los que entran en esta gran casa
han la salida dudosa y no cierta."

I beseech you to be my guide   195
into this great house that appears before us,
which I believe is all the more obedient
to you—whose holy name I invoke—
than to Fortune, who has little authority there,
using a name that is not rightly hers."   200

26 *Answer*

She answered: "Young man, straight away
you should follow my road, come and draw closer.
I will reveal to you a measure of that which
can be grasped by the human intellect.
You will at least know what is the type,   205
vice, and rank of every person,
and with what you see be happily satisfied
and do not demand more from one who is more than
    perfect."

27 *The Story Continues*

And toward the place where a gateway showed
she went, leading me by the hand.   210
She soon bade me note how its entrance
was large and open to all.
"But a trap is hidden within,"
she said, "that burns more fiercely than embers,
for all who enter into this great house   215
have a doubtful and uncertain exit."

28 *Petición del autor*

"Angélica imagen, pues tienes poder,
dame tal ramo por dónde me avises,
cual dio la Cumea al hijo d'Anchises
cuando al Erebo tentó descender,"
le dije yo luego y le oí responder:
"¡Quien fuere constante al tiempo adversario
y más no buscare de lo necesario
ramo ninguno no habrá menester!"

29 *Prosigue su historia*

Así razonando, la puerta pasamos,
por do confluía tamaño gentío
que allí do el ingreso más era vacío
unos a otros estorbo nos damos,
ca por la cosa que mucho andamos
cuanto deseo común más se esfuerza,
más nuestra prisa nos daña y nos fuerza,
y lo que queremos menos acabamos.

30 *Comparación*

Como el herido de aquella saeta,
que trae consigo, la cruel engorra,
mientras más tira, por bien qu'el ocorra,
más el retorno lo hiere y aprieta,
así mi persona que'staba sujeta:
cuando pugnaba por escabullirme,

28 *The Author's Petition*

"Angelic vision, since you have the power,
give me such a branch to forewarn me,
like the one the Cumaean Sibyl gave to the son of Anchises
when he attempted his descent into Erebus," 220
I then remarked and heard her respond:
"Whoever holds constant in times of trial
and does not seek for more than is needful
will have no need of any such branch!"

29 *He Continues His Story*

Arguing in this manner, we entered the gate 225
where a great crowd was converging,
for even at that spot where the entry seemed easier
we hindered each other,
for the thing after which we greatly strive,
when common desire increases its efforts, 230
our haste hinders and blocks us even more,
and what we want we never obtain.

30 *Comparison*

Like one wounded by that arrow
that he still bears, the cruel barb,
the more that he pulls, as much as he tries to avoid it, 235
the more its withdrawal hurts and torments him;
so my being was caught:
Whenever I tried to escape,

mi prisa y la de otros me tenía más firme,
240 no gobernándome de arte discreta.

31 *De cómo la Providencia metió al autor en la casa de la Fortuna*

Mas la sabia mano de quien me guiaba,
viéndome triste y tanto perplejo,
hubo por bueno de dar a mi quejo
un tal reparo cual yo deseaba:
245 Es a saber, de prisión tan brava
me toma y de dentro me pone tan libre,
cual el Penatígero entrando en el Tibre
fue de los griegos de quien recelaba.

32 *Escribe el altura de la casa*

¡Mas preguntadme ya de cuanta aína
250 estoy en lo más alto de aquella posada
dónde podía ser bien divisada
toda la parte terrestre y marina!
¡Aspira ya Febo, pues de tu doctrina
módulo tanto, que cante mi verso
255 lo que allí vimos del orbe universo
con toda la otra mundana maquína!

33 *Protestación*

Si coplas, o partes, o largas dicciones
no bien sonaren d'aquello que hablo,

so my haste and that of others bound me more tightly,
because I was not ruled by right reason.   240

31 *Of How Providence Took the Author into the House of Fortune*

However, the wise hand of my guide,
seeing me despondent and so perplexed,
judged it useful to give my complaint
a relief such as I desired:
To wit, from such brutal imprisonment   245
she takes and puts me within its walls, as free
as the bearer of the Penates upon entering the Tiber
was from the Greeks he mistrusted.

32 *He Describes the Height of the House*

But ask me straightaway how quickly
I found myself on the heights of that dwelling   250
from which one could well see
all the parts of the earth and the sea!
Readily inspire me, Phoebus, because I am such a follower
of your doctrine, so that my verse can sing
of what we saw there of the orb of the universe   255
with all the other worldly machinery!

33 *Protestation*

If songs, or discourses, or lengthy poems
are discordant with the subject I speak of,

miremos al seso, mas no al vocablo,
260 si salran los dichos según las razones,
las cuales inclino so las correcciones
de los entendidos, a quien sólo teman,
mas no de groseros, que siempre blasfeman
según la rudeza de sus opiniones.

34 *Muestra el autor cinco zonas en que la tierra es partida*

265 De allí se veía el esférico centro
y las cinco zonas, con todo el austral,
brumal, aquilón y la equinoccial,
con la que solsticia contiene de dentro;
vi más contra mí venir al encuentro
270 bestias y gentes d'estrañas maneras,
monstruos y formas fingidas y veras,
cuando adelante la casa más entro.

35 *Asia la Mayor*

La mayor Asia, en la zona tercera,
y tierra de Partia vi entre los ríos
275 Tigris e Indo, de reinos vacíos,
mucho espaciosa cada cual ribera;
allí la provincia d'Acursia vi que era
junta con Persia y más con Asiria,
y tierra de Media, do yo creería
280 la mágica haberse hallado primera.

let us look at the sense but not at the word,
if the terms adequately express their meaning; 260
for I submit them subject to the corrections
of the learned, whom alone you should fear,
and not of the loutish, who always blaspheme
according to their boorish opinions.

34 *The Author Shows Five Zones in Which the Earth Is Divided*

From there one could see the spherical center 265
and the five zones, consisting of the Austral,
Brumal, Aquilonial, and Equinoctial,
within which the Solstitial is contained;
and I saw coming toward me
more beasts and peoples of strange appearance, 270
monsters and shapes feigned and true,
as I ventured deeper into the house.

35 *Asia Major*

In the third zone, Asia Major
and the land of Parthia I saw between the rivers
Tigris and Indus, unencumbered by states, 275
each of their banks very wide;
there I saw the province of Arcusia
close to Persia and closer to Assyria,
and the land of the Medes, where I might have reason to believe
the magical arts were first found. 280

36

Y cerca de Eufrates vi los moabitas,
y Mesopotamia como se tendía,
Arabia y Caldea (do el astronomía
primero hallaron), gentes amonitas,
285 y los idumeos y medianitas,
y otras provincias de gentes mayores,
las cuales pasando concedan lectores
perdón a mi mano si no son escritas.

37

Vi, de Eufrates al Mediterráneo,
290 a Palestina y Fenicia la bella,
dicha de fénix, que se cría en ella,
o quizá de Fenis, de Cadmo hermano,
el Líbano monte do nace el Jordano,
do fue bateado el hijo de María,
295 y vi Comagena con toda Siría
y los nabateos que ahora no explico.

38 *Egipto*

De parte del Austro vi cómo se llega
la tierra de Egipto al Rubro Nereo
(de Egisto así dicha, padre de Linceo),
300 la cual cerca Nilo, que toda la riega,
do el cielo sereno jamás no se ciega,
ni el aire padece nubíferas glebas,
do vi a Mauricia y la antigua Tebas
más desolada que Estacio no alega.

36

And near to Euphrates, I saw the Moabites
and how Mesopotamia stretched out before me,
Arabia and Chaldea, where astronomy
was first found, Ammonite peoples,
and the Idumaeans and Medianites, 285
and other more populated provinces
which I pass over; readers, graciously concede
a pardon to my hand if they are not written!

37

I saw, from Euphrates to the Mediterranean,
Palestine and Phoenicia the beautiful, 290
called Phoenix, because it is raised there,
or perhaps because of Phoenix, brother to Cadmus;
Mount Lebanon, where the Jordan is born
and where the son of Mary was baptized;
and I saw Commagene with all of Syria 295
and the Nabataeans, of whom I will say nothing more now.

38 *Egypt*

In the Austral region, I saw how adjacent
the land of Egypt is to the Red Sea
(so called because of Aegisthus, father of Lynceus),
which is encircled by the Nile, which irrigates it all, 300
where the clear sky is never overcast,
nor the air is stricken by dark clouds,
where I saw Mauricio and ancient Thebes
more desolate than Statius claims.

39

305 Vi, de la parte que el Noto se enciende,
el Cáucaso monte cómo se levanta
con altitud y grandeza tanta
que hasta cerca de Europa se tiende,
de cuyas faldas combate y ofende
310 la gente amazona, menguada de tetas,
los sármatos, colcos y los masagetas,
y aun los hircanos que son más allende.

40

Vi luego los montes Hiperbóreos,
Armenia y Siria con toda Albanía;
315 aunque, por cuanto prolijo sería,
dejo más otros rincones de hebreos,
de los capadocios y los amorreos,
y de Nicea, do juntada fue
la sínodo santo que libró la fe
320 de otros peores que los maniqueos.

41 *Asia la Menor*

En la menor Asia mis ojos tornados
vieron aquella Galacia do fueron
las gentes que al rey Bitinio vinieron
dando socorros bien galardonados;
325 los campos de Frigia tanto llorados;
Caria y Cilicia vimos en pronto,
Licia, Panfilia y tierra de Ponto
do Naso y Clemente fueron relegados.

39

I saw, in the direction from which Notus blows,　　　　305
how the Caucasus Mountain soars
with such altitude and great might
that it extends nearly to Europe,
on whose flanks fight and clash
the Amazon people (shorn of breasts),　　　　310
the Sarmatians, Colchians, and Massageteans,
and even the remoter Hyrcanians.

40

Then I saw the Hyperborean mountains,
Armenia and Syria, with all of Albania;
however—because it would be very prolix—　　　　315
I do not tell more of other areas that belong to the Hebrews,
to the Cappadocians and the Amorreans,
and of Nicaea, where gathered
the holy synod that delivered the faith
from others worse than the Manichaeans.　　　　320

41 *Asia Minor*

My eyes turned to Asia Minor
and saw that Galatia, where
the people who came to the aid of the Bithynian king went,
giving well-rewarded assistance;
the Phrygian fields mourned with such fervor;　　　　325
we suddenly saw Caria and Cilicia,
Lycia, Pamphylia, and the land of Pontus,
where Naso and Clement were banished.

42 *Europa*

    E vi más aquella que Europa dijeron,
330 de la que robada en la taurina fusta
    lanzó los hermanos por causa tan justa
    en la demanda que fin no pusieron;
    y contra Trión luego parecieron
    los montes Rifeos y lagos Metoes,
335 los cuales te ruego, lector, que tú loes,
    porque vecinos de Gótica fueron.

43 *Alemania alta y baja*

    Y vi la provincia muy generosa
    que es dicha Gothia, según nuestro uso,
    de allí donde Júpiter alto dispuso,
340 cuando al principio formó cada cosa,
    saliese de tierra tan mucho famosa
    la gótica gente que el mundo vastase,
    porque la nuestra España gozase
    d'estirpe de reyes atán gloriosa.

44 *Alemania alta y baja*

345 Del agua del Tanais contra mediodía
    hasta Danubio, vi Cisia la baja
    y toda Alemania, que es una gran caja,
    con los pueblos dacios, en tierra muy fría;
    y hasta los Alpes se ya parecía
350 Germanía y Rocia la superior,
    Mesia, Panonia e, para mejor,
    todas las partes del reino d'Hungría.

42 *Europe*

I also saw the one they called Europa,
who, kidnapped by the bullheaded galley, 330
flung her brothers on a quest so just
in its demand that there was no end to it;
and from the direction of the Trion there appeared
the Riphaean Mountains and the Meotian lakes,
which I urge you, reader, to praise, 335
because they neighbored the Gothic lands.

43 *Higher and Lower Germany*

And I saw the very generous province,
called Gothia in our language,
the place where high Jupiter ruled—
when he first created everything— 340
that the Gothic people, destined to devastate the world,
should abandon so famous a land,
so that our Spain could enjoy
such a glorious lineage of kings.

44 *Higher and Lower Germany*

From the waters of the Tanais, south 345
to the Danube, I saw lower Scythia
and all of Germany, which is shaped like a great drum,
with the Dacian people—in a bitterly cold land—
and, toward the Alps one could glimpse
Germany and Upper Rhaetia, 350
Messia, Pannonia and, even better,
all the lands of the kingdom of Hungary.

45 *Grecia*

Del Mediterráneo hasta la gran mar,
de parte del Austro, vimos toda Grecia:
355 Cahonia, Molosia, Eladia, Boecia,
Epiro y su fuente muy singular,
en la cual si hachas queriendo quemar
muertas metieren, se encienden de fuego,
si vivas las meten, amátanse luego
360 ca pueden dar fuegos y fuegos robar.

46 *Tesalia e Italia*

La gran Tesalía nos fue demostrada,
y el Olimpo monte que en ella reside,
el cual en altura las nubes excede,
Arcadia Corintio teniendo abrazada;
365 y desde los Alpes vi ser levantada
hasta las lindes del gran Océano
Italia, la cual del pueblo romano
Saturnia fue dicha en la era dorada.

47 *Francia*

Y vi las tres Galias, conviene a saber,
370 Ludunia y Aquitania y la de Narbona,
que del primero franco que tuvo corona
en Francia su nombre les quiso volver.
Aquesta comienza de proceder
del monte de Jovis y tanto resalta
375 que tiende sus fines hasta la mar alta
que con los britanos tienen que hacer.

45 Greece

From the Mediterranean to the great sea,
where the South Wind blows, we saw all of Greece:
Chaeonia, Molossia, Helos, Boeotia, 355
Epirus and its wondrous fountain,
in which those who want to set torches ablaze
immerse them when dead, and they ignite;
if alive when submerged, they are smothered,
because it can both start and quench fires! 360

46 Thessaly and Italy

Great Thessaly was shown to us,
and the Olympian mountain sited on it,
which towers in height over the clouds,
embracing Corinthian Arcadia;
and from the Alps to the borders of the 365
great Ocean, I saw Italy raised,
who by the Roman people was called
Saturnia during the Golden Age.

47 France

And I saw the three Gallic lands, to wit,
Lugdunum and Aquitania and the land of Narbonne, 370
names which the first Frank to bear the crown
wished to change into France.
This one gets its start
at Mount Jovis and is so large
that its borders extend to the high sea 375
that it shares with the Britons.

48 *España*

    Vi las provincias de España y poniente:
la de Tarragona y la de Celtiberia,
la menor Cartago que fue la de Hesperia,
con los rincones de todo el occidente.
Mostróse Vandalia, la bien pareciente,
y toda la tierra de la Lusitania,
la brava Galicia con la Tingitania,
donde se cría feroce la gente.

49 *África*

Vimos allende lo más de Etiopia,
y las provincias de África todas;
las suertes de Amón do son las tripodas,
con lo que confina la tierra de Lopia.
Marmárida toda, do es la gran copia
de gente veloce de los trogloditas;
las áforas, gentes atán imperitas
que de casas y hierros padescen inopia.

50

El Cáucaso monte fue luego patente;
la Cirenaica, región de paganos,
y toda la tierra de los numidanos,
allí do Jugurta se hizo valiente.
Pentapolín conocimos siguiente,
Getulia, Bisante, con más de otra tanta
tierra que pueblan los de Garamanta,
desde que Juba les fue prepotente.

48 *Spain*

I saw the provinces of Spain and of the setting sun:
that of Tarragona and that of Celtiberia,
lesser Carthage, which belonged to Hesperia,
with all the nooks and crannies of the west. 380
Vandalia the beautiful appeared,
and all the land of Lusitania,
brave Galicia with the Tingitania,
where ferocious people are reared.

49 *Africa*

Beyond, we saw most of Ethiopia 385
and all the provinces of Africa;
the Syrtes of Amon, where the tripods are,
with all that is bounded by the land of Leptis.
All Marmarica, where the numerous
and fast Troglodyte people are; 390
the Africans, peoples so simple
that they lack houses and implements.

50

The Caucasus Mountain was then visible;
Cyrenaica, a pagan region,
and all the land of the Numidians, 395
there where Jugurtha came into power.
Pentapolis we spotted next,
Gethulia, Bisante, with as many other
lands settled by the Garamantes
from the time that King Juba ruled over them. 400

51 *Islas particulares*

El mar así mismo se nos representa
con todas las islas en él descubiertas,
también de las aguas vivas como muertas,
y dónde bonanza no teme tormenta.
405 Las Estegades vi, nueve por cuenta,
Rodas y Creta la centipolea,
Cicladas, las cuales cualquier que las vea
seis verá menos para ver sesenta.

52

Naxón la redonda se quiso mostrar,
410 Colcos, Ortigia llamada Delos,
de la cual Delio se dijo aquel dios
que los poetas suelen invocar;
y vimos las islas Eolias estar:
Icaria, a la cual el náufrago dió
415 de Ícaro nombre, que nunca perdió,
el mal gobernador de sabio volar.

53

Mostróse Samos y las Baleares,
Corcega, Bozis y las Vulcaneas,
las Gorgonas, islas de las Meduseas,
420 y otras partidas que son por los mares.
Vimos a Trinacria con sus tres altares,
Peloro, Pachino y más Lilibeo,
donde los fuegos insufla Tifeo,
formando gemidos y voces dispares.

51 *Individual Islands*

The sea also appeared before us
with all the known islands found on it,
and its living and dead waters as well,
and where good weather does not fear storms.
I saw the Stechades, nine in number, 405
Rhodes and Crete of the hundred cities,
the Cyclades, regarding which, whoever sees them
will see six less in order to see sixty.

52

Naxos the round wished to appear,
Colchis, Ortygia called Delos, 410
from which Delius was the name given to that god
that poets usually invoke;
there we saw the Aeolian Islands:
Icaria, to which the castaway gave
the name of Icarus, which it never lost, 415
the one who failed to chart a sensible flight.

53

Samos and the Balearic Islands came into sight,
Corsica, Ebosus, and the Vulcaneas,
the Gorgons, islands of Medusa,
and other places that are on the seas. 420
We saw Trinacria with its three altars,
Pelorus, Pachinus, and also Lilybaeus,
where Typhoeus breathes on fires,
producing moans and weird voices.

54 *Comparación*

425 Según hacen muchos en reino extranjero,
si alguno viese lo que nunca vido,
si no lo desdeña y está detenido,
los otros retratan de tal compañero,
ca es reputado por mucho grosero
430 quien hace tal fiesta de lo nuevo a él.
Que entiendan los otros que son cerca d'él
que no hubo d'ello noticia primero.

55

Así retractado y redargüido
de mi guiadora sería yo, cuando
435 el mundo me vido que andaba mirando
con ojos y seso allí embebecido,
ca vi que me dijo en son afligido:
"Déjate d'esto, que no hace al hecho;
mas mira, veremos al lado derecho
440 algo de aquello por que eres venido."

56 *De las tres ruedas que vió en la casa de la Fortuna*

Volviendo los ojos a do me mandaba,
vi más adentro muy grandes tres ruedas.
Las dos eran firmes, inmotas y quedas,
mas la de medio voltar no cesaba;
445 y vi que debajo de todas estaba,
caída por tierra gente infinita,
que había en la frente cada cual escrita
el nombre y la suerte por donde pasaba,

54 *Comparison*

As many do in a foreign kingdom, 425
if anyone were to see what he never saw before,
if he does not scorn it and is charmed by it,
his friends speak ill of such a companion,
because a person who appreciates what is novel to him
is reputed to be very vulgar. 430
Let the others near him realize
that he had never been warned about it before!

55

Thus chastened and reprimanded
by my guide must I have been, when
she saw I was looking at the world 435
with spellbound eyes and mind,
for I noticed that she worriedly said:
"Leave this be, for it is not pertinent;
but look, we shall see on the right side
a little of what you have come for." 440

56 *Of the Three Wheels He Saw in the House of Fortune*

Turning my eyes toward the place she ordered,
I saw three large wheels further inside.
Two were steady, unmoving, and still,
but the one in the middle ceaselessly turned;
and I saw that below them 445
infinite people were cast to the ground
that had written on the forehead of each
the name and the fate meted to them,

57 *Pregunta el autor a la Providencia*

    aunque la una que no se movía,
450 la gente que en ella había de ser
    y la que debajo esperaba caer
    con túrbido velo su mote cubría.
    Yo, que de aquesto muy poco sentía,
    hice de mi duda cumplida palabra
455 a mi guiadora, rogando que abra
    esta figura que no entendía.

58 *Respuesta*

    La cual me respondió: "Saber te conviene
    que de tres edades te quiero decir:
    pasadas, presentes y de porvenir,
460 ocupa su rueda cada cual y tiene:
    las dos que son quedas, la una contiene
    la gente pasada, y la otra futura;
    la que se vuelve en el medio procura
    la que en el siglo presente detiene."

59 *Prosigue la Providencia*

465 "Así que conoce tú que la tercera
    contiene las formas y las simulacras
    de muchas personas profanas y sacras
    de gente que al mundo será venidera;
    por ende cubierta de tal velo era
470 su faz, aunque formas tú vieses de hombres,
    porque sus vidas aun ni sus nombres
    saberse por seso mortal no pudiera."

57 The Author Asks Providence

although the one that was motionless
covered the mottoes of the people who were 450
yet to be on it and those who awaited their fall
with a shadowy veil.
I, who grasped little of this,
expressed my doubts plainly
to my guide, pleading for her to explain 455
this image that I did not understand.

58 Answer

She answered me: "You should know
that I wish to speak to you about the three time periods:
past, present, and future;
each one occupies and maintains its own wheel; 460
the two that do not move, one contains
people of the past, and the other of the future;
the one that turns in the middle holds
those confined to the present."

59 Providence Continues

"Therefore, you should be aware that the third 465
contains the shadows and the simulacra
of many secular and sacred beings
that belong to people yet to come to the world;
for this reason, a veil of such nature covers
their faces, for even if you were to perceive human shapes, 470
their lives or even their names
could not be known to a mortal intellect."

60 *Razón de la Providencia por qué los hombres no pueden saber lo por venir*

"El humano seso se ciega y oprime
en las bajas artes que le da Minerva;
475 pues ve qué haría en las que reserva
aquel que los fuegos corruscos esgrime.
Por eso ninguno no piense ni estime,
prestigiando, poder ser ciente
de lo concebido en la divina mente,
480 por mucho que en ello trascienda ni rime."

61 *Amonestación de la Providencia*

"Mas esto dejado, ven, ven tú conmigo
y hazte a la rueda propincuo ya cuanto
de los pasados, si quieres ver espanto;
mas sey bien atento en lo que te digo:
485 que por amigo ni por enemigo,
ni por buen amor de tierra ni gloria,
ni finjas lo falso ni hurtes historia,
mas di lo que hubiere cada cual consigo."

62 *De siete órdenes que había en cada rueda*

A la rueda hechos ya cuanto cercanos,
490 de orbes setenos vi toda tejida
la su redondeza por orden debida,
mas no por industria de mortales manos;
y vi que tenía de cuerpos humanos
cada cual círculo de aquestos siete

60 *The Reason Given by Providence Why Men Cannot Know the Future*

"The human intellect is blinded and oppressed
by the lowly arts given to it by Minerva;
consider what it would do with those reserved by him   475
who wields the all-consuming fires.
That is why no one should think or believe
that he could come to know by magical means
about what is conceived by the divine mind,
no matter how deeply he thinks or writes about it."   480

61 *Providence's Warning*

"But leaving this behind, you should come, come with me
and quickly draw nearer to the wheel
of those who belong to the past if you are up for a fright;
but be very attentive to what I say:
Neither for friend nor for foe,   485
nor for good love of country or glory,
are you to portray what is false or misrepresent history,
but say what is to happen to each and every one."

62 *Of Seven Circles That Made Up Each Wheel*

As we drew nearer to the wheel,
I saw that its circumference was all woven   490
of seven orbs in their proper order,
but not by the industry of human hands;
and I saw that each of the seven circles
held so many and such prominent human bodies,

495 tantos y tales que no podría Lete
dar en olvido sus nombres ufanos.

63 *De los que eran en la primera rueda y orden de Diana, castos y cazadores*

Pues vimos al hijo de aquel que sobró,
por arte mañosa más que por instinto,
los muchos reveses del gran Laberinto
500 y al Minotauro a la fin acabó;
la buena Hipermestra nos apareció,
con vulto más puro que toda la Grecia,
y, sobre todas, la casta Lucrecia
con ese cuchillo que se disculpó.

64 *Cómo vió Artemisia, mujer de Mauseolo, y Penélope, mujer de Ulises*

505 A ti, mujer, vimos del gran Mauseolo,
tú que con lágrimas nos profetizas,
las maritales regando cenizas,
vicio ser viuda de más de uno solo;
y la compañera del lleno de dolo,
510 tú, Penélope, la cual en la tela
tardaste demientre recib'en la vela
los vientos negados a él por Eolo.

65 *Como vió a Argía y Alcidas, que es Hércules*

También en la rueda vimos sublevada,
llena de méritos muchos, a Argía;

that Lethe would not be able 495
to consign their proud names to oblivion.

63 *Of Those Who Were on the First Wheel, the Order of Diana: The Chaste and Hunters*

Then we saw the son of him who overcame,
by skillful art more than by instinct,
the many twists and turns of the great Labyrinth
and slew the Minotaur at the end. 500
Good Hypermnestra appeared before us,
with a purer face than existed in all of Greece,
and, over all, the chaste Lucretia
with that knife that buried her shame.

64 *How He Saw Artemisia, the Wife of Mausolus, and Penelope, Wife of Ulysses*

We saw you, wife of the great Mausolus, 505
you whose tears prophesize to us,
while moistening the marital ashes,
that it is sinful to be a widow of more than one;
and the companion of the cunning one,
you, Penelope, who lingered 510
over the cloth while his sail caught
the winds denied to him by Aeolus.

65 *How He Saw Argia and Alcides, Who Is Hercules*

We also saw raised on the wheel
Argia, full of many merits,

515 y vi que la parte derecha tenía
Alcides casi del todo ocupada,
a fuer de montero, con maza clavada,
bien como cuando libraba en el siglo
los calidones del bravo vestiglo
520 y la real mesa de ser ensuziada.

66

Yo, que veía ser oficiosos
los ya memorados en virtud diversa,
veyendo la rueda que en uno los versa,
los mis pensamientos no eran ociosos;
525 miró Providencia mis actos dudosos:
"No te maravilles a tanto," respuso,
"sabida la orden que Dios les impuso,
ni se te hagan tan maravillosos."

67

"Dispuso *ab inicio* la mente superna
530 que círculo d'estos aquí no parezca
sin que la gente de aquel obedezca
las constelaciones de quien lo gobierna;
pues tu juicio, si sabe, discierna
que cada cual de los siete planetas
535 sus operaciones influye perfectas
a cada cual orbe por gloria eterna."

and I saw that the entire right side was 515
almost completely occupied by Alcides
in a hunter's outfit, with a spiked mace,
like at the time he freed
the Calydonians from the fierce monster
and kept the royal table from being defiled. 520

66

I, who considered to be very dutiful
those already remembered for their various virtues,
seeing how the wheel cast them down in unison—
my thoughts were in turmoil;
Providence, seeing my confusion, 525
replied: "Do not be so surprised
once you know the order God imposed on them,
nor consider their cases so unusual."

67

"From the beginning, the supreme mind determined
that none of these circles were to appear here 530
without the people that obey
the constellations that govern that planet;
let your judgment, if able, discern
which one of the seven planets
perfectly influences the operations 535
of each orb, in glory forever."

68

"Así que la Luna, que es la primera,
en el primer cerco imprime su acto,
segunda en segundo conserva tal pacto;
540 tercero no menos, pues, con la tercera;
y todas de todas por esta manera
son inclinadas a disposición
de las virtudes y constelación
de la materia de cada una esfera."

69

545 "El cerco por ende que tienes ya visto,
llámale círculo, tú, de la Luna,
y haz así nombre, pues, de cada una,
porque no vuelvas el caso tan misto.
Ahora ya donde dudabas insisto:
550 si viste las castas con los cazadores,
es porque asignan aquí los autores,
de este planeta tal grado bien quisto."

70

"Hazte a la rueda, pues, de los presentes
por que las veas entreambas a dos,
555 y de las dudas requieras a nos;
solvértelas hemos en versos patentes;
y visto el un cerco de pasadas gentes,
verás el otro d'esa condición
de las personas modernas que son:
560 pues abre los ojos y para tú mientes."

68

"Therefore, the Moon, which is the first,
imprints her action on the first ring,
the second on the second ring keeps a similar pact;
the third does no less with the third; 540
and all by all in this way
are predisposed to the dominance
of the virtues and the constellation
of the matter of each sphere."

69

"For that reason, the ring that you have already seen 545
you should call the circle of the Moon
and then give a similar name to each one,
so that you do not render the subject so confusing.
Now, on the matter of your misgivings, I insist:
If you saw chaste women in the company of hunters, 550
it is because authors assign such
well-liked characteristics to this planet."

70

"Get nearer, then, to the wheel of those presently living
so that you can see both of them at the same time,
and direct your doubts to us; 555
we will answer them for you in plain verses;
and once you have seen the circle of previous people,
you will see another of a similar condition,
made up of contemporaries yet alive:
Therefore, open your eyes and pay attention." 560

71 *Como los tres Hados traían la rueda*

Atento, según me mandaba, mirando,
vi los tres Hados, y Cloto el primero,
Lachesis segundo, Atropos el tercero,
en veces alternas la rueda girando;
565 y vi sobre todas estar imperando
en el primero cerco de Diana,
una tal reina que toda la humana
virtud parecía tener a su mando.

72 *La reina difunta de Castilla*

De cándida púrpura su vestidura
570 bien denotaba su gran señorío;
no le ponía su fausto más brío,
ni le privaba virtud hermosura;
vencíase d'ella su ropa en albura,
y ramo de palma su mano sostiene,
575 don que Diana por más rico tiene:
más mesurada que toda mesura.

73

Vi de la parte del siniestro lado,
al serenísimo rey, su marido,
la misma librea de blanco vestido,
580 no descontento de tal bajo grado;
y vi de la parte del diestro costado
una tal reina muy esclarecida,
que de virtudes de muy clara vida
tenía lo blanco del manto bordado.

71 *How the Three Fates Moved the Wheel*

Attentively looking, according to her instructions,
I saw the three Fates — Clotho the first,
Lachesis second, Atropos the third —
taking turns at spinning the wheel;
and I saw holding sway over all 565
on the first circle of Diana,
such a queen that all human
virtue seemed to be at her command!

72 *The Dead Queen of Castile*

Of pure purple, her dress
well heralded her great authority, 570
but its magnificence did not enhance her person,
nor did its virtue diminish her beauty;
her attire yielded in splendor to her,
and her hand held a branch of a palm,
a gift that Diana cherishes most: 575
more modest than all of modesty itself.

73

I saw on the left side,
the most serene king, her husband,
dressed in the same white livery,
not displeased by such a lower standing; 580
and I saw on the right side
such a very illustrious queen,
who the virtues of her blameless life
had embroidered on the field of her mantle.

74 *Comparación*

585 Volvíme con aire de dudosa cara
a la ensolvedora de mis ignorancias,
como de niño que de sus infancias
la madre benigna no triste separa;
tal Providencia se me demostrara,
590 diciéndome tanto: "Conozco ya bien
que tu deseo será saber quien
pueda ser esta tal gente así clara."

75 *La reina de Castilla difunta*

"La que la silla más alta tenía
no la debieres haber por extraña:
595 era la ínclita reina de España,
muy virtuosa, doña María,
la cual, allende de su gran valía,
allende de reina de los castellanos,
goza de fama tan rica de hermanos,
600 Césares otros en la monarquía."

76

"Goza de mucha prudencia y verdad,
goza de don inmortal de justicia,
ha de virtudes aquella noticia
que en hembra demanda la honestidad.
605 Si fuese trocada su humanidad,
según que se lee de la de Ceneo,
a muchos haría, según que yo creo,
domar los sus vicios con su justidad."

74 *Comparison*

I turned, with a questioning countenance, 585
to the dispeller of my ignorances,
like a child who from his infancy
his benevolent mother not sadly separates;
in this way Providence behaved toward me,
saying these words: "I know full well 590
that you will desire to know
who these prominent people might be."

75 *The Dead Queen of Castile*

"The one who occupied the highest throne
should not be a stranger to you:
She was the most illustrious queen of Spain, 595
the very virtuous Lady Mary,
who in addition to her great worthiness,
in addition to being queen of the Castilians,
enjoys fame for her great wealth in brothers,
other Caesars in the kingdom." 600

76

"She possesses much prudence and truth;
she possesses the immortal gift of justice,
she has those features of virtue
that honesty demands of women.
If her human form were to be exchanged, 605
as one reads was that of Caeneus,
she would make many, according to what I believe,
curb their vices with her evenhandedness."

77 *Recomienda a la reina de Aragón reinante*

"La otra que vimos a la mano diestra,
610 era la reina de aragoneses,
la cual, mientras sigue su rey los arneses,
rige su reino la reina maestra.
Así, con la mucha justicia que muestra,
mientras más reinos conquista el marido,
615 más ella cela el ya conquerido:
¡Guarda qué gloria de España la vuestra!"

78 *Encarece más su virtud*

"Muy pocas reinas de Grecia se halla
que limpios hubiesen guardados los lechos
a sus maridos, demientra los hechos
620 de Troya no iban en fin por batalla;
mas una sí hubo, es otra sin falla,
nueva Penélope aquesta por suerte.
¡Pues piensa qué fama le debe la muerte,
cuando su gloria la vida no calla!"

79 *Recomienda a una dueña de Coroneles*

625 Poco más bajas vi otras enteras:
la muy casta dueña de manos crueles,
digna corona de los Coroneles,
que quiso con fuego vencer sus hogueras.
¡O quírita Roma, si d'esta supieras
630 cuando mandabas el gran universo,

77 *He Commends the Queen Regnant of Aragon*

"The other one that we saw on the right-hand side
was the queen of the Aragonese, 610
who, while her king pursues the call of war,
the skillful queen rules his kingdom.
In such a way, with the great fairness she shows
that while her husband conquers more kingdoms,
she more zealously guards those already conquered: 615
Behold what glory for Spain is yours!"

78 *He Praises Her Virtue More*

"One finds that very few queens of Greece
kept their beds undefiled
for their husbands while the deeds
of Troy went unresolved in battle; 620
but luckily there was another without failings,
a new Penelope.
Therefore, think of the fame death owes to her,
when life still proclaims her glory!"

79 *He Commends a Lady of the Coronels*

A little lower, I saw other honest women: 625
The very chaste lady of the cruel hands,
worthy crown of the Coronels,
who sought to extinguish her own fires with fire.
Oh, Roman citizens, if only you had known of her
when you ruled the great universe, 630

¡qué gloria, qué fama, qué prosa, qué verso,
qué templo vestal a la tal le hicieras!

80 *Recomienda a las bajas gentes*

De otras no hablo, mas hago argumento,
cuya virtud, aunque reclama,
635 sus nombres oscuros esconde la Fama
por la baja sangre de su nacimiento.
Mas no dejaré decir lo que siento,
es a saber, que las bajas personas
roban las claras y santas coronas
640 y han de los vicios menor pensamiento.

81 *Endereza la historia al rey*

A vos pertenece tal orden de dar,
¡rey excelente, muy grande señor!,
así como príncipe legislador
la vida política siempre celar,
645 por que pudicicia se pueda guardar
y tomen las gentes seguros los sueños:
¡punir a los grandes como a los pequeños,
a quien no perdona no le perdonar!

82 *Comparación*

Como las telas que dan las arañas
650 las leyes presentes no sean atales,

what glory, what fame, what prose, what verses,
what Vestal temple would you have made for such a one!

80 *He Commends the Lowborn*

I do not speak of others, but argue that,
although worthy by reason of their virtue,
Fame keeps their names hidden in darkness, 635
because of their base blood at birth.
I will not, however, be kept from saying what I believe,
to wit, that lowborn persons
can surpass flawless and saintly tonsures
and give little thought to the vices. 640

81 *He Directs the Story to the King*

To you pertains the right to give such an order—
excellent king, most great lord!—
as prince-legislator,
to always keep watchful eyes on political life
so that honesty can be preserved 645
and people take their slumbers in peace:
Punish the great like the low!
You should not forgive the unforgiving!

82 *Comparison*

Let present-day laws not be
like the cobwebs spun by spiders, 650

que prenden los flacos viles animales
y muestran en ellos sus lánguidas sañas.
Las bestias mayores, que son más extrañas,
pasan por ellas, rompiendo la tela;
655 así que no obra vigor la cautela
si no contra flacas y pobres compañas.

83 *Da consejo*

¡Aprendan los grandes vivir castamente,
no venzan en vicios los brutos salvajes
en vilipendio de muchos linajes!
660 ¡Viles deleites no vicien la gente,
mas los que presumen del mundo presente
huyan de donde los daños renacen!
¡Si lindos codician ser hechos, abracen
la vida más casta con la continente!

84 *Definición de Castidad*

665 Es abstinencia de vil llegamiento
la tal Castidad, después ya de cuando
se va la noticia del vicio dejando
remoto por obras y mal pensamiento;
y no solamente por castos yo cuento
670 quien contra las flechas de Venus se escuda,
mas el que de vicio cualquier se desnuda
y ha de virtudes novel vestimento.

for they capture the weak, vile animals
and inflict their languid cruelties on them.
The larger beasts, which are rarer,
pass through them, tearing the web;
therefore, rigid regulation is ineffectual 655
except against weak and poor classes of people.

83 *He Counsels*

Let great noblemen learn to lead lives of chastity,
let them not surpass brute savages in vices
to the detriment of many lineages!
Let vile delights not corrupt human beings, 660
but those who are suspicious of today's world
should flee from those places where dangers spring forth
    anew!
If they long to be spotless, let them pursue
a more chaste and continent way of life!

84 *Definition of Chastity*

Abstinence from such foul union 665
is the nature of Chastity; after a while,
the remnants of vice diminish,
made distant from deeds and damaging thoughts;
and I do not only count those as chaste
who shield themselves against the arrows of Venus, 670
but him who sheds all vices from his body
and dons a new vestment made up of virtues.

85 *Comienza la segunda orden de Mercurio*

Vi los que sano consejo tuvieron
y los que componen en guerra las paces,
675 y vimos a muchos fuera d'estas hazes
que justas ganancias mercando quisieron,
y otros que libres sus tierras hicieron,
y los que por causa de evitar más daños
han relevado los grandes engaños,
680 a muchos librando que no se perdieron.

86 *Alega con antiguos*

Nestor el antiguo se nos demostró,
y los oradores mejor recibidos
del hijo de Fauno que no despedidos,
y el rey que su hijo ya muerto mercó,
685 y Capis, aquel que siempre temió
los daños ocultos del Paladión,
con el sacro vate de Laocoón,
aquel que los dragos de Palas ciñó.

87 *Hasta aquí dijo los virtuosos y ahora los viciosos*

Debajo de aquestos yo vi derribados
690 los que las paces firmadas ya rompen,
y los que por precio virtudes corrompen,
metiendo alimentos a los renegados.
Ahí vi gran clero de falsos prelados

85 *The Second Order of Mercury Begins*

I saw those who had good counsel
and those who make peace in war,
and we saw many outside these forces, 675
who sought proper gains from trade,
and others who freed their lands,
and those who in order to prevent more dangers
have revealed great deceptions,
sparing many who would otherwise have been lost. 680

86 *He Offers Examples through the Ancients*

Ancient Nestor came into view;
and the orators better received
by the son of Faunus rather than dismissed;
and the king who purchased his already-dead son;
and Capis, the one who always feared 685
the hidden dangers of the Palladium;
with the sacred seer Laocoon,
the one who grabbed the dragons of Pallas.

87 *Up to Now He Spoke about the Virtuous and Now about the Vile*

Beneath them, I saw cast down
those who readily violate formal peace agreements, 690
and those who corrupt virtues for money
by giving encouragement to those who renege.
There, I saw a great multitude of false prelates,

que hacen las cosas sagradas venales.
695 ¡O religión religada de males,
que das tal doctrina a los mal doctrinados!

88

Pues vimos a Pándaro, el dardo sangriento,
hermano de aquel buen Eriteon de Roma,
que por Menesteo la libre paloma
700 hirió donde iba volando en el viento;
el cual a los nervios así del amiento
contra las dóricas gentes ensaña
que toda la tregua firmada les daña,
dándoles campo de paces exento.

89 *Habla de los que por codicia socorrieron en vicios*

705 Allí te hallamos, ¡o Polinestor!,
cómo traíste el buen Polidoro,
con hambre maldita del su gran tesoro,
no te membrando de fe ni de amor.
Yaces acerca, tú, vil Antenor,
710 triste comienzo de los paduanos;
allí tú le dabas, Eneas, las manos,
aunque Virgilio te dé más honor.

90

Estabas, Erifile, allí vergonzosa,
vendiendo la vida de tu buen marido,

who make sacred things venal.
Oh, religion so interwoven with evil 695
that you place such doctrine in the hands of the unlearned!

88

Then we saw Pandarus, with bloodied dart,
(brother to that good Eurytion of Rome,
who, on account of Mnestheus, wounded the freed dove
while she was flying on the wind), 700
the one who the sinews of the strap
angrily thrust against the Doric people,
so that he completely shattered their signed truce,
giving them a battlefield bereft of peace.

89 *He Speaks about Those Who on Account of Their Greediness Yielded to Vices*

We found you there — oh Polynestor! — 705
how you treated good Polydorus,
because of your cursed hunger for his great wealth,
forgetful of faith or of love.
You lie nearby, you, vile Anthenor,
sad origin of the Paduans; 710
there, Aeneas, you were shown greeting him,
although Virgil honors you better.

90

Eriphyle, you were there, shamefully
selling the life of your good husband,

715 de ricos collares tu seso vencido,
quisiste ser viuda, más no deseosa.
¡O siglo nuestro! Edad trabajosa,
si hallarían los que te buscasen
otras Erisífiles que deseasen
720 dar sus maridos por tan poca cosa.

91

No buenamente te puedo callar,
Opas maldito, e a ti, Julián,
pues sois en el valle más hondo de afán
que no se redime jamás por llorar;
725 ¿cuál ya crueza os pudo indignar
a vender un día las tierras y leyes
d'España, las cuales pujanza de reyes
en años a tantos no pudo cobrar?

92

A la moderna volviéndome rueda,
730 fondón del cilénico cerco segundo,
de vicios semblantes estaba el profundo
tan lleno que no sé hablar quien lo pueda.
Ved si queredes la gente que queda,
darme licencia que os la señale,
735 mas al presente hablar no me cale:
¡verdad lo permite, temor lo devieda!

your senses overwhelmed by the splendor of necklaces; 715
you wished to be widowed, but not wanting.
Woe to our time! Worrisome age,
if those searching for you
were to find other Eriphyles who wished
to sell their husbands for so little. 720

91

I can hardly pass you over in silence,
cursed Oppas, and you, Julian,
for you are in the deepest valley of shame,
which can never be redeemed with tears.
What cruelty so angered you 725
as to betray the lands and laws
of Spain, which the might of kings
could not reclaim for so many years?

92

Upon turning to the modern wheel,
the bottom of the second Cyllenic circle 730
was so full of similar vices
that I do not know who would be able to describe it.
Examine, if you want, those people that remain on it,
give me license to point them out to you,
but, at present, it is not convenient for me to speak of 735
    them:
Truth allows it, fear forbids it!

93 *Muestra el autor que por miedo de los presentes deja de decir sus vicios*

¡O Miedo mundano, que tú nos compeles
grandes placeres fingir por pesares,
que muchos Enteles hagamos ya Dares
740 y muchos de Dares hagamos Enteles!
Hacemos de pocos muy grandes tropeles,
buenos nos haces llamar los viciosos,
notar los crueles por muy pïadosos
y los pïadosos por mucho crueles.

94 *Comparación*

745 Bien como siervo que por la fe nueva
del su patrono se muestra más vivo,
porque le pueda huir de cautivo
dice por boca lo qu'él no aprueba,
semblantes temores la lengua nos lleva
750 a la mendacia de la adulación
así que cualquiera hará conclusión
que diga lo falso, mas no lo que deba.

95 *De los vicios de los religiosos*

¿Quién así mismo decir no podría
de cómo las cosas sagradas se venden
755 y los viles usos en que se despenden
los diezmos ofertos a Santa María?
Con buenos colores de la clerecía

93 *The Author Says That Because of Fear of Those Presently Alive, He Does Not Mention Their Vices*

Oh, Worldly Dread, that you compel us
to pretend that great worries are pleasures,
to transform many an Entellus into a Dares
and many a Dares into an Entellus! 740
We take a few to be a very great mob;
"good" you make us call those riddled with vice,
to note the cruel as exceedingly pious,
and the pious as exceedingly cruel.

94 *Comparison*

Just like a slave who, on account of the new faith 745
of his master, seems more spirited
so that he can escape from his captivity,
mouths words in which he does not believe,
similar fears bring our tongue
to the falsehoods of adulation; 750
consequently, anyone will finish
by saying untruths but not what he ought.

95 *Of the Vices of the Religious*

Who could also not speak in the same way
about how sacred things are sold
and of the vile purposes to which are put 755
the tithes offered to Saint Mary?
Under the good repute of the clergy,

disipan los malos los justos sudores
de simples y pobres y de labradores,
760 cegando la santa católica vía.

96 *Pone en ejemplo*

Cesárea se lee que con terremoto
fuese su muro por tierra caído,
las gentes y pueblo todo destruido,
que no quedó lienzo que no fuese roto;
765 mas sólo su templo hallamos inmoto,
y la clerecía con el su prelado
salvo: ¡seguro fue d'esto librado
por su honesto vivir y devoto!

97 *Aplicación*

Si tal terremoto nos acaeciese,
770 lo que la divina clemencia no quiera,
por lo contrario presumo que fuera
de cualquiera villa donde se hiciese,
y antes presumo que hoy se hundiese
la clerecía con todo su templo,
775 y que la villa quedase en ejemplo,
libre, sin daño ninguno que fuese.

98 *Endereza el autor la habla al rey*

La vuestra sacra y real majestad
haga en los súbditos tal beneficio

evil men squander the just sweat
of the simple and poor and of farmers,
obstructing the holy Catholic way. 760

96 *He Gives an Example*

Caesarea, one reads, had an earthquake
that brought its ramparts to the ground,
its people and town all destroyed,
so that no wall remained untouched;
but only its temple we found unshaken, 765
and its clergy along with its bishop
unharmed: Surely, they were spared from this
because of their honest and devout way of living!

97 *Application*

If a such an earthquake were to happen to us —
may divine clemency forbid! — 770
I presume the reverse would occur
in any town where it took place;
and rather, I take for granted that today the clergy
along with all of its temple would collapse,
and that the town would remain as an example, 775
secure, spared of any damage it might have had.

98 *The Author Addresses His Words to the King*

May Your Sacred and Royal Majesty
confer on your subjects such benefit

que cada cual use así del oficio.
780 Que queden las leyes en integridad,
así que codicia ni rapacidad
no os ofenda lo bien ordenado,
por que departa de cualquier estado
la vil avaricia su sagacidad.

99 *Definición de Avaricia*

785 Es Avaricia, doquiera que mora,
vicio que todos los bienes confonde,
de la ganancia, doquier que se esconde,
una solícita inquisidora,
sirve metales, metales adora.
790 De robos notorios golosa garganta,
que de lo ganado sufre mengua tanta
como de aquello que espera aun ahora.

100 *Comienza la tercera orden de Venus do se habla del amor
bueno y malo, y de la especies de el*

Venidos a Venus, vi en grado especial
los que en el fuego de su juventud
795 hacen el vicio ser tanta virtud
por el sacramento matrimonial.
Abajo de aquestos vi gran general
de muchos linajes caídos en mengua,
que no sabe cómo se diga mi lengua
800 tantas especies y formas de mal.

as to let each person work in his profession!
Let laws go unbroken, 780
so that neither greed nor acquisitiveness
can disturb what has been well-ordered by you,
so that any rank can be freed
from vile avarice by their wisdom!

99 *Definition of Avarice*

Avarice, wherever she dwells, is 785
a vice that undermines all that is good;
of profits, wherever she hides,
she is a solicitous seeker,
she serves bullion, adores bullion.
She is a gluttonous maw for notorious robberies, 790
who worries as much about what is earned
as about what she even now expects.

100 *The Third Order of Venus Begins, Which Treats Good and Bad Love, and Their Varieties*

Upon reaching Venus, I saw set apart
those who in the fire of their youth
consider lust to be a great virtue 795
because of the sacrament of matrimony.
Below those, I saw a great assortment
of lineages that had fallen into destitution,
so that my tongue does not know how to speak about
so many kinds and forms of evil. 800

101 *Argumento de esta orden*

Eran adúlteros y fornicarios,
y otros notados de incestuosos,
y muchos que juntan tales criminosos
y llevan por ello los viles salarios,
805 y los que en afectos así voluntarios
su vida deleitan en vano pecando,
y los maculados del crimen nefando,
de justa razón y de toda contrarios.

102 *Alega antiguos dados al mal amor*

Vimos en una vilmente abrazados
810 la compañera de aquel gran Atrides,
duque de todas las grecianas lides,
tomar con Egisto solaces hurtados;
y vimos a Mirra, con los derribados,
hermana ya hecha de quien era madre,
815 y madre del hijo de su mismo padre
en contra de leyes humanas y grados.

103

Allí era aquel que la casta cuñada
hizo por fuerza no ser más doncella,
comiendo su hijo en pago de aquella
820 que por dos maneras d'él fue desflorada;
y vimos en forma muy mal aviltada
ser con Macareo la triste Canace,
de los cuales ambos un hijo tal nace
que la humana vida dejó injuriada.

101 *This Order's Function*

There were adulterers and fornicators,
and others noted for being incestuous,
and many who serve such criminals
and receive vile salaries for it,
and those who in similar affections 805
spend their life in delight, vainly sinning,
and those stained by the unmentionable sin,
contrary to each and every just reason.

102 *He Offers Examples of Ancients Given to Bad Love*

We saw, disgustingly embraced as one,
the companion of that great Atreides 810
(chief of all the Greek forces)
gratify her hidden desires with Aegisthus;
and we saw Myrrha among the fallen,
already made a sister of one to whom she was mother,
and mother of the son of her own father 815
against human laws and degrees.

103

There was the one whom his virtuous sister-in-law
forced to be a virgin no more,
eating his son in payment to her
who was deflowered by him in two ways; 820
and we saw in a most shameful manner
sorrowful Canace lie with Macareus;
from them both was born such a son
as damaged human life forever.

104

825 De los Centauros el padre gigante
allí lo hallamos con muy poca gracia,
al que hizo Juno con la su falacia
en forma mintrosa cumplir su talante;
y vimos, movidos un poco adelante,
830 plañir a Pasifae sus actos indignos,
la cual antepuso el toro a ti, Minos.
¡No hizo Cila troque semejante!

105 *Como halló Macías*

Tanto anduvimos el cerco mirando
que nos hallamos con nuestro Macías,
835 y vimos que estaba llorando los días
con que su vida tomó fin, amando.
Llegueme más cerca turbado yo, cuando
vi ser un tal hombre de nuestra nación,
y vi que decía tal triste canción,
840 en elegíaco verso cantando:

106 *Cantar de Macías*

"Amores me dieron corona de amores
por que mi nombre por más bocas ande.
Entonces no era mi mal menos grande
cuando me daban placer sus dolores.
845 Vencen el seso los dulces errores,
mas no duran siempre según luego placen.
Pues me hicieron del mal que os hacen,
¡sabed al amor desamar, amadores!"

104

The giant father of the Centaurs 825
we found there very poorly depicted,
the one whom Juno with her deviousness made
to fulfill his desires fraudulently;
and we saw, when we moved a little ahead,
Pasiphae mourning her shameful acts, 830
she who preferred the bull to you, Minos.
Scylla did not make such an exchange!

105 *How He Found Macias*

We spent so much time examining the circle
that we came upon our Macias,
and saw that he was lamenting the days 835
that the course of his life, while loving, came to an end.
Distraught, I approached nearer to him and
saw that he was a man from our nation,
and noticed that he was uttering this sad song,
singing in elegiac verses: 840

106 *Song of Macias*

"Love gave me a crown made of love
so that my name could be invoked by more mouths.
Before, my grief was no less intense,
when the pain inflicted by her gave me pleasure.
Sweet sins overcome the mind, 845
but they do not last forever, as can be seen later.
Since they harmed me in the same way they do you:
Lovers, know how to spurn love!"

107

"¡Huid un peligro tan apasionado!
850 ¡Sabed ser alegres! ¡Dejad de ser tristes!
¡Sabed deservir quien tanto servistes;
a otros que amores dad vuestro cuidado,
los cuales, si diesen por un igual grado
sus pocos placeres según su dolor,
855 no se quejara ningún amador
ni desesperara ningún desamado!"

108 *Comparación*

"Y bien como cuando algún malhechor,
al tiempo que hacen de otro justicia,
temor de la pena le pone codicia
860 de allí adelante vivir ya mejor;
mas desque pasado por él el temor,
vuelve a sus vicios como de primero,
así me volvieron a do desespero
deseos que quieren que muera amador."

109 *Pregunta el autor a la Providencia*

865 Tan gran multitud turbada veyendo
por fuego vicioso de ilícito amor,
hablé: "Providencia, tú dime mejor
aquesta mi dubda que yo no entiendo:
estos a tanto discretos seyendo,
870 ¿por qué se quisieron amar ciegamente?

107

"Flee from a danger so passionate!
Know how to be cheerful! Cease being sad! 850
Know how to ignore the one you courted so much;
place your devotion on things other than love,
which, if its few pleasures
equaled its pains,
no lover would complain 855
nor any unloved despair of it!"

108 *Comparison*

"And as happens with any criminal
at the moment that justice is wrought on another,
fear of the punishment makes him eagerly wish
to lead a better life from then on 860
but, when that fear leaves him,
he reverts to his vices as before;
thus, I was brought back to the place where I despair
by desires that seek the death of the lover."

109 *The Author Asks Providence*

Seeing such a great multitude perturbed 865
by the vicious fire of illicit of love,
I spoke: "Providence, you should clarify
this unresolved doubt of mine:
These persons, being so wise,
why did they wish to love each other so blindly? 870

Bullada debieran tener en la frente
la pena que andan aquí padeciendo."

110 *Responde la Providencia mostrando algunas cosas que provocan amor por artificio*

Respondió riendo la mi compañera:
"Ni causan amores ni guardan su tregua
875 las telas del hijo que pare la yegua;
ni menos agujas hincadas en cera,
ni hilos de alambre ni el agua primera
del mayo bebida con vaso de yedra,
ni fuerza de yerbas, ni virtud de piedra,
880 ni vanas palabras de la encantadera.

111 *Otras razones que causan amor naturalmente*

"Mas otras razones más justas convocan
los corazones a las amistades:
virtudes y vidas en conformidades,
y sobre todo beldades provocan,
885 y delectaciones a muchos advocan,
y cuando los dones son bien recibidos,
o por linaje nacer escogidos,
o dulces palabras allí donde tocan."

112

"Val asímismo para ser amado
890 anticiparse primero en amar:

They should bear a mark on their forehead
announcing the punishment they are suffering here."

110 *Providence Answers, Showing Some Things That Provoke Love by Artificial Means*

Laughingly, my companion answered:
"Neither do the membranes of a colt born to a mare
cause love nor honor its truce, 875
nor any less needles thrust in wax,
nor iron filaments, nor the first waters
of May drunk in cups of ivy,
nor the strength of potions, nor the virtue of stones,
nor a sorceress's foolish incantations." 880

111 *Other Reasons That Naturally Cause Love*

"But other more justified reasons
join hearts in amity:
Virtues and lives in agreement,
and, above all, a desire for beautiful things
and pleasures attract many people, 885
and when boons are well received
or one is born to a worthy lineage,
or sweet words find their intended recipient."

112

"It is also helpful, in order to be loved,
to anticipate oneself in loving: 890

no es ninguno tan duro en el dar
que algo no diese si mucho ha tomado;
pues mucho debiera ser más que culpado
aquel corazón que si no querer
895 quiere, que quiera querido no ser,
o por ser querido viva despagado."

113 *Aquí responde la Providencia a la otra duda*
 que dijo "discretos seyendo"

"Entonces se puede obrar discreción
si amor es ficto, vanílocuo, pigro;
mas el verdadero no teme peligro
900 ni quiere castigos de buena razón,
ni los juicios de cuantos ya son
le estorban la vía de cómo la entiende:
¡ante[s] sus llamas mayores enciende
cuando le ponen mayor defensión!"

114 *Endereza el autor el habla al rey*

905 "Por ende, monarca, señor valeroso,
el regio cetro de vuestra potencia
hiera mezclando rigor con clemencia,
porque os tema cualquier criminoso,
los viles actos del libidinoso
910 fuego de Venus del todo se maten,
y los humanos sobre todo caten
el limpio católico amor virtuoso,"

No one is so begrudging of giving back
something, if he has taken much,
since greater blame should be given
to that heart that does not want
to love, yet seeks rejection, 895
or lives displeased because it is loved."

113 *Here Providence Responds to His Other Doubt, When He Said "Beings So Wise"*

"Therefore, one can act according to reason
if love is feigned, blustering, indolent;
but true love is not afraid of danger,
nor does it seek the advice of sound reason, 900
nor do the judgments of many
hinder the path as it sees it:
Rather, its flames burn more fiercely
when greater obstacles appear before it!"

114 *The Author Directs His Text to the King*

"Therefore, monarch, most brave lord, 905
let the royal scepter of your power
strike, mixing harshness with clemency,
so that every criminal is fearful of you.
Let the vile acts of the libidinous
fires of Venus be completely quenched, 910
and humankind abide above all by
the virtuous pure Catholic love,"

115 *Definición que cosa sea buen amor o malo*

"el cual es tal medio de dos corazones
que la voluntad, que estaba no junta,
915 la su dulcedumbre concuerda y ayunta,
haciéndoles una sus dos opiniones,
y dando tal parte de sus afecciones:
a los amadores sin gozo cadena,
y a los amados deleite sin pena.
920 ¡A los menos méritos más galardones!"

116 *Fenece la orden tercera de Venus, comienza la cuarta de Febo*

Aquí vi gran turba de santos doctores
y contemplativos de aquel buen saber
que para siempre nos puede valer,
haciéndonos libres de nuestros errores:
925 filósofos grandes y flor d'oradores,
aquí citaristas, aquí los profetas,
astrólogos grandes, aquí los poetas,
aquí cuadrivistas, aquí sabidores.

117 *Teólogos*

Está sobre todos gran turba compuesta
930 de claros maestros, doctores muy santos:
estaba Jerónimo alzando los cantos,
Gregorio, Agustino velando respuesta,
y vimos el santo doctor cuya fiesta
nuestro buen César jamás solemniza,

115 *Definition of What Is Good or Bad Love*

"which is a means by which two hearts
whose wills did not harmonize before
are joined and yoked by its sweetness, 915
making one of their two opinions
and rewarding their affections in this manner:
to joyless lovers, a chain,
and to those who are loved, delight without anguish.
To the less meritorious, greater rewards!" 920

116 *The Third Order of Venus Ends and the Fourth of Phoebus Begins*

Here I saw a great throng of saintly doctors
and contemplatives of that true knowledge
that can be eternally beneficial to us
by freeing us from our sins:
great philosophers and the flower of orators, 925
here citharists, here the prophets,
great astrologers, here the poets,
here scholars, here the wise.

117 *Theologians*

A great throng is above all, that is composed
of distinguished teachers, very saintly doctors: 930
Jerome was raising his songs,
Gregory, Augustine awaiting their answers,
and we saw the saintly doctor whose feast
our good Caesar always celebrates,

935 y otros doctores a quien canoniza
    la silla romana por vida modesta.

118 *Filósofos*

    Vi los filósofos Crato y Polemo,
    el buen Empedocles y do[c]to Zenón,
    Aristóteles cerca del padre Platón,
940 guiando a los otros con su dulce remo.
    Vi más a Sócrates tal que lo temo,
    con la ponzoña mortal que bebía,
    y vi a Pitágoras que defendía
    las carnes al mundo comer por extremo.

119 *Elocuentes*

945 Vi a Demóstenes y a Gabiano,
    y vi más a Tulio con su rica lengua,
    Casio Severo, sufriendo gran mengua,
    dado en exilio del pueblo romano.
    Mostróse Domicio, rector africano,
950 y vimos a Plucio con Apolodoro;
    y vimos la lumbre del claro tesoro
    del nuestro retórico Quintiliano.

120 *Músicos*

    Demostróse Júbal, primero inventor
    de cónsonas voces y dulce armonía;
955 mostróse el harpa que Orfeo tañía
    cuando al infierno lo trujo el amor;

and other doctors who are canonized 935
by the Roman See on account of their humble lives.

118 *Philosophers*

I saw the philosophers Cratylus and Polemon,
the good Empedocles and knowledgeable Zeno,
Aristotle near to Father Plato,
guiding the others with his sweet rowing. 940
I also saw Socrates as I feared,
with the poisonous draft he was drinking,
and I saw Pythagoras strongly forbidding
the world from excessive consumption of meat.

119 *Rhetoricians*

I saw Demosthenes and Gabinianus, 945
and ahead I saw Tully with his rich language;
Cassius Severus, suffering great want,
sent into exile by the Roman people.
Domitius was shown, the African rector;
and we saw Plotinus with Apollodorus; 950
and we saw the radiance of that exceptional treasure
of our rhetorician Quintilian.

120 *Musicians*

Displayed was Jubal, first inventor
of consonant voices and sweet harmony;
displayed was the harp that Orpheus was strumming 955
when love took him to hell;

mostrósenos Fíliris, el tañedor,
maestro d'Aquiles en citarizar,
aquel que por arte herir y domar
960 pudo a un Aquiles, tan gran domador.

121 *Profetas pone las diez Sibilas*

La compañía virgínea perfecta
vimos en alto de vidas tranquilas,
el décimo número de las Sibilas,
que cada cual pudo llamarse profeta:
965 estaba la Pérsica con la Dimeta,
y la Babilónica, gran Eritea,
y la Frigiana, llamada Albunea,
vimos estar con la Delfijineta.

122

Femonoé por orden la sesta
970 estaba, la cual en versos sutiles
tanto pregona las guerras civiles,
de quien hubo Apio la triste respuesta;
y vimos a Líbisa, virgen honesta;
estaba Vetona con el Amatea;
975 y era la décima aquella Cumea
de quien los romanos hacen hoy fiesta.

123 *Poetas*

Vimos a Homero tener en las manos
la dulce Ilíada con el Odisía;

displayed was Phillyrides the musician,
teacher of Achilles in playing the cither,
he who by artful means could strike and subdue
someone like Achilles, so a great tamer himself! 960

121 *He Turns the Ten Sibyls into Prophets*

The perfect virginal company
of tranquil lives we saw on high,
the Sibyls, ten in number;
each one could be deemed a prophet:
The Persian was there with Dimeta 965
and the Babylonian; great Erythrea,
and the Phrygian called Albunea,
we saw together with the Delphic.

122

Phemonoe, in order the sixth,
was there. She who, in difficult verses 970
reveals so much about the civil wars,
from whom Appius got the dismal answer;
we saw Libisa, an honest virgin;
Vetona was there with Amalthea;
and the tenth was that Cumaean, 975
whom the Romans today celebrate.

123 *Poets*

We saw Homer holding in his hands
the sweet *Iliad* with the *Odyssey;*

el alto Virgilio vi que lo seguía
980 Énio con otro montón de romanos:
trágicos, líricos, elegïanos,
cómicos, sátiros, con heroístas,
y los escritores de tantas conquistas
cuantas nacieron entre los humanos.

124 *Razón porque no loa los poetas de Córdoba*

985 ¡O flor de saber y de caballería!
Córdova madre, tu hijo perdona
si en los cantares que ahora pregona
no divulgar[e] tu sabiduría.
De sabios valientes loarte podría
990 que fueron espejo muy maravilloso
por ser de ti misma; seré sospechoso,
dirán que los pinto mejor que debía.

125 *Viene a los presentes*

Venimos al cerco de nuestros presentes,
donde hallamos muy pocos de tales:
995 hoy la doctrina mayor es de males
que no de virtudes acerca las gentes;
mas entre otros allí prefulgentes
vimos a uno lleno de prudencia,
del cual preguntada la mi Providencia
1000 respondió dictando los versos siguientes:

I saw that high Virgil was followed by
Ennius with another horde of Romans: 980
tragic, lyrical, elegiacal,
comic, satirical, and heroic poets,
and the writers of as many conquests
as could be made by humankind.

124 *Reason Why He Does Not Praise the Poets of Cordoba*

Oh, flower of knowledge and of chivalry! 985
Mother Cordoba, forgive your son
if in the songs he now intones,
he should fail to divulge your wisdom!
I could extol you for your valiant, wise sons,
who were a marvelous reflection 990
because they were yours; I will be suspected,
they will say I depict them better than I should.

125 *He Comes to the Presently Living*

We arrive at the circle of our contemporaries,
where we find very few such people:
The principal doctrine of today is about the sins 995
and not the virtues of people;
but, among others who shone there,
we saw one full of prudence,
about whom when asked, my Providence
answered by chanting the following verses: 1000

126

"Aquel que tú ves estar contemplando
el movimiento de tantas estrellas,
la obra, la fuerza, la orden de aquellas,
que mide los cursos de cómo y de cuándo,
1005 y hubo noticia filosofando
del Movedor y de los conmovidos,
de lumbres y rayos y son de tronidos,
y supo las causas del mundo velando,"

127

"aquel claro padre, aquel dulce fuente,
1010 aquel que en el Cástalo monte resuena,
es don Enrique, señor de Villena,
honra de España y del siglo presente.
¡O ínclito sabio, autor muy cïente!,
otra y aún otra vegada yo lloro
1015 porque Castilla perdió tal tesoro,
no conocido delante la gente."

128

"Perdió los tus libros sin ser conocidos,
y cómo en exequias te fueron ya luego
unos metidos al ávido fuego,
1020 otros sin orden no bien repartidos.
Cierto en Atenas los libros fingidos
que de Pitágoras se reprobaron,
con ceremonia mayor se quemaron,
cuando al senado le fueron leídos."

126

"He that you see busily contemplating
the movement of so many stars—
their fabric, their strength, and their order—
who measures the how and when of their courses,
and deduced through reasoning   1005
the existence of the Prime Mover and of the moved,
of the light and lightning, and the sound of thunder,
and knew the laws of the world by observation,"

127

"that well-known father, that fountain of sweetness,
he who echoes on the Castalian mountain,   1010
is Don Enrique, Lord of Villena,
honor of Spain and of present times.
Oh, outstanding sage, most erudite of writers!
I cry again and again,
because Castile lost such a treasure,   1015
unknown to the people."

128

"It lost your books without being known,
and how, as in exequy, some were immediately
cast into the ravenous fire,
others were poorly dispersed without order.   1020
I know for a fact that in Athens, the forged books
of Protagoras were condemned,
burned with great ceremony,
when they were read to the senate."

129 *Artes dañadas*

1025 Fondón de estos cercos vi ser derribados
los que escudriñaban las dañadas artes,
y la su culpa vi hecha dos partes,
de los que demuestran y de los demostrados:
magos, sortílegos mucho dañados,
1030 prestigïantes vi luego siguiente,
y los matemáticos que malamente
tientan objetos a nos devedados.

130

Los ojos dolientes al cerco bajando,
vimos la forma del mago Tyrrheo,
1035 con la de Ericto que a Sesto Pompeo
dio la respuesta, su vida fadando.
Estaba sus hijos despedazando
Medea, la inútil nigromantesa,
herida de flecha mortal de deesa,
1040 que no supo darse reparos amando.

131

Estaban las hembras Licinia y Publicia,
dando, en oprobio de los sus linajes,
a sus maridos mortales potajes
mezclados con yerbas llenas de malicia;
1045 ca, desque se pierde la gran pudicicia—
virtud necesaria de ser en la hembra—
tal furia crece, tal odio se siembra,
que han los maridos en inimicicia.

129 *Damned Arts*

At the base of these circles, I saw cast down
those who scrutinized the damned arts,
and their sin split them into two kinds:
those who teach and those who are taught:
Mages, severely punished sorcerers,
prestidigitators, I then saw,
and mathematicians who maliciously
touch upon subjects forbidden to us.

130

Lowering our doleful eyes further down the circle,
we saw the figure of the magician Tiresias
with that of Erictho, who gave Sextus Pompeus
an answer foretelling his life.
Tearing her children apart was
Medea, the worthless necromancer,
mortally wounded by a goddess's deadly arrow,
so that in love, she knew no restraint.

131

The women Licinia and Publicia were there
giving—to the shame of their descent—
mortal potions to their husbands,
mixed with herbs full of malice;
because, when great modesty is lost—
a virtue that is necessary in females—
such fury arises, such hate is engendered,
that they treated their husbands as enemies.

132

Por ende vosotros, algunos maridos,
si sois trabajados de aquella sospecha,
nunca os sienta la vuestra derecha,
ni menos entiendan que sois entendidos;
sean remedios enante venidos
que necesidades os traigan dolores:
¡A grandes cautelas, cautelas mayores,
más vale prevenir que no ser prevenidos!

133 *Comparación*

Para quien teme la furia del mar
y las tempestades recela de aquella,
el mejor reparo es no entrar en ella,
perder la codicia del buen navegar;
mas el que de dentro presume de andar
sin que padezca miseria ninguna,
a la primera señal de fortuna
debe los puertos seguros tomar.

134 *Endereza el autor la materia al rey*

A vos, poderoso gran rey, pertenece
hacer destruir los falsos saberes
por donde los hombres y malas mujeres
asayan un daño mayor que parece;
una gran gente de la que perece
muere secreto por arte malvada,
y fingen que fuese su muerte causada
de mal que a los malos pensar no fallece.

132

Therefore, you married few,
if you are troubled by the same suspicion, 1050
never let your right hand know,
nor let them suspect that you are aware;
let remedies come before
hardships cause you pain:
To great tricks, greater trickery, 1055
for it is better to prevent than to be unaware!

133 *Comparison*

For the one who fears the sea's fury
and is fearful of its tempests,
the best remedy is not to embark on it at all,
to lose all hope of good sailing; 1060
but, he who dares to venture from land
without suffering any distress,
at the earliest signs of misfortune
should take shelter in ports!

134 *The Author Directs the Subject to the King*

To you, mighty great king, belongs 1065
the duty of having all false knowledge destroyed,
by which men and wicked women
seek to cause a greater harm than at first is evident;
a great many of the people who perish
die in secret from this malevolent art, 1070
and they pretend their death was caused
by an ailment that the wicked claim not to know.

135

Magnífico príncipe, no lo demanda
la gran honestad de los vuestros siglos
sufrir que se crían mortales vestiglos
que matan la gente con poca vianda.
La mucha clemencia, la ley mucho blanda
del vuestro tiempo no cause malicias
de nuevas Medeas y nuevas Publicias:
¡Baste la otra miseria que anda!

136

Las lícitas artes con vuestra clemencia
crezcan a vueltas los rectos oficios.
Caigan los daños, fenezcan los vicios,
no disimule más mal la paciencia,
porque contemplen en vuestra presencia
los años quietos de vuestra gran vida,
el arte malvada por vos destruida,
y más restaurada la santa Prudencia.

137 *Definición de la Prudencia*

Es la Prudencia ciencia que mata
los torpes deseos de la voluntad;
sabia en lo bueno, sabida en maldad,
mas siempre las vías mejores acata.
Destroza los vicios, el mal desbarata;
a los que la quieren ella se convida;

135

Magnificent prince,
the great integrity of your times does not require
condoning the creation of deadly monsters 1075
that murder people with little reason.
Do not let the great compassion, the great leniency of
    the law
of your times cause the malice
of new Medeas and new Publicias:
Our current misery should be enough! 1080

136

Let the lawful arts with your merciful approval
grow together with the uncorrupted office holders!
Let troubles decrease, vices die,
and patience no longer turn a blind eye to further iniquities,
so that, while living, 1085
the peaceful years of your great life can witness
the destruction of the cursed arts
and the further restoration of holy Prudence!

137 *Definition of Prudence*

Prudence is a science that kills
the base desires of the will; 1090
Aware of the good, knowing of malice,
but always looking for the best courses of action.
She destroys vices, routs wickedness;
she willingly keeps company with those who desire her;

1095 da buenos fines, seyendo infinida,
y para el ingenio más neto que plata.

138 *Fenece la cuarta orden de Febo; comienza la quinta de Marte*

Ya reguardamos el cerco de Mares,
do vimos los reyes en la justa guerra
y los que quisieron morir por su tierra
1100 y los enemigos sobraron a pares.
Y vimos debajo, sufriendo pesares,
los belicosos en causas indignas,
y los que murieron en ondas marinas,
y de otros soberbios muy muchos millares.

139 *Alega con antiguos*

1105 Los fuertes Meteles allí se mostraban,
sepulcro rabioso de cartaginenses;
allí relumbraban los claros arneses
de aquellos Camilos que a Francia vastaban;
los dos compañeros acordes estaban,
1110 Petreo y Feneo, vedando con saña
la gente de César entrar en España,
según que de Lérida lo porfiaban.

140

Vimos a Craso, sangrienta el espada
de las batallas que hizo en Oriente,

she gives good endings, being infinite herself; 1095
and is more valuable than silver to the intellect.

138 *The Fourth Order of Phoebus Ends; the Fifth of Mars Begins*

We then approached the circle of Mars,
where we saw the kings in just wars,
and those who chose to die for their land
and bested their enemies. 1100
And we saw below them, suffering woes,
those who fought for vain causes,
and those who perished under the waves of the sea,
and very many thousands of arrogant others.

139 *He Offers Examples through the Ancients*

The hardy Metelluses were shown there, 1105
rabid sepulcher of the Carthaginians;
there gleamed the noble armors
of those Camilluses who ravaged France;
the two companions were in accord,
Petreius and Afranius, forcefully preventing 1110
the people of Caesar from entering Spain,
as they resisted him from Lerida.

140

We saw Crassus, his sword bloodied
by the battles he held in the Orient,

1115 aquel de quien vido la romana gente
su muerte plañida, mas nunca vengada;
y vimos la mano de Mucio quemada,
al cual la salud del fuerte guerrero
más triste lo deja que no placentero
1120 le hace la vida por él otorgada.

141 *Invocación*

¡Belígero Mares, tú sufre que cante
las guerras que vimos de nuestra Castilla,
los muertos en ellas, la mucha mancilla
que el tiempo presente nos muestra delante!
1125 ¡Dame tú, Palas, favor ministrante,
a lo que se sigue depara tal orden
que los mis metros al hecho concorden
y goce verdad de memoria durante!

142 *Como estaba el rey*

Allí sobre todos Fortuna pusiera
1130 al muy prepotente don Juan el Segundo,
d'España no sola, mas de todo el mundo,
rey se mostraba según su manera:
de armas flagrantes la su delantera,
guarnida la diestra de fúlmina espada,
1135 y él de una silla tan rica labrada
como si Dédalo bien la hiciera.

he whose death the Roman people saw 1115
mourned but never avenged;
and we saw the burned hand of Mucius,
whose strong warrior's health
left him more unconsolable, not at all pleased
by the life it granted to him. 1120

141 *Invocation*

Belligerent Mars, allow me to sing
about the wars that we witnessed in our Castile,
those who died in them, the great disgrace
that the present time forecasts for us!
You, Pallas, give me your ministering help, 1125
impose such order on what follows
that my verses correspond to the facts
and truth enjoys everlasting remembrance!

142 *How the King Was Portrayed*

There, above all, Fortune placed
the very prepotent Don Juan the Second, 1130
shown as king not only of Spain but of all the world,
according to the manner in which he was depicted:
his front clad in shining armor,
his right hand armed with a quick-striking sword,
and he on a throne so richly wrought 1135
that Daedalus could well have made it.

143

    El cual reguardaba con ojos de amores,
como haría en espejo notorio,
los títulos todos del gran abolorio
de los sus ínclitos progenitores,
los cuales tenían en ricas labores
ceñida la silla de imaginería,
tal que semblaba su masonería
iris con todas sus vivas colores.

144 *Comparación*

    Nunca el escudo que hizo Vulcano
en los etneos ardientes hornaces,
con que hacía temor a las hazes
Aquiles delante del campo troyano,
se halla tuviese pintadas de mano
ni menos esculpas entretalladuras
de obras mayores en tales figuras
como en la silla yo vi que desplano.

145 *Pinturas de la silla*

    Allí vi pintados por orden los hechos
de los Alfonsos, con todos sus mandos,
y lo que ganaron los reyes Fernandos,
haciendo más largos sus reinos estrechos;
allí la justicia, los rectos derechos,
la mucha prudencia de nuestros Enriques,
porque los tales tú, Fama, publiques,
y hagas en otros semblantes provechos.

143

The said king was looking with fondness,
as one would do in any goodly mirror,
at all the titles of the great pedigree
of his exceptional progenitors,
which in rich works of imagery
profusely ornamented the throne,
so much so, that its fashioning resembled
a rainbow in its vivid gamut of colors.

144 *Comparison*

Never was the equal of the shield made by Vulcan
in the fiery forges of Etna,
with which Achilles instilled fear in the troops
before the battlefield of Troy,
found to have been painted by hand,
or even sculpted in relief
with major deeds made up of such images,
until the throne that I saw and describe now.

145 *The Throne's Paintings*

There I saw painted in sequence the deeds
of the Alfonsos, with all the forces under their command,
and what the kings named Fernando won,
expanding the confines of their small kingdoms;
there, the justice, the valid rights,
the boundless prudence of our Enriques,
so that you, Fame, can make them known far and wide,
and bestow on others similar benefits.

146

Escultas Las Navas están de Tolosa,
triunfo de grande misterio divino,
con la morisma que de África vino
pidiendo por armas la muerte sañosa;
1165 están por memoria también gloriosa
pintadas en uno las dos Algeciras;
están por espada domadas las iras
de Almohacén, que nos fue mayor cosa.

147 *Dijo de los reyes pasados; ahora dice del rey presente*

Crecían los títulos frescos a vueltas
1170 de aqueste rey nuestro muy esclarecido,
los cuales habrían allende crecido
si no recrecieran algunas revueltas,
las cuales, por paces eternas disueltas
presto nos vengan a puerto tranquilo,
1175 por que Castilla mantenga en estilo
toga y oliva, no armas con peltas.

148 *De la Vega de Granada*

Con dos cuarentenas y más de millares
le vimos de gentes armadas apunto,
sin otro más pueblo inerme allí junto,
1180 entrar por la vega talando olivares,
tomando castillos, ganando lugares,
haciendo por miedo de tanta mesnada

146

Carved is Las Navas de Tolosa,
a triumph of great divine mystery
against the Moorish tide that came from Africa
seeking their terrible death by arms;
also for the sake of glorious memory   1165
the two Algeciras are painted as one;
tamed by the sword are the ires
of Abu al-Hasan, who gave us such sorrow.

147 *He Talked about the Past Kings; He Now Talks about the Present King*

Growing by the moment were the new-won titles
of this, our very illustrious king,   1170
which would have further increased,
were it not for the rekindling of some rebellions
which, by eternal peace resolved,
should quickly bringing us to a haven of calm,
in which Castile can once again dress in   1175
toga and olive wreath and not weapons with small shields.

148 *Of the Vega de Granada*

With twice forty and more thousands of
armed soldiers we saw him ready—
without counting other unarmed people assembled there—
to enter by the orchard, cutting down olive groves,   1180
taking castles, conquering towns,
making all of the land of Granada tremble

con toda su tierra temblar a Granada,
temblar las arenas fondón de los mares.

149

1185 Mucha morisma vi descabezada
que, más que reclusa detrás de su muro
ni que gozosa de tiempo seguro,
quiso la muerte por saña d'espada;
y mucha más otra por piezas tajada,
1190 quiere su muerte tomarla más tarde:
huyendo no huye la muerte cobarde,
que más a los viles es siempre llegada.

150 *Comparación*

Como en Sicilia resuena Tifeo,
o las herrerías de los milaneses,
1195 o como guardaban los sus entremeses
las sacerdotisas del templo lieo,
tal vi la vuelta d'aqueste torneo;
en tantas de voces prorrumpe la gente
que no entendía sino solamente
1200 el nombre del hijo del buen Zebedeo.

151

Y vimos la sombra d'aquella higuera
donde a deshoras se vido criado
de muertos en piezas un nuevo collado,
tan grande que sobra razón su manera;
1205 y como en arena do momia se espera,

in fear of the immense forces,
tremble down to the sand at the bottom of the sea.

149

I saw many Moors beheaded 1185
who, rather than take shelter behind its walls
or be joyous of a measure of safety,
sought death by the wrath of the sword;
and many others cut into pieces
had wanted to delay their death: 1190
A coward does not escape death by fleeing
for it always comes to the scum!

150 *Comparison*

Like Typhoeus rumbles in Sicily,
or the forges of the Milanese,
or how rites were celebrated by 1195
the priestesses of Lyaeus's temple,
I interpreted the back-and-forth of this tourney:
The people roared out so many shouts,
that I could hear only one,
the name of the son of good Zebediah. 1200

151

And we saw the shadow of that fig tree
where all of a sudden one witnessed a new hill
created from parts of the dead,
so large in size that words fail to describe it;
and, as in sands where one expects to find mummies, 1205

súbito viento levanta gran cumbre,
así del otero de tal muchedumbre
se espanta quien antes ninguno no viera.

152 *Recomienda la guerra con los moros*

¡O virtuosa, magnífica guerra!
1210 En ti las querellas volverse debían,
en ti do los nuestros muriendo vivían
por gloria en los cielos y fama en la tierra,
en ti do la lanza cruel nunca yerra
ni teme la sangre verter de parientes:
1215 ¡revoca concordes a ti nuestras gentes
de tales cuestiones y tanta desferra!

153

No convenía por obra tan luenga
hacer esta guerra, mas ser ella hecha,
(aunque quien viene a la vía derecha
1220 no viene tarde, por tarde que venga).
Pues no se dilate ya más ni detenga,
mas hayan envidia de nuestra victoria
los reinos vecinos, y no tomen gloria
de nuestra discordia mayor que convenga.

154 *Real de Ariza*

1225 Otros entalles no tanto bruñidos
con epitafios de títulos ciertos
vi cómo eran deletos y muertos,
unos testados y otros raídos.

a gale suddenly lifts a great mountain,
so, at the sight of these never-before-seen corpses,
anyone would be horrified.

152 *He Recommends War with the Moors*

Oh virtuous, magnificent war!
Quarrels should turn into you! 1210
Into you, where our dead lived after death
in heavenly glory and earthly fame!
Into you, where the cruel lance never fails to hit its target
nor fears to shed the blood of relations!
Turn our people toward you and away 1215
from such issues and so many disagreements!

153

It was inconvenient to wage this war,
because of its difficulty, but let it be completed.
(Even though the person who comes to the rightful path
does not come late, however late he comes). 1220
Therefore, it should no longer be delayed or halted,
but let our victory cause envy in
the neighboring kingdoms, and let them not profit
from our discord more than is needful.

154 *Real de Ariza*

I saw other carvings, not so beautifully burnished 1225
with inscriptions of clear titles,
how they were deleted and rubbed out,
some in poor shape and others scraped off.

>   En los que pudieron por mí ser leídos
> 1230 las guerras que hubo Aragón hallarán,
>   real de Ariza y Belamazán,
>   do no vencedores hallé ni vencidos.

155 *Del Real de Medina del Campo*

>   Vi más la furia civil de Medina,
>   y vi los sus muros no bien horadados,
> 1235 vi despojadores y vi despojados
>   hechos acordes en paz muy aína;
>   vi que a su rey cada cual inclina
>   yelmo, cabeza, con el estandarte,
>   y vi dos extremos hechos una parte,
> 1240 temiendo la justa real disciplina.

156 *Comparación*

>   Bien como cuando respondió en el huerto
>   el Sumo Maestro de nuestras mercedes
>   aquel mote santo de "¿A quién queredes?"
>   a hijos de los que libró del desierto,
> 1245 y como aquel pueblo cayó casi muerto,
>   así en Medina, siguiendo tal ley,
>   vista la cara de nuestro gran rey,
>   le fue todo llano y allí descubierto.

157 *Otra comparación*

>   Según que se hacen el viso más fiero
> 1250 los que entran en juego llamado palestra,

In those that could be read by me
you will find the wars with Aragon, 1230
Real de Ariza, and Velamazán,
where I found no winners or losers.

155 *Of the Real of Medina del Campo*

I also saw the civil fury of Medina,
and I saw its walls not very well breached;
I saw despoilers and despoiled, 1235
very soon united in peace;
I saw each faction bow to its king
helmet, head, and pennant,
and I saw two extremes become one
for fear of the just royal authority. 1240

156 *Comparison*

As when the Supreme Teacher of our mercies
answered in the garden
with those holy words, "Whom do you seek?"
to the children of those he freed from the desert,
and when that nation fell almost dead, 1245
so it happened in Medina, following a similar precedent—
once the face of our great king appeared,
everything was made clear and disclosed to him.

157 *Another Comparison*

Just like the men who fight in an arena
make their face look more ferocious, 1250

en cuanto son dentro su saña se muestra,
mas fuera se ríen como de primero,
así hacen muchos en lo postrimero:
los ínclitos reyes y grandes señores
1255 vuelven en gozo sus muchos rigores,
y nunca el enojo les es duradero.

158

Mirad a los fines, vosotros, por ende,
si sois de diversas cuestiones secuaces;
no os engañen los vultos minaces,
1260 ca uno a las veces por otro se entiende.
Yerra quien habla do se reprehende;
en dichos y hechos vivid mesurados,
ca vuelven acordes los desacordados
y queda ofendido quien antes ofende.

159 *La muerte del conde de Niebla*

1265 Bajé más mis ojos, mirando las gentes
que vi sublimadas del trono mavorcio,
dignas del mucho famoso consorcio
donde hallamos los muy prepotentes.
Yo, que mirábalos tan inocentes
1270 en un caballero tardanza más hiz,
del cual preguntada por mí la ductriz
respondió dictando los metros siguientes:

to show their savagery as soon as they are inside,
but once outside, they laugh as before;
many behave the same way at the end:
Prominent kings and great lords
turn their many rigors to joy
and their anger never lasts long.

158

For this reason, you should look at the goals,
if you are followers of different factions;
do not be fooled by threatening faces,
because one thing can be confused with another.
He who speaks where he could be rebuked errs;
in deeds and words always be measured,
for those in disagreement with each other will reach an accord,
and the one who caused the offense ends up offended.

159 *The Death of the Count of Niebla*

I lowered my eyes some more, looking at the people
that I saw sublimated on Mars's throne,
worthy of that very famous gathering
where we find the very prepotent.
I, who saw them so blameless,
lingered longer on a knight,
about whom, when I asked her, my guide
responded by singing the following verses:

160

"Aquel que en la barca parece asentado,
vestido de engaño de las bravas ondas,
en aguas crueles ya más que no hondas
con una gran gente en el mar anegado,
es el valiente, no bien fortunado,
muy virtuoso, perínclito conde
de Niebla, que todos sabéis bien adonde
dió fin, el día del curso fadado."

161

"E los que lo cercan por alderredor,
puesto que fuesen magníficos hombres,
los títulos todos de todos sus nombres,
el nombre los cubre de aquel su señor,
ca todos los hechos que son de valor
para mostrarse por sí cada uno,
cuando se juntan y van de consuno,
pierden su nombre delante el mayor."

162 *Comparación*

"Arlanza, Pisuerga y aún Carrión
gozan de nombres de ríos, empero,
desque juntados, llamámoslos Duero:
hacemos de muchos una relación.
Oye, por ende, pues, la perdición
de sólo el buen conde sobre Gibraltar;

160

"He who appears sitting on a skiff,
deceptively dressed in roiling waves—
in cruel rather than deep waters— 1275
drowned in the sea with a great many people.
He is the brave, but unfortunate,
very virtuous prominent Count
of Niebla, of whom you all well know where
he came to an end, on that fated day." 1280

161

"And those who encircle him,
even though they were magnificent men,
all the labels attached to all of their names
are covered by that of their lord,
because all deeds that are worthy 1285
of being celebrated by themselves,
when joined and appearing as one,
lose their uniqueness before one that is greater."

162 *Comparison*

"Arlanza, Pisuerga, and even Carrion
possess the names of rivers; however, 1290
after joining, we call them Duero:
We make one of many.
Well, listen, therefore, to the loss
of the good count in the assault on Gibraltar;

1295 su muerte, llorada de digno llorar,
provoque tus ojos a lamentación."

163

"En la su triste fadada partida
por muchas señales que los marineros
han por auspicios y malos agüeros
1300 fueron mostradas negar su venida,
las cuales veyendo, con voz dolorida,
el cauto maestro de toda su flota
al conde amonesta del mal que denota,
por que la vía fuese resistida."

164 *Señales agoreras que denuncian tempestad según los agüeros*

1305 "Ca he visto," dice, "señor, nuevos yerros
la noche pasada hacer las planetas:
con crines extendidas arder las cometas,
y dar nueva lumbre las armas y hierros,
gritar sin herida los canes y perros,
1310 triste presagio hacer de peleas
las aves nocturnas y las funéreas
por los collados, alturas y cerros."

165 *Dijo de los agüeros de las aves, dice de la nave*

"Vi que las gúmenas gruesas quebraban
cuando las áncoras quise levantar,

his death, properly bewailed,   1295
should bring tears to your eyes."

163

"At his ill-fated departure
many signs that sailors believe
to be auguries and bad omens
were shown to oppose his going;   1300
on seeing these, with a glum voice,
the cautious quartermaster of all his fleet
admonishes the count about the adversities he sees
that indicate the expedition should be abandoned."

164 *Warning Signs That Portend a Tempest According to Auguries*

"For I have seen," he says, "my lord, new baleful signs   1305
made last night by the planets:
comets that burn with extended manes,
armor and iron implements that cast a strange glow,
mastiffs and dogs that howl without being wounded,
sad omen of battles foreshadowed by   1310
nocturnal and funereal birds
on the hills, heights, and mountains."

165 *He Spoke of the Omens of Birds, and He Now Speaks about the Ship*

"I saw that the heavy cables were splitting
when I tried to raise the anchors;

1315 vi las entenas por medio quebrar,
aunque los cárbasos no desplegaban,
los másteles fuertes en calma temblaban,
los flacos trinquetes con la su mesana
vi levantarse de no buena gana
1320 cuando los vientos se nos convidaban."

166 *Alega la historia a su propósito*

"En la partida del resto troyano
de aquella Cartago del bírseo muro,
el voto prudente del buen Palinuro
toda la flota loó de más sano;
1325 tanto que quiso el rey muy humano,
cuando lo vido, pasado Acheronte
con Leucaspis acerca Oronte,
en el Averno tocarle la mano."

167

"Ya pues si debe en este gran lago
1330 guiarse la flota por dicho del saje,
vos dejaredes aqueste viaje
hasta ver día no tan aciago.
Las deidades llevar por halago
debedes, veyendo señal de tal plaga:
1335 ¡no dedes causa a Gibraltar que haga
en sangre de reyes dos veces estrago!"

I saw the lateen yards split in half,
even though their sails were unfurled,
mainmasts trembling in calm weather;
and smaller foremasts with their mizzen sails
I saw halfheartedly filled
when winds favored us."

166 *He Connects the Story to His Purpose*

"When the remnants of the Trojans departed
from that Carthage of the Birsean wall,
good Palinurus's prudent vote was hailed
as the most judicious by all the fleet;
so much so, that the very human king wanted,
when he crossed the Acheron
with Leucaspis near Orontes,
to touch his hand in Avernus."

167

"Therefore, if in this great lake
the fleet were to be guided by the words of a sage,
you should abandon this journey
until you witness a day not so baneful.
You should be mindful of pleasing the gods
upon seeing signs of such perils:
Do not give Gibraltar a chance to wreak
havoc twice on the blood of kings!"

168

      El conde, que nunca de las abusiones
creyera, ni menos de tales señales,
dijo: "No apruebo por muy naturales,
1340 maestro, ninguna d'aquestas razones;
las que me dices ni bien perfecciones
ni veros pronósticos son de verdad,
ni los indicios de la tempestad
no veemos fuera de sus opiniones."

169 *Señales de tempestad según los naturales*

1345 "Aun si yo viera la menstrua luna
con cuernos oscuros mostrarse fuscada,
muy rubicunda o muy colorada,
creyera que vientos nos diera Fortuna;
si Febo, dejada la delia cuna,
1350 ígneo viéramos o turbulento,
temiera yo lluvia con fuerza de viento:
en otra manera no sé qué repuna."

170

      "Ni veo tampoco que vientos delgados
muevan los ramos de nuestra montaña,
1355 ni hieren las ondas con su nueva saña
la playa con golpes más demasiados;
ni veo delfines de fuera mostrados,
ni los merinos volar a lo seco,
ni los caístros hacer nuevo trueco,
1360 dejar las lagunas por ir a los prados."

168

The count, who never believed
in superstitions, much less omens,
said: "I do not accept as very natural,
master, any of these signs; 1340
those you mention are not correct,
nor are they real portents in truth,
nor any signs of the tempest
we see beyond your own estimations."

169 *Traces of a Tempest according to the Natural Signs*

"Even if I were to see the waning moon 1345
show itself shrouded with darkened horns,
very ruddy or very red,
I would think that we were favored with wind by Fortune;
if we were to see Phoebus rise from his Delian cradle,
ablaze or turbulent, 1350
I would fear rain with strong gusts of wind:
I do not know of any other interpretation."

170

"Neither do I see that gentle breezes
sway the branches of our forests,
nor waves renew their attack 1355
on the beach with excessive force,
nor dolphins jump out of the sea,
nor cormorants fly to dry land,
nor swans make an unusual trade,
leaving ponds in favor of fields." 1360

171

"Ni baten las alas ya los alciones,
ni tientan jugando de se rociar,
los cuales amansan la furia del mar
con sus cantares y lánguidos sones,
1365 y dan a sus hijos contrarias sazones,
nido en invierno con grande pruina,
do puestos acerca la costa marina
en un semilunio les dan perfecciones."

172

"'Ni la corneja no anda señera
1370 por el arena seca paseando,
con su cabeza su cuerpo bañando
por ocupar el agua venidera;
ni vuela la garza por alta manera,
ni sale la fúlica de la marina
1375 contra los prados, ni va nin declina
como en los tiempos adversos hiciera."

173 *Concluye el conde, aconsejando la partida*

"Despliega las velas, pues, ¿ya qué tardamos?
y los de los bancos levanten los remos,
a vueltas del viento mejor que perdemos,
1380 no los agüeros, los hechos sigamos,
pues una empresa tan santa llevamos
que más no podría ser otra ninguna,
presuma de vos y de mí la Fortuna,
no que nos fuerza, mas que la forzamos."

171

"Nor do halcyons beat their wings any longer,
nor playfully seek to spray themselves;
they pacify the fury of the sea
with their songs and languid sounds,
and give their children in the opposite season　　　1365
a nest in frost-laden winter,
where, placed near the seacoast,
in fourteen days they reach perfection."

172

"Nor does the crow make its way alone,
promenading through the dry sand,　　　1370
bathing its body with bobbing head,
taking on the approaching waters;
nor does the heron fly very high,
nor does the coot abandon the seashore
for the fields; it does not leave or depart　　　1375
as it might have done in hazardous times."

173 *The Count Concludes, Advising the Departure*

"Unfurl the sails, therefore—why do we delay any longer?
And those seated on the benches man the oars
to replace the better winds that are lost to us;
let us not be ruled by omens but deeds,　　　1380
since we are called to a holier venture
than any other could be.
Let Fortune be proud of you and of me,
not because she forces us, but because we force her!"

174

1385 Tales palabras el conde decía
que obedecieron el su mandamiento
y dieron las velas infladas del viento,
no padeciendo tardanza la vía.
Según la Fortuna lo ya disponía,
1390 llegaron acerca de la fuerte villa
el conde con toda la rica cuadrilla,
y por el agua su flota seguía.

175

Con la bandera del conde tendida
ya por la tierra su hijo viniera
1395 con mucha más gente qu'el padre le diera,
bien a caballo y a punto guarnida,
por que a la hora que fuese la grida,
súbitamente, en el mismo deslate,
por ciertos lugares hubiese combate
1400 la villa que estaba desapercebida.

176

El conde y los suyos tomaron la tierra
que era entre el agua y el bordo del muro,
lugar con menguante seco y seguro,
mas con la creciente del todo se cierra;
1405 quien llega más tarde presume que yerra,
la empavesada ya junta sus alas,

174

Such forceful remarks were spoken by the count 1385
that those under his command obeyed
and unfurled the sails to the swelling wind,
not suffering any delay in undertaking the course.
According to what Fortune had already decreed,
the count with all of the excellent squad 1390
neared the fortified town,
and his fleet remained on the water.

175

When the count's flag was already displayed,
his son came by land
with many more men that his father had provided, 1395
well mounted on horses and rightly appareled,
so that, whenever the call to arms might be sounded,
suddenly, at the very same time,
fights would break out in predetermined places
in the still-unsuspecting town. 1400

176

The count and his men landed on a beachhead
between the sea and the edge of the city wall,
a place that was dry and secure at low tide,
but at high tide was completely submerged—
he who reaches it later, realizes his error; 1405
the shield wall was bringing up its protective wings,

levantan los troceos, crecen las escalas,
crecen las artes mañosas de guerra.

177

Los moros, sintiendo crecer los engaños,
veyéndose todos cercados por artes
y combatidos por tantas de partes,
allí socorrieron do iban más daños,
y con necesarios dolores extraños
resisten con saña las fuerzas ajenas;
botan los cantos desde las almenas,
y lanzan los otros que no son tamaños.

178 *Comparación*

Bien como médico mucho famoso
que tiene el estilo por manos seguido,
en cuerpo de golpes diversos herido
luego socorre a lo más peligroso,
así aquel pueblo maldito, sañoso,
sintiendo más daños de parte del conde,
a grandes cuadrillas juntado, responde
allí do el peligro más era dañoso.

179

Allí disparaban lombardas y truenos,
y los trabucos tiraban ya luego

stones and darts together with flaming arrows,
so that they mowed down our forces.
Some Moors with the reputation of being skilled
shakily throw their spears; 1430
they overshot the frontlines, palisades, and perimeters,
doubling their efforts, beset by strange fears.

180

While they were dying and while they were killing,
the waves were increasing apace on the side of the ocean,
and the haughty and deep seas covered 1435
the fields that lay before the walls,
so much that, if those who were fighting there
were to attempt to retreat to the ships,
the increasing tide would already have prevented them
from reaching the galleys they had left on the sea. 1440

181

With a dangerous and vain effort,
a boat was able to rescue its count,
which would have securely carried him away,
if at that moment fate had not frowned on him—
bear with me, if you want me to speak of it. 1445
When those left behind saw him leave,
from the many who could not go with him,
you could imagine there arose a painful cry!

182 *Palabras de los del conde*

Entrando tras él por el agua, decían:
"Magnánimo conde, ¿y cómo nos dejas?
nuestras finales y últimas quejas
en tu presencia favor nos serían;
las aguas la vida nos ya desafían:
si tú no nos puedes prestar el vivir,
danos linaje mejor de morir;
daremos las manos a más que debían,"

183

"y volveremos a ser sometidos
a aquellos adarves, aunque no debamos,
por que los tuyos muriendo podamos
ser dichos muertos, mas nunca vencidos;
sólo podremos ser redargüidos
de temeraria, inmensa osadía,
mas tal infamia mejor nos sería
que no en las aguas morir sepelidos."

184 *De cómo el conde, volviendo por los que dejaba, se anegó con ellos*

Hicieron las voces al conde a desora
volver la su barca contra las saetas
y contra las armas de los mahometas,
ca fue de temor piedad vencedora.
Había Fortuna dispuesto la hora,

182 *Words of the Count's Men*

Wading in the water behind him, they said:
"Magnanimous count, how can you leave without us?   1450
Our last and final complaints
should be graced by your presence;
our lives are already threatened by water,
if you cannot grant us life,
you should at least give us a better way of dying;   1455
we will then sell our lives dearly,"

183

"and we would once more be under
those ramparts—even though we should not—
so that your vassals in dying can
be deemed dead, but never defeated;   1460
we could only be blamed
for audacious, immense resolve,
but such notoriety would better befit us
than dying entombed in these waters."

184 *Of How the Count, Returning for Those Left Behind, Drowned with Them*

Their voices made the count   1465
turn his boat around quickly against the hail of arrows
and against the weapons of the Mohammedans,
for pity vanquished fear.
Fortune had decreed the hour

1470 y como los suyos comienzan a entrar,
la barca con todos se hubo anegar,
de peso tamaño no sostenedora.

185 *La manera que tienen los que se ahogan en
la agonía que hacen*

Los míseros cuerpos ya no respiraban,
mas so las aguas andaban ocultos,
1475 dando y trayendo mortales singultos
de aguas, la hora que más anelaban;
las vidas de todos así litigaban
que aguas entraban do almas salían;
la pérfida entrada las aguas querían,
1480 la dura salida las almas negaban.

186 *Recomienda y alaba el autor la muerte
del conde*

¡O piedad fuera de medida!
¡O ínclito conde, quisiste tan fuerte
tomar con los tuyos enantes la muerte
que no con tu hijo gozar de la vida!
1485 Si fe a mis versos es atribuida,
siempre la tu fama, siempre la tu gloria
darán a los siglos eterna memoria;
será muchas veces tu muerte plañida.

and, as his men started to climb aboard, 1470
the boat with all of them had to founder,
being unable to sustain such weight.

185 *The Way Those Who Drown Look in Their Agony*

The miserable bodies were no longer breathing,
but went unseen beneath the waves,
gasping in and gasping out mortal gulps 1475
of water at the time they craved more;
the lives of all struggled this way,
for waters entered where souls departed;
the waters sought the treacherous ingress,
the souls refused the harsh exit. 1480

186 *The Author Recommends and Praises the Death of the Count*

Oh measureless piety!
Oh illustrious count, you wanted so deeply
to share death with your men,
rather than enjoy life with your son!
If my verses are held to be true, 1485
forever your fame, forever your glory
will be consigned to time's eternal memory;
your death will be mourned again and again.

187 *Fenece la historia del conde y prosigue adelante*

    Después que yo vi que mi guiadora
1490 había ya dado su fin a la historia,
yo le suplico me haga notoria
la vida de otros que allí son ahora;
la cual, mis plegarias oídas, implora
el divino nombre con más sumo grado,
1495 el cual humilmente por ella invocado,
respóndeme breve como sabidora:

188 *La muerte del conde de Mayorga*

"Las claras virtudes, los hechos extremos,
la viva victoria que Mares otorga
al conde bendito don Juan de Mayorga,
1500 razón no lo sufre que nos lo callemos.
Alce Fortuna sus pérfidos remos,
la Fama sus alas doradas levante,
porque la vida de aqueste se cante
jamás por el modo que nos cantaremos."

189

1505 "Primero su vida muy leda cantamos,
su mano feroz, potente, famosa;
segundo la su juventud virtuosa;
tercero su muerte tan presta lloramos;
mas con los que tanto sus hechos amamos
1510 usó de clemencia la divina mano:
dejónos en prendas a un tal hermano
con cuya vida su muerte olvidamos."

187 *The Story of the Count Ends and He Proceeds Further*

Once I've seen that my guide
has already concluded her story, 1490
I plead with her to tell me plainly
about the lives of others presently there;
my prayers heard, she implores
the divine name with the greatest respect,
which, humbly invoked by her, 1495
answers me in a few sage words:

188 *The Death of the Count of Mayorga*

"The excellent virtues, the extreme deeds,
the most excellent victory that Mars bestows
on the blessed Count Don Juan de Mayorga,
reason does not want us to silence. 1500
Let Fortune raise her perfidious oars,
Fame lift up her golden wings,
so that the life of this one may be sung
always in the manner that we will sing it."

189

"First, we will sing about his very carefree life, 1505
his fierce hand, potent, famous;
second, about his virtuous youth;
third, we will mourn his too-sudden death;
but, with those who loved his deeds so much,
the divine hand was merciful: 1510
she left us as a pledge such a brother
with whose life we are forgetful of his death."

190 *La muerte del adelantado Diego de Ribera, que murió sobre Alora*

"Aquel que tú ves con la saetada,
que nunca más hace mudanza del gesto,
1515 mas por virtud de morir tan honesto
deja su sangre tan bien derramada
sobre la villa no poco cantada,
el adelantado Diego de Ribera
es, el que hizo la vuestra frontera
1520 tender las sus faldas más contra Granada."

191 *Compáralo a Esceva, otro valiente que murió así*

"Dentro en Ematía más Esceva no pudo
mostrarse animoso, allí donde quiso
sacarse aquel hasta de medio del viso
quel' diera Gortyn con hierro tan crudo;
1525 ni tanto constante aquel no estudo
donde aquel triste de Aulo, creyendo
que la virtud le faltase muriendo,
más lo hallaba feroce, sañudo."

192

"Tú adelantaste virtud con estado,
1530 muriendo muy firme por la santa ley;
tú adelantaste los reinos al rey,

190 *The Death of the Adelantado Diego de Rivera, Who Died in the Siege of Alora*

"He whom you see pierced by an arrow,
who never again will change his expression,
but, by virtue of his honest death, 1515
leaves his blood so well spilled
over the town not little celebrated in song:
he is the *adelantado* Diego de Rivera,
the one who made your border
spread its skirts more toward Granada." 1520

191 *She Compares Him to Scaeva, Another Courageous Man Who Died in This Manner*

"In Emathia, Scaeva could not
show himself to be braver, there where he wanted
to remove that stake from the middle of his face,
that the very cruel Gortinian iron gave to him;
nor was he as steady 1525
in that place where that sad Aulus, believing
that death had robbed him of manly virtue,
still found him ferocious, enraged."

192

"You advanced virtue with status,
dying very firmly for the holy Commandments; 1530
you advanced the king's dominions

seyéndole firme, leal y criado;
tú adelantaste tu fama, finado,
en justa batalla muriendo como hombre;
1535 pues quien de tal guisa adelanta su nombre,
¡ved si debía ser adelantado!"

193 *La muerte de Rodrigo de Perea, adelantado de Cazorla, comparándolo a Curio*

"El que de días parece mayor,
por ira tan justa su gesto sañudo,
que preso y herido demuestra que pudo
1540 enantes matarlo pesar que dolor,
aquel que tú ves con tan gran honor
el adelantado es aquel de Perea,
que hubo victoria de tanta pelea
que bien lo podemos llamar vencedor."

194 *Comparación que hace d'este a Curio, que murió de pesar cerca de Cartago*

1545 "Así como Curio perdió la codicia
de toda su vida, veyendo el estrago
cerca los rotos muros de Cartago
que hizo en su gente Juba con malicia,
porque con falso color de justicia
1550 Curio, quiriendo a Juba gran mal,
quisiera tirarle la silla real
cuando mandaba la ley tribunicia."

as his firm, loyal retainer;
you advanced your fame in dying,
perishing in just war like a man!
Therefore, whoever advances his fame in such manner, 1535
see whether he ought to be made an *adelantado!*"

193 *The Death of Rodrigo de Perea, Adelantado of Cazorla, Comparing Him to Curio*

"He who appears to be older in days,
his brow furrowed by such righteous anger,
shows that, when taken prisoner and wounded,
sorrow could kill him before pain! 1540
That one that you see with such great honor,
he is the *adelantado* of Perea,
who won victory over so many battles
that rightly we can call him victorious."

194 *A Comparison She Makes between This Man and Curio, Who Died of Grief near Carthage*

"Just as Curio completely lost his lust 1545
for life, upon seeing the devastation
around the ruined walls of Carthage
that Juba maliciously wrought on his people,
since it was under a false pretense of justice,
Curio, wishing great ills on Juba, 1550
wished to drive him out of the royal seat,
according to the dictates of the tribunal law."

195

 "Pues bien como Curio no pudo sufrir
el ánima contra la falsa fortuna,
1555 así él de Perea, veyendo la puna,
muertos los suyos, no quiso vivir;
antes comienza, muriendo, a decir:
'Sobro a quien hizo sobrar mi virtud;
pues la vergoñosa no es buena salud,
1560 purgue la falta el honesto morir.'"

196 *La muerte de Pedro de Narbáez comparándolo a Palante, y a su padre Rodrigo a Evandro*

 "El otro mancebo de sangre hirviente,
que muestra su cuerpo sin forma ninguna,
par en el ánimo, no en la fortuna,
con las virtudes del padre valiente,
1565 Narbáez aquel es, el cual agriamente
muriendo, deprende vengar la su muerte,
la cual, infortunio de no buena suerte,
saltea con manos de pagana gente."

197

 "Según lo que hizo su padre Rodrigo,
1570 bien lo podemos hacer semejante,
Evandro a su padre, su hijo a Palante,
al cual el comienzo fue fin enemigo;
mas es otorgada, sin esto que digo,

195

"Just as Curio could not endure
the suffering of his spirit against false fortune,
so he of Perea, seeing the battle,   1555
his men already dead, no longer wished to live;
but rather, before dying, begins to say:
'I rise above him who overcame my virtue,
for there is no good health in a shameful life.
Let an honest death purge this fault!'"   1560

196 *The Death of Pedro de Narbáez, Comparing Him to Pallas, and His Father Rodrigo to Evander*

"The other young man of seething blood,
who shows his body without any form,
is equal in valor, not in fortune,
to the virtues of his brave father.
Narbáez is that one who, bitterly   1565
dying, undertakes to avenge his death,
which, by ill luck's misfortune,
is ambushed by the hands of pagan people."

197

"We can certainly do something similar
to what was done by his father Rodrigo—   1570
as with Evander for his father, for his son as with Pallas.
for whom the beginning led to a disastrous end;
however, the crown of heaven and earth

a él la corona del cielo y la tierra
1575 que ganan los tales en la santa guerra,
do fin semejante les es más amigo."

198 *La muerte de Juan de Merlo*

Allí, Johan de Merlo, te vi con dolor;
menor vi tu fin que no vi tu medio,
mayor vi tu daño que no el remedio
1580 que dio la tu muerte al tu matador.
¡O porfioso, pestífero error!
¡O Hados crueles, soberbios, rabiosos,
que siempre robades los más virtuosos,
y perdonades la gente peor!

199 *Comienza las armas que hizo en Bala y en Ras*

1585 Bien te creemos que tú no pensaste
semejante finida de todo tu bien,
cuando al Enrique ya de Remestén
por armas y trances en Bala sobraste;
pues no menos hiciste cuando te hallaste
1590 en Ras con aquel señor de Charní,
donde con tantos honores así
tu rey y tus reinos y manos honraste.

200

Ya de más gentes diversas que viera
tanto hallaba sus letras de fuertes

is granted to him, needless to say,
that such men win in holy war, 1575
where a similar end can be kinder to them."

198 *The Death of Juan de Merlo*

There, Juan de Merlo, I saw you in pain;
I saw your end as lesser than I saw your life's middle,
I saw your injury greater than the relief
that your death gave to your killer. 1580
Oh obstinate, pestiferous error!
Oh cruel Fates, proud, raging,
you always steal from the most virtuous
and pardon worse people!

199 *Here Begin His Battles in Basel and Arras*

We can well believe that you did not anticipate 1585
a similar end to all your goodness,
when in Basel you straight away surpassed
Henry of Ramstein in arms and combat;
you did no less later when you found yourself
in Arras with that Lord of Charny, 1590
where with so many honors
you honored your king and your kingdoms and people.

200

Now, upon beholding many diverse people,
I found their emblems so valiant to see,

1595 que hizo que me diese sus nombres y suertes
puestos por historia la mi compañera;
la cual, inclinada como placentera
a las plegarias del mi simple voto,
con harmonía de estilo devoto
1600 respondió cantando por esta manera:

201 *La muerte de Lorenzo d'Avalos*

"Aquel que tú ves al cerco tornado,
que quiere subir y se halla en el aire,
mostrando su rostro robado donaire
por dos deshonestas heridas llagado,
1605 aquel es el d'Avalos mal fortunado,
aquel es el limpio mancebo Lorenzo,
que hizo en un día su fin y comienzo;
aquel es el que era de todos amado";

202

"el mucho querido del señor infante,
1610 que siempre le fuera señor como padre;
el mucho llorado de la triste madre,
que muerto ver pudo tal hijo delante.
¡O dura Fortuna, cruel tribulante!
Por ti se le pierden al mundo dos cosas:
1615 la vida, y las lágrimas tan piadosas
que ponen dolores de espada tajante."

that it made my companion include 1595
their names and fortunes in this story.
She, inclined to be benevolent
to the pleadings of my simple request,
with the harmony of a devout style,
replied, singing in this manner: 1600

201 *The Death of Lorenzo de Avalos*

"He whom you see on returning to the circle,
who wants to climb and finds himself in the air,
showing his face robbed of poise,
injured by two dishonest wounds,
he is the misfortunate Dávalos, 1605
he is the noble young Lorenzo,
who in one day made his end and beginning;
he is the one who was loved by all,"

202

"the one very beloved by the lord prince,
who always acted as a fatherly lord to him, 1610
the one greatly mourned by his sad mother,
who was able to see such a son dead before her.
Oh cruel Fortune, pitiless cause of affliction!
Because of you the world loses two things:
life and the very pious tears 1615
caused by the agonies of a cutting sword."

203 *Las endechas que hace su madre por él*

"Bien se mostraba ser madre en el duelo
que hizo la triste, después ya que vido
el cuerpo en las andas sangriento tendido
1620 de aquel que criara con tanto recelo:
ofende con dichos crueles al cielo
con nuevos dolores su flaca salud,
y tantas angustias roban su virtud
que cae por fuerza la triste por suelo,"

204

1625 "y rasga con uñas crueles su cara,
y hiere sus pechos con mesura poca;
besando a su hijo la su fría boca,
maldice las manos de quien lo matara,
maldice la guerra do se comenzara,
1630 busca con ira crueles querellas,
niega a sí misma reparo de aquellas
y tal como muerta viviendo se para."

205

"Decía, llorando, con lengua rabiosa:
'O matador de mi hijo cruel,
1635 mataras a mí y dejaras a él,
que fuera enemiga no tan porfiosa;
fuera la madre muy más digna cosa
para quien mata llevar menor cargo;
no te mostraras a él tan amargo,
1640 ni triste dejaras a mí querellosa.'"

203 *The Laments That His Mother Makes for Him*

"She showed herself well to be a mother in the grief
expressed by the sorrowful woman after she saw
the bloodied body laid out on the bier
of him whom she had nurtured with such zeal;   1620
she pierces the heavens with cruel words,
her ill-health wracked with new pains,
and so much anguish robs her vitality
that the sorrowful woman is driven to the ground"

204

"and with cruel nails scratches her face,   1625
and strikes her chest violently
while kissing the cold mouth of her son.
She curses the hands of his murderer,
curses the war where it all began,
searches with rage for cruel complaints,   1630
denies herself respite from them
and stands like a living dead woman."

205

"She weepingly said with a furious tongue,
'Oh cruel murderer of my son,
would that you had killed me and let him live;   1635
then I would have been a less determined enemy.
His mother would have been a much more worthy thing,
an easier kill for a murderer;
you should not have shown yourself so bitter to him,
nor left me to be wretched and mournful.'"   1640

206

"'Si antes la muerte me fuera ya dada,
cerrara mis ojos con estas sus manos
mi hijo, delante de los sus hermanos,
y yo no muriera más de una vegada;
1645 así morré muchas, desaventurada,
que sola padezco lavar sus heridas
con lágrimas tristes, más no agradecidas,
aunque lloradas por madre cuitada.'"

207 *Comparación*

"Así lamentaba la pía matrona
1650 al hijo querido que muerto tú viste,
haciéndole encima semblante de triste,
según al que pare hace la leona;
¿pues dónde podría pensar la persona
los daños que causa la triste demanda
1655 de la discordia del reino que anda,
donde no gana ninguno corona?"

208 *La muerte del clavero que murió en el Convento*

E vi por lo alto venir ya volando
el ánima fresca del santo clavero,
partida del cuerpo del buen caballero
1660 que por su justicia murió batallando;
si fe merecieren mis versos trobando,

206

"'If an early death were granted to me,
my son would have closed my eyes
with his hands, in front of his brothers,
and I would not have died more than once.
This way I will die many times, ill-fated,   1645
for I experience alone the cleaning of his wounds
with sorrowful but not welcomed tears,
though shed by a grief-stricken mother.'"

207 *Comparison*

"In this manner, the pious matron lamented
the beloved son whom you saw dead,   1650
looking upon him with sad countenance
as does the lioness to a newborn.
So where, might a person think, dwell
the troubles caused by the wretched demands
of the discord that exists in the realm,   1655
where no one wins a crown?"

208 *The Death of the Keeper of the Keys, Who Died in the Convent*

And I saw come through the sky, already in flight,
the recent soul of the holy keeper of the keys,
having just left the body of the goodly knight
who died fighting for his justice;   1660
if my song shall be held to be true,

siempre en los siglos será muy perfecto
el nombre famoso de aquel buen electo,
que bien yo no puedo loar alabando.

209

1665 Electo de todos por noble guerrero,
electo maestro por muy valeroso,
electo de todos por muy virtuoso,
por mucho constante, fiel, verdadero,
al cual un desastre mató postrimero
1670 con piedra que hizo de honda reveses;
por que maldigo vos, Mallorqueses,
vos que las hondas hallastes primero.

210

Veyendo yo gentes allí tan apuestas,
dije: "Entre tanto valiente varón,
1675 ¿cómo no vemos al fuerte Milón
que al templo llevaba un gran toro a cuestas?"
La mi guiadora con dulces respuestas
respondió: "La rueda de Mares presenta
los que por fuertes virtud representa;
1680 de fuerza desnuda no hace ella fiestas."

211 *Qué cosa sea fuerza y fortaleza,*
y pone las diferencias

"Fuerza se llama, mas no fortaleza,
la de los miembros o gran valentía;

time will always consider extremely perfect
the famous name of that goodly chosen one,
whom I cannot suitably extol with praise.

209

Considered by all as a noble warrior,   1665
chosen as master for his extraordinary valor,
chosen by all for his many virtues,
for being ever constant, faithful, true,
whom a disaster nevertheless killed,
with a stone sling that upset his fortune;   1670
for that reason I curse you, Mallorcans,
you who first found the use of slings.

210

Seeing people there who were so dashing,
I said, "Among so many courageous men,
how can we not see strong Milo,   1675
who carried a great bull to the temple on his shoulders?"
My guide with sweet responses
replied: "The wheel of Mars holds
those in whom the virtue of strength is represented;
she does not celebrate brute force."   1680

211 *What Sort of Thing is Strength and Fortitude, and She Lists the Differences*

"Strength it is called, but not fortitude,
that which is of bodily members or great bravery.

la gran fortaleza en el alma se cría
que viste los cuerpos de rica nobleza,
1685 de cuerda osadía, de gran gentileza,
de mucha constancia, de fe y lealtad;
a tales esfuerza su autoridad
que débiles hizo la naturaleza."

212 *Endereza el sermón al señor rey*

Muy claro príncipe, rey escogido
1690 de los que son fuertes por esta manera,
la vuestra corona magnífica quiera
tener con los tales el reino regido;
ca estos más aman con justo sentido
la recta justicia que no la ganancia,
1695 y rigen y sirven con mucha constancia
y con fortaleza en el tiempo debido.

213 *Qué cosa sea fortaleza virtuosa*

Es fortaleza un grande denuedo
que sufre las prósperas y las molestas;
salvo las cosas que son deshonestas,
1700 otras ningunas no le hacen miedo;
huye, desdeña, depártese cedo
de las que disformes por vicio se hacen;
las grandes virtudes inmenso le plazen:
hacen el ánimo firme ser quedo.

Great fortitude is nurtured in the soul,
for she adorns the bodies with rich nobility,
with reasoned daring, with great gentility,   1685
with much constancy, with faith and loyalty.
Such men her authority fortifies,
who were made weak men by nature."

212 *He Directs His Speech to the Lord King*

Very illustrious prince, chosen king
among those who are strong in this manner,   1690
with such men may your magnificent crown
seek to keep the kingdom well governed,
because they love with right reason
righteous justice rather than profit,
and they govern and serve with great fealty   1695
and with strength at the required time.

213 *What Sort of Thing Is Virtuous Fortitude*

Fortitude is a great hardiness
that persists through prosperous and troubled times;
except for things that are dishonest,
nothing else ever instills fear in it.   1700
It flees, disdains, it quickly breaks away
from things that are deformed by vice;
great virtues please it immensely:
they quiet the steady.

214 *Fenece la quinta orden de Mares; comienza la sexta de Júpiter*

1705 Y vi los que reinan en paz gloriosa,
y los muy humanos a sus naturales,
y muchos de aquellos que siendo mortales
viven celando la pública cosa;
y vi bajo d'estos gran turba llorosa
1710 de los invasores y grandes tiranos,
que por exceso mortal de sus manos
dejan la fama cruel, monstruosa.

215 *Alega antiguos*

Vimos sin armas a Octaviano,
que hubo los tiempos así triunfales
1715 y tanto pacífico el mundo de males
que tuvo cerradas las puertas de Jano;
y vimos la gloria del bravo romano,
guarda fiel de la tarpea torre,
aquél que con todas sus fuerzas acorre
1720 contra el hambre del nuevo tirano.

216

Y vimos a Codro gozar de la gloria,
con los constantes y muy claros Decios,
los cuales tuvieron en menores precios
sus vidas delante la noble victoria;
1725 estaba Torquato, con digna memoria,
siendo del hijo cruel matador,

214 The Fifth Order of Mars Ends; the Sixth of Jupiter Begins

And I saw those who reign in glorious peace 1705
and those very humane to their people,
and many of those who, being mortals,
spend their lives watching over public matters;
and I saw beneath these a great, sorrowful mass
of invaders and great tyrants, 1710
who by the deadly excess of their hands
leave behind a cruel, monstrous fame.

215 He Offers Ancient Examples

We saw Octavian without weapons,
whose times were triumphant,
and the world so untroubled by evils 1715
that he kept shut the gates of Janus;
and we saw the glory of that brave Roman,
faithful guard of the Tarpeian tower,
he who with all his might renders succor
against the hunger of the new tyrant. 1720

216

And we saw Codrus enjoy the glory
together with the constant and very illustrious Deciuses,
those who placed a lesser value
on their lives than on noble victory;
there was Torquatus, of worthy memory, 1725
being the cruel murderer of his son,

aunque lo vió venir vencedor,
porque pasara la ley ya notoria.

217

Dos vengadores de la servidumbre
muy animosos estaban los Brutos,
de sangre tirana sus gestos polutos
no permitiendo mudar su costumbre;
están los Catones encima la cumbre,
el buen uticense con el censorino,
los cuales se dieron martirio condigno
por no ver la cuita de tal muchedumbre.

218

Estaba la imagen del pobre Fabricio,
aquel que no quiso que los senadores
oro nin plata de los oradores
tomasen, ni otro ningún beneficio,
probando que fuese más hábil oficio
al pueblo romano querer poseer
los que poseían el oro que haber
todo su oro con cargo de vicio.

219

¡O siglo perverso, cruel, engañoso,
pues das a señores tan grandes oficios,
danos entre ellos algunos Fabricios

even though he saw him come victorious,
because he had already implemented the notorious law.

217

Two avengers of the people
were the very spirited Brutuses, 1730
their faces sullied by tyrant blood,
not permitting their nature to change;
the Catos, the good Uticensis and the Censor,
are above the summit,
they who fittingly martyred themselves 1735
so as not to see the unhappiness of such a multitude.

218

The image of poor Fabricius was there,
he who did not want the senators
to take gold or silver from the orators,
or any other benefit, 1740
proving that it was a more proper
for the Roman people to want to hold power
over those who were in possession of gold, than
to have all the gold they unscrupulously obtained.

219

Oh perverse times, cruel, deceitful, 1745
since you give lords such great offices,
give us some Fabriciuses among them

que hagan al pueblo bien provechoso;
y los que presumen con acto glorioso
1750 de más animosos que nuestros mayores
hiciésense dignos o merecedores
del nombre de alguno que fue virtuoso!

220. *Hablado de los pasados,*
viene a los presentes

Alzamos los ojos ya contra la gloria
del cerco constante de nuestros presentes,
1755 donde hallamos las insignes gentes
de los que no muere jamás su memoria;
y vimos la fama vulgar y notoria—
¡o loor de los reyes d'España la clara!—
con la trábea real y tiara
1760 que son los insignias de noble victoria.

221

Al nuestro rey magno bienaventurado
vi sobre todos en muy firme silla,
digno de reino mayor que Castilla,
velloso león a sus pies por estrado;
1765 vestido de múrice ropa de estado,
ebúrneo cetro mandaba su diestra
y rica corona la mano siniestra,
más prepotente que el cielo estrellado.

who would benefit the people greatly;
and those who presume with a glorious act
to be more valiant than our ancestors, 1750
would that they might make themselves worthy and
    deserving
of the renown of anyone who was virtuous!

220 *Having Spoken of Those Who Had Passed,*
    He Comes to Those Present

We now raise our eyes toward the glory
of the constant circle of our contemporaries,
where we find the renowned individuals 1755
whose memory never dies;
and we saw the widely acknowledged public fame —
oh praise of the kings of illustrious Spain! —
with the royal garb and crown
that are the regalia of noble victory. 1760

221

Our great, fortunate king,
I saw above all, seated on a very firm throne,
worthy of a greater kingdom than Castile,
a maned lion serving at his feet as a dais,
dressed in purple state clothes, 1765
an ivory scepter wielded by his right hand
and a rich crown in his left hand,
more prepotent than the starry sky.

222

    Atal lo hallaron ya los oradores
1770 en la su villa de fuego cercada,
    cuando le vino la gran embajada
    de bárbaros reyes y grandes señores;
    y tal lo dejaron los que con honores
    vuelven alegres de dones honustos,
1775 don Juan alabando sobre los Augustos
    por sus facundos interpretadores.

223 *Sigue un razonamiento que el autor hace consolatorio contra las pobres gentes que desde la su bajeza acatan el estado de los reyes en el su triunfo*

    ¡Perded la codicia, vos, pobres mortales,
    de aqueste triunfo y de todas sus leyes;
    do veredes los grandes señores y reyes!
1780 Envidia no os hagan sus grandes caudales,
    los cuales son una simiente de males
    que debe huir cualquier entendido,
    ya mayormente que bien discutido
    las vuestras riquezas son más naturales.

224

1785 Envidia más triste padecen aquellos
    de bienes diversos a vosotros dados
    que no la codicia que por sus reinados
    todos vosotros podéis haber d'ellos;

222

In this manner the envoys found him
in his town encircled by flame, 1770
when the great embassy came to him
of barbarian kings and great lords;
and so they left him, those who with honors
return joyfully laden with gifts,
praising Don Juan above the Augustuses 1775
for his eloquent negotiators.

223 *What Follows Is the Reasoning That the Author Makes in Consolation against the Pitiable People Who from Their Lowly Station Consider the State of Kings in Their Triumph*

Lose your covetousness, you, poor mortals,
of this triumph and of all its laws,
where you will see great lords and kings!
Do not be envious of their great riches 1780
from which evils germinate,
which everyone in the know ought to flee,
especially now that (being well discussed)
your own riches are more natural.

224

A more sorrowful greed afflicts them, 1785
for the many possessions bestowed upon you,
and not the envy about their reigns
that all of you could have toward them;

ca todos vosotros queredes ser ellos
1790 por uso sólo de la su riqueza,
y ellos vosotros, do naturaleza
vos hizo cumplidos de dones más bellos.

225

Hanvos envidia de la hermosura
cuando la suya no bien se conforma
1795 hanvos envidia la hermosa forma,
y muchas vegadas la desenvoltura ;
hanvos envidia prudencia y mesura,
fuerza, coraje, y más la salud;
pues ved ser en ellos no tanta virtud,
1800 ni toda en riquezas la buena ventura.

226 *Comparación*

Demás que Fortuna con grandes señores
estando tranquilo los menos escucha,
y más a menudo los tienta de lucha,
y anda jugando con los sus honores;
1805 y como los rayos las torres mayores
hieren enante que no en las bajuras,
así dan los Hados sus desaventuras
más a los grandes que a los menores.

227 *Alaba la pobreza con paciencia recebida*

¡O vida segura la mansa pobreza,
1810 dádiva santa desagradecida !

for all of you want to replace them
only for the use of their wealth, 1790
and they you, whereas nature
endowed you with more bountiful gifts.

225

They are envious of your beauty,
when their own does not compare well to it;
they envy your beautiful form 1795
and, on many occasions, its gracefulness;
they envy your prudence and moderation,
force, courage, and even more your health.
You should recognize that there is not so much virtue
    in them,
nor every good fortune in riches. 1800

226 *Comparison*

For Fortune with great lords,
in times of peace, heeds them less,
and more frequently tempts them to strife,
and is playful with their honors;
and as lightning bolts strike 1805
great towers first and not low-lying places,
so the Fates mete out their misfortunes
more to the great lords than to commoners.

227 *He Praises the Patient Acceptance of Poverty*

Oh sheltered life, meek poverty,
unappreciated holy gift! 1810

Rica se llama, no pobre, la vida
dél que se contenta vivir sin riqueza;
la trémula casa, humil en bajeza,
de Amiclas el pobre muy poco temía
la mano del César qu'el mundo regía,
maguer que llamase con gran fortaleza.

228 *Hasta aquí dijo de los que vivían o regían justamente;
ahora comienza a tratar de los que por tiranía
ocupan lo no suyo*

La gran avideza de la tiranía
vimos, venidos al ínfimo centro,
do muchos señores están tan adentro
que no sé qué lengua los explicaría;
vimos entre ellos, sin ver alegría,
los tres Dionisios siracusanos,
con otro linaje cruel de tiranos
que Dios en el mundo por plagas envía.

229

Yonus primero halló la moneda,
y hirió de cuño los mixtos metales,
al cual yo maldigo, pues tantos de males
causa la simiente que nunca va queda;
por esta justicia se nos deshereda,
los reinos por esta nos escandalizan,
por esta los grandes así tiranizan
que no sé quien viva seguro nin pueda.

Rich, not poor, one calls the life
of him who is content to live without wealth;
the modest house, humble in its lowliness,
of poor Amyclas had little to fear
from the hand of Caesar who ruled the world,   1815
although he knocked with great power.

228 *Up to Now He Spoke of Those Who Lived and Ruled Justly; Now He Begins to Treat Those Who by Tyranny Occupy What Is Not Theirs*

The great thirst of tyranny
we saw, when we arrived at the lowest point of the center,
where many lords are so far inside
that I know not what words would be enough to explain   1820
    them to you;
we saw among them, without seeing any sign of joy,
the three Dionysiuses of Syracuse,
with another lineage of cruel tyrants
that God sends as plagues to the world.

229

Ionos first discovered coinage   1825
and minted mixed metals—
whom I curse, because so many ills
are caused by that never-still seed.
Because of its rule we are dispossessed,
our kingdoms are scandalized because of it,   1830
because of it the powerful readily tyrannize,
so that I do not know who is or could be secure.

230 *Endereza la habla al rey*

Sanad vos los reinos de aqueste recelo,
¡o príncipe bueno, o novel Augusto,
o lumbre d'España, o Rey mucho justo!,
pues rey de la tierra os hizo el del cielo;
y los que os sirven con malvado celo,
con hambre tirana, con no buena ley,
haced que aprendan temer a su rey,
por que justicia no ande por suelo.

231 *Definición de justicia*

Justicia es un cetro que el cielo crió,
que el gran universo nos hace seguro,
hábito rico del ánimo puro,
introducido por público pro;
y por igual peso siempre conservó
todos estados en los sus oficios;
es más azote que pune los vicios,
no corruptible por sí ni por no.

232 *Fenece la sexta orden de Júpiter; comienza la última de Saturno*

Y vimos, al último cerco venidos,
las grandes personas en sus monarquías,
y los que rigen las sus señorías
con moderada justicia temidos;
y vimos debajo los que no punidos
sufren que pasen males y vicios

230 *He Directs His Words to the King*

It is up to you to heal the kingdoms of this distrust—
Oh good prince! Oh new Augustus!
Oh light of Spain! Oh king ever just!—   1835
for you were made an earthly king by the heavenly one.
And those who serve you with evil intent,
with tyrannical hunger, with no good law,
you should teach to fear their king,
so that justice might not be trampled in the dirt!   1840

231 *Definition of Justice*

Justice is a scepter that heaven created
to secure the great universe for us,
a rich habit of the pure soul,
introduced for public benefit;
and it always gave equal weight to keeping   1845
all the social estates in their proper roles;
it is more of a whip that punishes vices,
not corruptible by assent or denial.

232 *The Sixth Order of Jupiter Ends; Here Begins the Last, of Saturn*

And we saw, having arrived at the last circle,
the great personages in their kingdoms   1850
and those who rule their domains,
feared for their measured justice;
and we saw below them those who, without punishment,
allow evils and vices to exist

1855 y los que pigros en los sus oficios
dejan los crímenes mal corregidos.

233 *Pregunta del condestable*

"O tú, Providencia, declara de nuevo
quién es aquel caballero que veo,
que mucho en el cuerpo parece a Tideo,
1860 y en el consejo Nestor el longevo;
por que yo hable d'aquel lo que debo,
si libre pudiere salir d'este valle,
no sufras tal ignorancia que calle
lo que notorio por ojos apruebo."

234 *Comparación*

1865 Así como hacen los enamorados
cuando les hablan de lo que bien quieren,
alegran los ojos, doquier que estuvieren,
y cobran semblantes muy más alterados,
no hizo menos alegres estados
1870 la Providencia a la cual preguntara,
y luego repuso con alegre cara,
pospuestos los otros divinos cuidados:

235

"Este cabalga sobre la Fortuna
y doma su cuello con ásperas riendas;
1875 aunque d'él tenga tan muchas de prendas,
ella no le osa tocar a ninguna;

and those who, apathetic to their offices,   1855
allow crimes to go uncorrected.

233   *He Asks about the Constable*

"Oh Providence, declare once again
who is that knight I see,
who closely resembles Tydeus in body
and in counsel Nestor the long-lived;   1860
so that I may speak about him as I should,
if I were to exit this valley freely,
do not allow such ignorance to silence
what my eyes single out and approve!"

234   *Comparison*

Just as lovers do   1865
when others speak to them about what they most cherish—
they make their eyes joyous wherever they might be
and their faces are very affected—
no less joyful a state was shown by
Providence, to whom I addressed my questions,   1870
whereupon she replied with a radiant expression,
postponing the other divine cares:

235

"This one rides over Fortune
and curbs her neck with harsh reins;
although she has in her possession many of his valuables,   1875
she dares not touch anything of his;

míralo, míralo en plática alguna,
con ojos humildes, no tanto feroces;
¿cómo, indiscreto, y tú no conoces
1880 al condestable Alvaro de Luna?"

236

"Ahora," repuse, "conozco mejor
aquel cuyo ánimo, virtud y nombre
tantas de partes le hacen de hombre
cuantas estado le da de Señor,
1885 las cuales le hacen ser merecedor
ser hecho de mano de nuestro gran rey,
y clara experiencia de su firme ley,
y de la Fortuna siempre vencedor."

237

Aunque la contra creo que sentían
1890 los que quisieron haber confianza
más en el tiempo que en buena esperanza,
cuando los mundos se nos revolvían;
digo de algunos que así lo hacían
en el comienzo de aquellas cuestiones,
1895 que so color de ciertas razones
al condestable se le despedían.

238

Fueron movidos a esto hacer,
según argumento de lo que presumo,

behold, behold him in any discussion,
with humble, not-so-fierce eyes;
how is it—indiscreet one—that you cannot recognize
the constable Álvaro de Luna?" 1880

236

"Now," I responded, "I better recognize
that one whose spirit, virtue, and name
clearly are due to the many qualities that make him a man,
as many as are due to his lordly estate,
which make him deserving 1885
of being ennobled by the hand of our great king
and the clear experiences of his firm beliefs,
and by being always victorious over Fortune."

237

Even though a different belief was held
by those who wanted to have more 1890
confidence in time than in good hope
when our worlds were in turmoil,
I speak about some who dealt with him in this way
at the onset of those disputes,
when, under the guise of certain justifications, 1895
they were abandoning the constable.

238

The ones who were moved to do this—
according to the reasons I surmise—

los que cegaron del túrbido humo
1900　y fama que entonces se pudo entender
　　　de algunos que mucho quisieron saber,
　　　por unas palabras de hembra mostrada
　　　en cercos y suertes de arte vedada,
　　　la parte que había de prevalecer.

239

1905　Según la respuesta, parece, que hubieron,
　　　juzgaron por menos allí favorable
　　　el hecho y la vida del su condestable,
　　　y quizá por esto se le despidieron;
　　　mas si los hechos según los hicieron
1910　os place, lectores, que os lo relate,
　　　sufrid que mis versos un poco dilate,
　　　por que vengamos a lo que vinieron.

240

　　　Por mucho qu'el sabio prudente, discreto,
　　　encubre por cabo sus hechos y cela,
1915　más son las cosas que Fama revela
　　　que no las que sabe callar el secreto.
　　　Estos, habiendo medroso respeto,
　　　con una persona muy encantadera
　　　tuvieron secreto lugar y manera
1920　donde sus suertes hubieron efecto.

were those blinded by the turbid smoke
and the reputation, generally known,
of those few individuals who very much wanted to know
through some utterances of a woman shown
through circles and divinations of the forbidden arts
which faction was to prevail.

239

It seems that, according to the answer they received,
they judged the deeds and life of their constable
to be less advantageous,
and perhaps for this reason they abandoned him;
but, readers, if you are pleased
with my account of their acts,
allow me to spin out my verses some more,
so that we can know what happened to them.

240

However much a wise, prudent, discrete man
tries to conceal and guard his actions,
there are more things revealed by Fame
than those she knows to keep to herself.
These men, imbued with a fearful respect
for a person very knowledgeable in sorcery,
had a method and secret meeting place
where her divinations were to take place.

241

Pulmón de lince allí no fallece,
de hiena no menos el nudo más tuerto,
de sierpe formada d'espina de muerto,
y ojos de loba después que encanece,
médula de ciervo que tanto envejece
que traga culebra por rejuvenir,
y aquella piedra que sabe adquirir
el águila cuando su nido fornece.

242

Allí es mezclada gran parte de equino,
el cual, aunque sea muy pequeño pez,
muchas vegadas y no una vez
retiene las fustas que van de camino;
pues no menos falta la que quimerino
se engendra por yerro de naturaleza,
y piezas de aras que por gran alteza
son dedicadas al culto divino.

243

Espuma de canes que el agua recelan,
membranas de líbica sierpe cerrasta,
ceniza de fénix, aquella que basta,
huesos de alas de dragos que vuelan,
de otras vipéreas sierpes que velan
dando custodia a las piedras preciosas,
y otros diversos millares de cosas
qu'el nombre no saben aun los que las celan.

241

The lung of a lynx is not lacking there,
nor is the crookedest bone of the hyena,
of a serpent formed in the spine of a dead man,
and eyes of a she-wolf after having gone gray,
marrow of a stag that grows so old 1925
that it swallows a serpent to rejuvenate,
and that stone the eagle knows
to acquire when building its nest.

242

Mixed in that place is a lot of remora,
which, although a very small fish, 1930
many times — and not just once —
impedes galleys from going their way;
neither is the chimera lacking,
generated by nature's mistake,
nor parts of an altar that, because of their great height, 1935
are dedicated to the divine cult.

243

Drool from the mouths of dogs that fear water,
membranes of the Libyan serpent cerastes,
ash of the phoenix (whatever suffices),
bones of wings of dragons that fly 1940
and other viperous serpents that keep
watchful eyes over precious stones,
and other many thousands of things
whose names even their keepers do not know.

244

1945 No fue tal mixtura con fuego mezclada,
según presunciones de lo que yo arguyo,
mas en las aguas que hierven de suyo,
por venas sulfúreas haciendo pasada,
la tal decocción fue conglutinada;
1950 así que cualquiera cuerpo ya muerto
ungido con ella pudiera despierto
dar a los vivos respuesta hadada.

245

Y busca la maga ya hasta que halla
un cuerpo tan malo que por aventura
1955 le fuera negado de haber sepultura,
por haber muerto en no justa batalla;
y cuando de noche la gente más calla,
pónelo ésta en medio de un cerco,
y desde allí dentro conjura en el huerco,
1960 y todas las sombras ultrices sin falla.

246

Ya comenzaba la invocación
con triste murmuro y dísono canto,
fingiendo las voces con aquel espanto
que meten las fieras con muy triste son,
1965 ora silbando como dragón,
y como tigre haziendo estridores,
ora ladridos formando mayores
que forman los canes que sin dueño son.

244

This mixture was not combined with fire— 1945
following the presumptions of my argument—
but in waters that boil on their own
while passing through sulfurous veins
was that concoction agglutinated,
so that any human body already deceased, 1950
anointed with it, could readily waken
to give a supernatural answer to the living.

245

And the sorceress searches until she finds
a body of one so evil that
it was denied burial by fate 1955
for having died in unjust battle;
and when people are most quiet at night,
she places it at the center of a circle,
and from inside it conjures up Orcus
and all the vengeful shades without fail. 1960

246

She was already starting her spell
with a gloomy murmur and dissonant chant,
mimicking the frightful howls of wild animals
with the same mournful sound,
now hissing like a dragon 1965
or making strident sounds like a tiger,
or greater barkings
than are made by stray dogs.

247

Con ronca garganta ya dice: "Conjuro,
Plutón, a ti, triste, y a ti, Proserpina,
que me enviedes entrambos aína
un tal espíritu, sútil y puro,
que en este mal cuerpo me hable seguro,
y de la pregunta que le fuere puesta
me satisfaga de cierta respuesta,
según es el caso que tanto procuro."

248

"Dale salida, velloso Cervero,
por la tu triste trifauce garganta,
pues su tardanza no ha de ser tanta,
y dale pasada, tú, vil marinero.
¿Pues ya qué hacedes? ¿A cuándo os espero?
Guardad no me ensañe, sino otra vez
haré descenderos allá por juez
a aquel que os trajo ligado primero."

249

Tornándose contra el cuerpo mezquino,
cuando su forma vido ser inmota,
con viva culebra lo hiere y azota
por que el espíritu traiga maligno;
el cual quizá teme d'entrar, aunque vino,
en las entrañas heladas sin vida,

247

With a throaty voice she intones, "I conjure
you, Pluto, dire one, and you, Proserpina, 1970
so that both of you might quickly send me
such a spirit, subtle and pure,
that from this evil corpse can speak to me truthfully,
and to the question placed before it
satisfy me with a definite answer, 1975
according to the circumstance I so readily pursue."

248

"Give vent, shaggy Cerberus,
to your mournful triple throat,
for its delay should not be too long,
and grant it passage, vile boatman. 1980
For what are you doing now? When can I expect you?
Be careful that you not infuriate me, otherwise
I will send down to you as judge
the one who first brought you bound."

249

She turned toward the wretched body; 1985
when she saw its inert form,
she wounds and whips it with a live snake
so that the malignant spirit can be summoned;
who—although he came—fears stepping
into the frigid, lifeless viscera, 1990

o si viene el alma que d'él fue partida,
quizá y tarda más en el camino.

250

La maga, veyendo crecer la tardanza,
por una abertura que hizo en la tierra:
1995 "Hécate," dijo, "¿no te hacen guerra
más las palabras que mi boca lanza?
Si no obedeces la mi ordenanza,
la cara que muestras a los del infierno
haré que demuestres al cielo superno
2000 tábida, lúrida, sin alabanza."

251

"¿Y sabes tú, triste Plutón, que haré?
Abriré las bocas por do te gobiernas,
y con mis palabras tus hondas cavernas
de luz subitánea te las heriré.
2005 Obedecedme, sino llamaré
a Demogorgón, el cual invocado
treme la tierra, ca tiene tal hado
que a las Estigias no mantiene fe."

252

Los miembros ya tiemblan del cuerpo muy fríos,
2010 medrosos de oír el canto segundo;

or perhaps if the soul that parted from it
is further delayed in coming.

250

The sorceress, seeing that the wait was being prolonged,
using a breach she made in the earth,
said, "Hecate, don't the words 1995
flung from my mouth vex you?
If you disobey my orders,
the face that you show to the dwellers of hell
I will make you expose to the supreme heaven
as rotten, lurid, without praise." 2000

251

"And do you know, gloomy Pluto, what I will do?
I will unseal the cave mouths in the regions you rule,
and with my words I will pierce
your deep caverns with sudden flashes of light.
Obey me; if not I will call 2005
on Demogorgon, who, when invoked,
makes the earth quake, because such is his power
that he does not fear even the Stygian waters."

252

The very cold extremities of the body suddenly tremble,
fearful of hearing the second chant; 2010

ya forma sus voces el pecho iracundo,
temiendo la maga y sus poderíos;
la cual se le llega con besos impíos,
y hace preguntas por modo callado
al cuerpo ya vivo, después de finado,
por que sus actos no salgan vacíos.

253

Con una manera de voces extraña
el cuerpo comienza palabras atales:
"Irados y muchos son los infernales
contra los grandes del reino d'España,
porque les hacen injuria tamaña,
dando las treguas a los infieles,
ca mientras les fueron mortales crueles
nunca tuvieron con ninguno saña."

254

"Animas muchas hacen que no hayan
en hacer paces con aquella seta,
mas ellos ya vuelven con arte secreta
otros lugares por donde les vayan;
y porque hicieron las paces, asayan
sembrar tal discordia entre castellanos
que fe no se guarden hermanos a hermanos,
por donde los tristes fenezcan y cayan."

its irate chest is already forming voices,
fearful of the sorceress and her powers,
she who approaches him with impious kisses
and asks questions in a hushed tone
of the body, now quickened after expiring,   2015
to make her efforts not be in vain.

253

With an altered, strange way of speaking,
the body began to utter these words:
"Wrathful and many are the inhabitants of hell
opposing the powerful lords of the kingdom of Spain,   2020
because they do them great harm,
granting truces to the infidels,
because, while they were mortally cruel to them,
they never battled with any."

254

"Many souls are opposed   2025
to peace treaties with that sect,
but instead they readily turn to other secret
opportunities for provoking them:
and because they made peace, they try
to sow seeds of discord among the Castilians,   2030
so that brothers cannot keep faith with brothers,
thereby coming to their sad end and fall."

255

"Y quedarán d'ellos tales indignidades,
y sobre partir tales discordanzas,
que por los puños romper muchas lanzas
veréis, y revuelta de muchas ciudades.
Por ende, vosotros, esos que mandades,
la ira, la ira volved en los moros;
no se consuman así los tesoros
en causas no justas como las edades."

256

"Y del condestable juzgando su hecho,
así determino su hado y pregono:
será detraído del sublime trono
y aun a la fin del todo deshecho.
Pues ya venir en un tal estrecho,
según lo que hallo, forzado conviene,
finja color el que la no tiene,
y cada cual busque temprano provecho."

257

¡Cuántas licencias y despedimientos
al buen condestable fueron demandadas!
¡Cuántos hicieron palabras osadas,
con vana soberbia de los mudamientos!
Fortuna, que nunca nos tuvo contentos,
hacía a muchos partirse, dejando

255

"And such foul deeds will be remembered of them,
and such discords over divisions,
that you will see clenched fists break many lances
and revolts in many cities.
Therefore, you who command these men,
their wrath, their wrath you should turn toward the Moors;
so that treasures and time might not be squandered in this
    manner
on unjust causes."

256

"And judging by the deeds of the constable,
I foretell his fate and proclaim:
He will be cast down from his sublime throne,
and will be completely destroyed even at the end.
So those who come to such straits,
according to what I have found, should pretend
to have a reason, even when they do not,
and each one should seek early profit."

257

How many absences and leaves
were requested of the good constable!
How many uttered bold words
about changes in fate with vainglorious arrogance!
Fortune, whose wont was never to keep us satisfied,
made many go away, leaving

2055 al su señor propio, no bien acatando
qué fin habrían sus merecimientos.

258

Los que se parten por tal novedad
licencia por muchas razones pretenden:
unas alegan, mas otras entienden,
2060 y cubren con falsa color la verdad.
Pues ya deteneos, siquier' esperad,
porque entre buenos razón no admite
causas que ponga ninguno ni quite,
cuando el señor es en necesidad.

259 *Comparación*

2065 Al camaleón que en el aire se cría
son semejantes los tales efectos,
que tantos y cuantos tocare de objectos
de tantas colores se vuelv'en el día.
¡O rica nobleza! ¡O gran hidalguía!
2070 ¡O ínclita sangre! Tú, ¿cómo sostienes
por vana codicia de mundanos bienes
tocar los humanos tal vil villanía?

260

Fama vos mueva de justo deseo:
pues tanto que a César siguió Labiëno
2075 siempre le dieron el nombre de bueno,

their natural lord, not considering well
what would be the end of their doings.

258

Those who depart due to such a turn of events
seek leave for many reasons:
they put forth some, while intending others,
and cloak the truth under false colors.
So stop at once or at least hesitate,
because among good people reason does not allow
anyone to excuse themselves or run off
when their lord is in need.

259 *Comparison*

Such reasons can be compared
to the chameleon, who is nourished on air,
because it takes on as many colors in a day
as the many and plentiful objects it touches.
Oh rich nobility! Oh great pedigree!
Oh renowned blood! How can you tolerate
that a vain covetousness of worldly goods
taints people with such vile villainy?

260

Fame, righteous desire should move you,
for as long as Labienus followed Caesar
he was always considered good,

hasta que tuvo señor a Pompeyo;
así los señores, según lo que veo,
los que a dos partes así prevarican
menos los precian si más los platican;
2080 danles partido, mas no buen arreo.

261 *Comparación*

Como los árboles presto se secan
que muy a menudo las gentes remudan,
así los que a muchos señores ayudan
en vicio semejante presumo que pecan;
2085 y como las peñas que de alto derruecan
hasta lo hondo no son detenidas,
así acaece a los que sus vidas
con muchos señores descojen y truecan.

262

¡O vil codicia, de todos errores
2090 madre, y carrera de todos los males,
que ciegas los ojos así de mortales
en las condiciones de los servidores;
tú que endureces así los señores,
y que los méritos tanto fatigas
2095 de vana esperanza, que muchos obligas
a tales miserias hacer y mayores!

until he switched to Pompey as master;
so it is with lords, according to my experience;
those who waver between two factions
value them less the more they do business with them;
they support them, but not very well. 2080

261 *Comparison*

Like trees that quickly wither
when people with great frequency transplant them,
thus are those who are in the service of many lords—
I consider them to be afflicted with similar vice
and, like stones that fall from above 2085
to the depths without hindrance,
so it happens with those who choose
to share and apportion their lives with many masters.

262

Oh vile covetousness, of all errors
mother, and pathway to every sin, 2090
for in this way you blind the eyes of mortals
to the conditions of followers,
you that thus harden the hearts of lords,
you that so weaken what is meritorious
with elusive hopes, that you compel many 2095
to behave in boundless miserable ways!

263

Después ya del caso del todo pasado,
hechos los ya nuevamente adversarios,
veyendo los fines del todo contrarios
al triste juicio que estaba hadado,
vuelven a aquella que les había dado
las execrables y duras respuestas,
diciéndole cómo no fueran aquestas
las grandes fortunas que había memorado.

264

"Si las palabras," responde, "al vero
sobre el condestable vos bien acatasteis,
y las fortunas venidas mirasteis,
veréis que ha salido todo verdadero:
ca así le fuera hadado primero
que presto deshecho sería del todo;
mirad en Toledo, que por este modo
lo ya deshicieron con armas de acero."

265

"Ca un condestable armado, que sobre
un gran bulto de oro estaba asentado,
con manos sañosas vimos derribado,
y todo deshecho fue tornado cobre.
¿Pues cómo queredes que otra vez obre
Fortuna, tentando lo que es importuno?
Basta que pudo derribar el uno,
que al otro más duro lo halla que robre."

263

Now after the matter was fully concluded,
the newly created adversaries,
seeing the outcome completely different
from the sorrowful outcome that had been predicted, 2100
turned to her who had given to them
the awful and harsh answers,
telling her how such were not
the great misfortunes that she had foretold them.

264

"If, in truth," she replied, "the words 2105
concerning the constable you did study well,
and the predictions of the future you did examine,
you will see that all truly has come to pass,
for it was first predicted
that he would soon be completely destroyed; 2110
look how in Toledo, in this manner,
he was completely dismantled with weapons of steel."

265

"Because an armed constable, who on
a great cushion of gold was seated,
we saw was brought down by spiteful hands, 2115
and, all destroyed, was turned back to copper.
So how is it that you want Fortune to revisit the case,
attempting to change what is inopportune?
It is enough that she could bring down one,
for the other she finds harder than oak." 2120

266 *Comparación*

Así como hacen los bravos leones
cuando el ayuno les da grandes hambres,
comen las carnes heladas, fiambres,
porque las vivas les dan evasiones,
bien así hacen las constelaciones
cuando a sus hados hallan un obstante:
hartan sus iras en forma semejante
donde executan las sus impresiones.

267

Por ende, magnífico gran condestable,
la ciega Fortuna, que había de vos hambre,
harta la deja la forma de alambre;
de aquí en adelante vos es favorable.
Pues todos notemos un caso mirable,
y nótenlo cuantos vinieren de nos,
que de vos y d'ella, y d'ella y de vos
nunca se parte ya paz amigable.

268 *Descripción del tiempo*

El lúcido Febo ya nos demostraba
el don que no pudo negar a Faetonte:
subiendo la falda del nuestro horizonte,
del todo la fusca tiniebla privada;
sus crines doradas así dilataba
que todas las selvas con sus arboledas,
cumbres y montes y altas roquedas,
de más nueva lumbre los iluminaba.

266 *Comparison*

Like ferocious lions behave,
when fasting makes their hunger pains stronger—
they eat frozen carrion,
because live prey evades them—
so the constellations behave in this way: 2125
whenever they find an obstacle to their predictions,
they satisfy their ire in a similar form:
on it they can exert their influences.

267

Therefore, magnificent great constable,
blind Fortune, who hungered after you, 2130
was satisfied by the bronze simulacrum;
from here on out she is favorable to you.
For let us all note an admirable case,
and let all who follow us note,
that between you and her, and her and you 2135
never again will an amicable peace fail.

268 *Description of Time*

Radiant Phoebus already was showing us
the gift that he could not deny to Phaethon:
climbing the edges of our horizon,
divesting all of the obscuring darkness. 2140
His golden tresses spread in such manner
that all the forests with their tree groves,
summits and mountains, and rocky heights
he illumined in a newer light.

269

Yo, que las señas vi del claro día,
pensé si los hechos de lo relatado
hubiese durmiendo ya fantaseado,
o fuese veraz la tal compañía;
dispuse conmigo que demandaría,
por ver más abierta la información,
quier fuese vera, quier ficta visión,
a la Providencia que siempre me guía.

270

Así que propuse por esta manera:
"O gran profetisa, quienquier que tú seas,
con ojos iguales suplico que veas
mi duda, y le prestes razón verdadera:
yo te demando, gentil compañera,
me digas del nuestro grand rey y fiel
qué se dispone en el cielo d'aquél."
E luego con boca habló placentera:

271

"Será rey de reyes y rey de señores,
sobrando, venciendo los títulos todos,
y las hazañas de reyes de godos,
y rica memoria de los sus mayores;
y tal y tan alto favor de loores
sus hechos ilustres al tu rey darán
qu'en su claro tiempo del todo serán
con él olvidados sus antecesores."

269

I, who saw the signals of a clear day, 2145
wondered whether I might have fantasized
the events just related while sleeping,
or whether it could be that such company was real;
I thought to myself that I would ask
Providence, who is always my guide, 2150
in order to better understand whether
the information was a true or fictive vision.

270

So I inquired in this manner:
"Oh great prophetess, whoever you may be,
with gentle eyes I plead that you resolve 2155
my doubt, and grant it true reason:
I request that you, noble companion,
speak to me about our great and faithful king,
what is decreed for him in the heavens."
And then she spoke with a pleasing voice: 2160

271

"He will be king of kings and sovereign of lords,
overcoming, triumphing over all kingdoms
and the deeds of Gothic kings
and the rich memory of his forebears;
and such an exalted bestowal of praises 2165
will be granted to your king for his illustrious acts
that with him, in his splendid time,
his predecessors will be completely forgotten."

272

"Será Gerión con los olvidados;
será como muerta la fama de Cindo,
rey de los godos magnífico, lindo,
uno primero de los bateados;
serán adormidos y no relatados
los hechos de Bamba con el nuevo uso,
rey de Castilla que primero puso
términos justos a los obispados."

273

"Será olvidado lo más de lo antigo,
veyendo su fama crecer atán rica;
serán olvidados los hechos d'Egica,
bisnieto de Sindo y hijo de Eurigo;
será Vitisauris, según lo que digo,
morirá la memoria según que su dueño;
y ante los suyos serán como sueño
los hechos mayores del godo Rodrigo."

274

"A este los hechos del pobre Pelayo
reconocerán, aunque feroce,
tanta ventaja cuanta reconoce
el triste diciembre al hermoso mayo;
en este no miedo pondrán ni desmayo
los enemigos a él capitales,
antes más recio vendrá por los tales
que viene la llama d'encima de rayo."

272

"Geryon will join the forgotten;
the fame of Chinda will be as if dead, 2170
magnificent king of the Goths, righteous,
among the first to be baptized;
laid to rest and not recounted will be
the acts of Wamba with his new consuetude,
the king of Castile who first placed 2175
appropriate boundaries to bishoprics."

273

"Forgotten will be most of the ancient,
seeing his fame grow so richly;
forgotten will be the acts of Egica,
grandnephew of Chinda and son of Erwig; 2180
the same will happen to Witiza, according to my words:
his memory will die in tandem with its owner;
and before his, the major deeds
of the Goth Rodrigo will seem like a dream."

274

"Compared to this one, poor Pelayo's deeds, 2185
although ferocious, will be acknowledged to be
like those that gloomy December
acknowledges to be greater in beautiful May;
in this one, faintheartedness or fearfulness
will not be instilled by his foremost enemies, 2190
but rather he will come for them more boldly
than the flame comes after lightning."

275

"Favila olvidado será en aquel hora,
y los claros hechos de Alfonso el Primero,
aquel que a Segovia ganó de guerrero,
Braganza, Flavia, Ledezma, Zamora,
y Salamanca nos dio hasta ahora,
Astorga, Saldaña, León y Simancas,
Amaya y Viseo, haciéndolas francas
de moros con mano siempre vencedora."

276

"Conquistó Sepúlveda con lo ganado,
Orenés, Portugal, y poblólas luego
de gente de Asturias y mucho gallego,
gentío que vino de vuelta mezclado,
y de vizcaínos fue parte poblado;
mas cuanto tú oyes que hizo aquel rey
mediante de todo la divina ley
será con lo d'este siempre olvidado."

277

"Entonces Fruela por los sus errores
callará los casos de su triste muerte,
el cual a su hermano fue tanto de fuerte
que su homicida lo hacen autores;
si los hechos buenos ante los mejores
se olvidan, y callan por grandes los chicos,
¡cuánto más deben los inicos
callar ante hechos de grandes valores!"

275

"Favila will be forgotten at that time,
and the illustrious acts of Alfonso the First,
he who won Segovia in battle, and gave us 2195
Braganza, Iria Flavia, Ledesma, Zamora,
and Salamanca till now;
Astorga, Saldaña, León, and Simancas,
Amaya and Viseo, he freed
from Moors with an ever-victorious hand." 2200

276

"He conquered Sepúlveda, added to
Orense, Portugal, and then settled them
with people from Asturias and many Galicians,
people who again were mixed,
and in part it was settled with Basques; 2205
but whatever else you might hear that king did,
according to divine law,
all by comparison will be forgotten forever."

277

"Then Fruela, on account of his errors,
will be quiet about matters relating to his sad demise, 2210
he who was so ill-disposed toward his brother
that authors take him for his murderer;
if good actions, in the presence of better ones,
are forgotten, and small things are silenced for larger ones,
how much more so should the wicked 2215
hush before deeds of great value!"

278

"Ante los suyos serán adormidos
los hechos del casto Alfonso el Segundo,
que hizo en Oviedo por quien hizo el mundo
2220 templo do sean sus santos servidos;
ni menos los hechos serán repetidos
de Calvo Laín y de Nuño Rasuera,
antes darán más abierta carrera
a los que ser deben por este cumplidos."

279

2225 "Callarse han los hechos del magno Fernando,
de Sancho su hijo, y Alfonso el Tercero,
que al fuerte Toledo ganó de primero,
e irán do fueren, ante este callando;
la fama que fuere aqueste cobrando,
2230 el cuarto Alfonso que fue emperador
la irá perdiendo, y por su valor
al segundo Sancho irán olvidando."

280

"Del quinto Alfonso no será membranza,
que la de las Navas venció de Tolosa,
2235 una batalla tan mucho famosa,
do' fue más el hecho que no la esperanza;
nin será memoria de la malandanza
del primer Enrique que en adolescencia
la teja, o Fortuna, mató en Palencia,
2240 y sobre todo divina ordenanza."

278

"Compared to his acts, those of Alfonso the Second
the Chaste will be put to sleep,
he who in Oviedo made for the creator of the world
a temple where his holy saints might be served;   2220
nor will the deeds be repeated
of Calvo Laín and of Nuño Rasura,
but rather they will clear a wider path
for those that are yet to be done by this one."

279

"The deeds of Fernando the Great must be muted,   2225
of Sancho his son, and Alfonso the Third,
who first won fortified Toledo,
and, wherever they go, they would hush before this one;
the fame that would be acquired by
the fourth Alfonso, who was emperor,   2230
he will slowly lose; and on account of his value,
the second Sancho will be forgotten."

280

"Of the fifth Alfonso there will be no remembrance,
he who won the Navas de Tolosa,
a battle so very famous,   2235
that the deed surpassed expectations;
nor will the misfortunes be remembered
of the first Enrique, who in adolescence
a roofing tile or Fortune killed in Palencia,
and above all heaven's decree."   2240

281

"Y no tan nombrado será don Fernando,
en quien se hicieron los reinos más juntos,
rey y corona de reyes difuntos,
que tanto su mano ganó batallando;
2245 este conquistó por fuerza ganando
el reino de Murcia con toda su tierra;
este conquistó por fuerza de guerra
allende de cuanto diré relatando."

282

"Ubeda, Andújar, y más a Montiel,
2250 Vilches y Baños ganó con Baeza,
cortando de moros muy mucha cabeza,
así como bravo señor y fiel;
Iznatoraf y a Martos con él,
y con Salvatierra ganó Medellín,
2255 sufriendo muy poco criar el orín
en la su espada tajante, cruel."

283

"Conquistó las villas de Castro y Baena,
Córdoba y Écija, Palma y Estepa,
tanto que no me membrava donde quepa
2260 la su fortaleza con gran dicha buena;
ganónos Espejo, Trujillo y Marchena,
ganó Hornachuelos, a Luque, Montoro;

281

"And less renowned will be Don Fernando,
during whose reign the kingdoms were brought closer
    together,
king and crowning glory of departed kings,
whose hand won so much in battle;
he conquered by force, gaining 2245
the realm of Murcia with all of its land;
he conquered by force of arms
more than I could say."

282

"Ubeda, Andujar, in addition to Montiel,
Vilches and Baños he won with Baeza, 2250
cutting off so very many Moorish heads,
just like a fierce and faithful lord should;
Castrotorafe and Martos with it,
and with Salvatierra, he won Medellín,
letting very little tarnish form 2255
on his sharp, cruel sword."

283

"He conquered the towns of Castro and Baena,
Córdoba and Écija, Palma and Estepa,
so many that I could not recall where his fortitude,
known for its great goodness, would fit; 2260
he won Espejo, Trujillo, and Marchena for us,
he won Hornachuelos, Luque, Montoro;

por tales lugares sembró su tesoro,
no cobardeando fatiga ni pena."

284

2265 "Ganó Almodóvar y a Moratilla,
ganó a Zuheros y más Albendín,
ganó los Gazules, después a la fin
ganó sobre todos la grande Sevilla;
ganó a Jerez con la su cuadrilla,
2270 Cádiz y Arcos, Béjar y Lebrija;
y por que no sea mi habla prolija,
callo hazañas de gran maravilla."

285

"Mas según aquello que está ya dispuesto
del tu claro rey y de su majestad,
2275 ante sus hechos y prosperidad
en poco tendredes lo mucho d'aquesto;
tendredes en poco los hechos del sexto
Alfonso, persona de tanto misterio,
que fue de Alemania llamado al imperio,
2280 según que leyendo nos es manifiesto";

286

"aunque conquistó Hellín y Chinchilla,
las Peñas y Cuenca por fuerza d'espada,
Montánchez y Mérida la despoblada,

in such places he scattered his treasure,
not exhibiting cowardly fatigue or discomfort."

284

"He won Almodóvar and Moratilla, 2265
won Zueros in addition to Albendín,
won the Gazules; then at the end of his life,
he won above all great Seville;
won Jerez with his troops,
Cadiz and Arcos, Vejer and Lebrija; 2270
and so that my words be not prolix,
I say no more about other deeds of great wonder."

285

"But according to what already has been predicted
about your illustrious king and his majesty,
beholding his acts and good fortune, 2275
you will think not enough has been said;
you will look down on the deeds of the sixth
Alfonso, a person of so much mystery,
who was called by Germany to head the empire,
according to what our reading has made manifest"; 2280

286

"although he conquered Hellín and Chinchilla,
Las Peñas and Cuenca at sword point,
Montánchez and the depopulated Mérida,

Badajoz y Niebla juntó con Castilla,
y hizo rescate de gran maravilla:
al emperador de Constantinopla
libró de los Turcos, mejor que mi copla
lo dice trobando por habla sencilla."

287

"Iredes a Sancho Tercero callando,
aquel que la fuerte Tarifa conquiso;
irá ya dejando de ver nuestro viso
todos los hechos del tercer Fernando,
áquel que Alcaudete ganó batallando,
del que se dice morir emplazado
de los que de Martos hubo despeñado,
según dicen rústicos d'esto cantando."

288

"El séptimo Alfonso, su rebisabuelo,
querrá ser vencido de su rebisnieto,
y por que más sea famoso, perfecto,
habrá mayor gloria do goza en el cielo;
no embargante que puso por suelo
todos los reyes de Benimerín,
ganó más las Cuevas y a Locubín
con muy animoso, magnífico celo."

Badajoz and Niebla he joined with Castile,
and paid a ransom of wondrous size: 2285
The emperor of Constantinople he
rescued from the Turks, in a better way than my verses
can tell in plain words."

287

"You will go on to Sancho the Third in silence,
he who conquered strong Tarifa; 2290
your vision will already barely distinguish
all the deeds of the third Fernando,
that one who won Alcaudete in battle,
of whom it is said he died summoned
by those whom he had thrown off the cliff in Martos, 2295
according to what the rustics say when singing about this."

288

"The seventh Alfonso, his great-great grandfather,
will be defeated by his great-great grandson,
and so that he could be more famous, perfect,
he will have greater glory where he delights in the heavens; 2300
notwithstanding the fact that he consigned to the dirt
all the Marinid kings,
in addition to conquering Las Cuevas and Locubín
with a very spirited, magnificent zeal."

289

2305 "A Teba y Cañete ganó conquiriendo,
a Rute y Priego y a Carcabuey,
haciendo hazañas conformes a rey,
a todos peligros remedio poniendo;
prolija fatiga por gloria sufriendo,
2310 conquistó de moros la gran Algecira;
conquistó Bencaide, tomada por ira,
y Benamejí más a punto siendo."

290

"Entonces veredes escura la fama
del bravo don Pedro, según la clemencia
2315 que d'este se muestra por fe d'experiencia,
siendo constante siempre a quien ama;
veredes cesada la muy clara fama
de aquel don Enrique, su buen bisabuelo;
veredes con este callar el abuelo,
2320 aunque por nombre semejante se llama."

291

"Tú, don Enrique, querrás ser callado,
tú que concordia de toda tu tierra
pudiste ser dicho sin punto de guerra,
teniendo tu reino tan bien sosegado;
2325 aunque tu hijo más aventurado
reinar en la tierra desd'el cielo veas,
asaz es a ti que por padre tú seas
de aqueste muy alto don Juan pregonado."

289

"Teba and Cañete, Rute and Priego, and Carcabuey, he gained through conquest,
accomplishing deeds worthy of a king,
finding remedies for all dangers;
suffering untold fatigue in exchange for glory,
he conquered great Algeciras from Moors,
conquered Benzaide, taken with fury,
and Benamejí, being more to the point."

290

"Then you will see darkened the fame
of the fierce Don Pedro, such is the clemency
he showed by experience,
being constant always to his beloved;
you will see halted the preeminent fame
of that Don Enrique, his good great-grandfather;
with this one you will see his grandfather silenced,
although he is called by a similar name."

291

"You, Don Enrique, will want to be silenced,
you who could be hailed as the peacemaker of all your land,
never waging a single war,
keeping your kingdom so much at peace;
even though you were to see from the heavens
your most fortunate son reigning on earth,
it is sufficient for you to be proclaimed
father to this very exalted Don Juan."

292

    Así profetizando la mi guiadora,
rey soberano, las vuestras andanzas,
dándovos alto favor d'esperanzas
con lengua fatídica y boca sonora,
y más abajando su voz sabidora,
representaba ya, como callando,
los tiempos futuros de cómo y de cuándo
será vuestra mano siempre vencedora.

293

    Yo que quisiera ser certificado
d'estas andanzas y cuándo serían,
y cuándo los tiempos se nos mudarían,
o cuándo veríamos el reino apaciguado,
ítem quisiera ser más informado
de toda la rueda que dije futura,
y de los hechos que son de ventura
o que se rigen por curso hadado.

294

    Mas el imagen de la Providencia
hallé de mis ojos ser desvanecida,
y vi por lo alto su clara subida
hacer afectando la divina excelencia;
yo deseando con gran reverencia
tener abrazados sus miembros garridos,
hallé con mis brazos mis hombros ceñidos,
y todo lo visto huyó a mi presencia.

292

My guide so prophesizing
your endeavors, sovereign king, 2330
bestowing high favor to your hopes,
with a fateful tongue and a resounding mouth,
and further lowering her voice full of wisdom,
as if in a hush, at once spoke of
the coming times, and how and when 2335
your hand will be always victorious.

293

I, who wished to be reassured
about these matters, and when they would come to pass,
and when the times would be favorable to us,
or when we would see the kingdom at peace, 2340
also wanted to be more informed
about all of the future wheel I spoke of,
and of the outcomes that are up to chance
or that are governed by a predestined course.

294

But the image of Providence, 2345
I found, disappeared from before my eyes,
and I saw her make a splendid ascent on high,
taking on the impression of divine excellence;
I, desiring with great reverence
to embrace her elegant limbs, 2350
found that my arms clasped around my shoulders,
and all that I had previously seen fled from my presence.

295 *Comparación*

Como los niños o los ignorantes,
veyendo los átomos ir por la lumbre,
2355 tienden sus manos por su muchedumbre,
mas húyenles ellos, su tacto negantes,
por modos atales o por semejantes
la mi guiadora huyó de mis manos;
huyeron las ruedas y cuerpos humanos,
2360 y fueron las causas a mi latitantes.

296

Pues si los dichos de grandes profetas
y los que demuestran las veras señales,
y las entrañas de los animales,
y todo misterio sutil de planetas,
2365 y vaticinio de artes secretas
nos profetizan triunfos de vos,
haced verdaderas, señor rey, por Dios,
las profecías que no son perfectas.

297

Haced verdadera la gran Providencia,
2370 mi guiadora en aqueste camino,
la cual vos ministra por mando divino
fuerza, coraje, valor y prudencia,
por que la vuestra real excelencia
haya de moros pujante victoria,
2375 y de los vuestros así dulce gloria
que todos vos hagan, señor, reverencia.

295 *Comparison*

As happens when children or the ignorant,
upon seeing particles move through blazing light,
reach out with their hands on account of their number, 2355
but these retreat from them, refusing their touch,
so in a similar way,
my guide evaded my hands,
the wheels and human bodies vanished,
and the causes of things were hidden from me. 2360

296

For, if the sayings of great prophets
and those who reveal true portents,
and the entrails of animals,
and all the subtle mystery of planets,
and the predictions of occult arts 2365
prophesize your triumphs to us,
by God, lord king, make true
the prophesies that are not perfect.

297

Make true what great Providence has said
(my guide in this journey, 2370
she who provides force, courage,
valor, and prudence by divine order),
so that Your Royal Excellence
may inflict crushing victory over the Moors,
and receive sweet praise from your subjects; 2375
may they all, lord, be reverential to you.

298

La flaca barquilla de mis pensamientos,
veyendo mudanza de tiempos oscuros,
cansada ya toma los puertos seguros,
temiendo discordia de los elementos.
Tremen las ondas y luchan los vientos;
cansa mi mano con el governalle;
las nueve Musas me mandan que calle;
fin me demandan mis largos tormentos.

299

Y ya fin les daba con gesto placiente,
en ocio trocando mi dulce fatiga,
no porque mengua ni falta que diga,
mas yerra quien dice, si dice y no siente.
El largo trabajo secuestra la mente,
así que hablando no siento que digo,
por ende dispuso mi seso conmigo
dar fin callando al libro presente.

300

Mas voz de muy sublime autoridad
súbito luego me fue presentada:
"Escribe, tú," dijo, "no des fin nada,
cresca tu obra, diciendo verdad,

THE LABYRINTH OF FORTUNE

298

The frail ship of my thoughts,
seeing the mutability of storm-darkened times,
already wearily seeks anchor in safe ports,
fearing the clash of the elements. 2380
The waves tremble and the winds fight;
my hand tires of holding the helm of the ship;
the nine Muses command me to be silent;
my long torments demand that I come to an end.

299

And I came to the end of my travails with an affable face, 2385
exchanging for leisure my sweet fatigue,
not because of any insufficiency or want of words,
but because one errs in speaking if one speaks and does not listen.
Prolonged labor isolates the mind;
therefore, when speaking, I do not hear what I say; 2390
for that reason my common sense ordered me
to end this book with silence.

300

However, a voice of very sublime authority
suddenly appeared before me:
"Keep writing," she said. "Don't think that you are done; 2395
let your work grow larger by telling the truth,

ca vicio no hace la prolijidad
do' trae buen modo de satisfacer;
si pueden favores prestarte placer,
2400 favor es el mundo de mi majestad."

because prolixity is not a vice
when its intentions are good;
if help can bring relief to you,
granting succor is the sphere of my majesty."

Note on the Text

The Labyrinth of Fortune survives in eighteen manuscripts belonging to two textual families, labeled A and B, respectively, that stem from the same manuscript. The best version of A (Paris, Bibliothèque nationale de France, Espagnol MS 229, better known by its Dutton designation as PN7) is not only the basis of this edition but also of most modern critical editions. It was copied by four scribes, and two commenter-correctors glossed it. Some of these glosses are early and may have been written by Mena himself, others are subsequent additions, and some were later copied from the first edition of *Las Trezientas*. See Maxim P. A. M. Kerkhof, "Notas de crítica textual sobre el *Laberinto de Fortuna* de Juan de Mena," *Neophilologus* 77, no. 4 (1993): 573–86, and Maxim P. A. M. Kerkhof, "El Ms. 229 (PN7) de la 'Bibliothèque nationale' de París; base de las ediciones modernas del *Laberinto de Fortuna* de Juan de Mena," *Medievalia* 50 (2018): 217–31.

The Labyrinth of Fortune also appeared in three related print editions (Salamanca, ca. 1481?; Zaragoza, 1489; and Seville, 1496) and was newly edited by Hernán Núñez in 1499 and reedited with changes in 1505. See Julian Weiss and Antonio Cortijo Ocaña, eds., *Glosa sobre las "Trezientas" del famoso poeta Juan de Mena* (Madrid, 2015); all of our references to *Las Trezientas* are to their edition. Although we do not incorporate any of the glosses from PN7 or *Las Trezientas,* we adopt some of PN7's scribal corrections and an occasional reading from *Las Trezientas,* in keeping with earlier editors. Deviations from and corrections to PN7 are indicated in the Notes to the Text.

As mentioned in the Introduction, our text is modernized as long as it does not interfere with the syllable count of a line or violate the rhyme scheme of a stanza. However, we have left some archaic words and poetic expressions that can still be understood by readers of modern Spanish who are familiar with such conventions in literary texts. It is also our belief that an edition of an exhortatory poem like *El Laberinto* should make use of exclamations more frequently than has been done by past editors. Also note that although the translation attempts to replicate the distribution of Mena's verses in the prose translation for ease of comparison, this is only possible approximately ninety percent of the time, because otherwise the syntax would become disruptively awkward. Likewise, note that Spanish and English punctuation norms do not always coincide (see our Introduction) and that we do not adopt PN7's initial capitalization of each line of verse. Finally, PN7 does not number the poem's stanzas from 1 to 300, but we follow the practice accepted since *Las Trezientas* and do so. In addition, we enumerate each fifth verse consecutively as other modern editors have done.

Notes to the Text

25   As many editors have done, we add *que* to the first verse of this stanza, although PN7 reads, *Commo que creo no fuessen menores.*

32   This is the reading of PN7. Other readings make *dañada* plural to agree with *hazañas.*

41   PN7 *desrama* (to unbranch); Núñez, *Las Trezientas, derrama* (to spill or flow unto). We also accept the insertion by the corrector of PN7 of an *E* before *ya.*

43   PN7 inserts *a* before *spira.*

46   PN7 incorrectly writes *Tetis.* As Núñez, *Las Trezientas,* notes, Mena refers to Thespiae. (See Notes to the Translation.)

48   PN7 *suplid cobdiçiando,* as do all other manuscripts, but the glosser of Núñez, *Las Trezientas,* inserts *cobijando* above it, which makes better sense.

56   PN7 *más una*: A syncope for *más unida* for the sake of the rhyme.

69   The scribe or glosser of PN7 inserts the conjunction *o* before *muestra,* which we translate as "either show."

71   PN7 *nos fatigas*: An error for *nos fatigues.*

126   PN7 *allí con aquesto deseo*; Núñez, *Las Trezientas, asy con este deseo.*

130   PN7 *se mire de derecho en drecho*; Núñez, *Las Trezientas, se mire derecho en derecho.*

147   PN7 *ad'aquellos que son*; Núñez, *Las Trezientas, en aquellos que son.*

150   PN7 *de poder mirar*; Núñez, *Las Trezientas, de dialogar.*

235   *por bien qu'el ocorra*: We do not modernize *ocorra* because of the rhyme.

260   PN7 *salran los dichos según las razones*; Núñez, *Las Trezientas,* writes *sobran* instead of *salran,* but *salran* is an attested form.

NOTES TO THE TEXT

272   PN7 *cuando delante*; Núñez, *Las Trezientas, cuanto adelante*.

297   PN7 *como se llega*; Núñez, *Las Trezientas, como se allega*; however, both mean the same thing.

319   PN7 *sancto*; Núñez, *Las Trezientas, sancta*.

327   PN7 writes *lo lidia*. We correct as others do to *Licia*, an area in Asia Minor.

343   PN7 *porque la nuestra España*; Núñez, *Las Trezientas, por que la tierra de España*.

348   PN7 *en tierra muy fría*; Núñez, *Las Trezientas, que es tierra muy fría*.

387   PN7 *suertes de Amon do son los tripodas*; Núñez, *Las Trezientas, Sirtes de Amon do son las tripodas*. The former makes better sense.

418   PN7 has an interlinear insertion of an *e* before *Bosis*.

530   PN7 *aquí non perezca* (will not perish here); Núñez, *Las Trezientas, aquí non parezca* (were not to appear here).

560   PN7 *para tú mientes* (stop your hesitation); Núñez, *Las Trezientas, para bien mientes* (pay attention).

563   PN7 inserts *an* before *Tropus*; Núñez, *Las Trezientas, Atropos*.

577–92   PN7 inverts stanzas 73 and 74, but this order makes little sense given the flow of the conversation with Divine Providence. We follow the order of Núñez, *Las Trezientas*, in the Spanish text and in the translation.

595   PN7 *era ínclita reina*; Núñez, *Las Trezientas, era la ínclita reina*.

603   PN7 *mas de virtudes aquella noticia*; Núñez, *Las Trezientas, ha de virtudes aquella noticia* (in addition to those features of virtue).

621   PN7 *una siona* with the scribal insertion of an *e*, to read *esiona*; Núñez, *Las Trezientas, una sy ovo es otra sin falla* (she is doubtless another). Although both verses refer to Penelope, the last is the reading favored by Maxim P. A. M. Kerkhof, ed., *El laberinto de Fortuna* (Madrid, 1995), and by our translation.

637   PN7 reads *Mas no dejaré decir,* but we accept the insertion by Kerkhof, *El laberinto*, of *de* after *decir*.

660   PN7 *non vieçan la gente*; Núñez, *Las Trezientas, no envicien la gente*.

686   PN7 *de Paladión*; Núñez, *Las Trezientas, del Paladión*.

687   PN7 *de lacahón*; Núñez, *Las Trezientas, de Laocoón*.

698   Kerkhof, *El laberinto, ermano de aquel buen archero de Roma*.

709   PN7 *ya se t'acerca aquel vil Anthenor*; Kerkhof, *El laberinto, yaces*

NOTES TO THE TEXT

	açerca, tú, vil Anthenor, with a note stating why he prefers this reading, which we accept.
828	PN7 *en forma monstruosa*; we accept, as Kerkhof, *El laberinto,* does, the variant found in other manuscripts, *en forma mintrosa.*
961	PN7 *la compañía virgen e perfecta*; we opt like Kerkhof, *El laberinto,* for *la compañía vírginea perfecta.*
962	PN7 *vimos en alto de vidas tranquilas,* which makes most sense given the context; Núñez, *Las Trezientas, acto,* which other manuscripts render as *auto.*
1100	PN7 *e los enemigo sobaro[n] apares*; Núñez, *Las Trezientas, y los enemigos sobraron a pares.*
1135	PN7 *de una silla*; Núñez, *Las Trezientas, en una silla,* which we choose.
1173	PN7 *hazes* ("troops" or "forces"); Núñez, *Las Trezientas, pazes.*
1252	PN7 *mas fuera serían*; Núñez, *Las Trezientas, fuera se ríen,* which is preferable.
1297	PN7 *Si la su triste partida*; Núñez, *Las Trezientas, En la su triste partida,* which we follow.
1360	PN7 *plados* is a common vacillation between *r* and *l.*
1378	PN7 *levanten*; we follow Núñez, *Las Trezientas,* as it maintains the imperative mood.
1414	PN7 *con su sañ*; Núñez, *Las Trezientas* omits *su,* since it adds a thirteenth syllable.
1440	PN7 *dejara*; Núñez, *Las Trezientas* writes *dejaban,* which agrees with the consonant rhyme scheme and maintains the imperfect tense of the phrase.
1445	PN7 *que lo diga,* as does Núñez, *Las Trezientas*; we maintain the extra syllable, as do a majority of editors (not omitting *que* or *lo*).
1525	We do not modernize *estudo* (antique for *estuvo*) because of the rhyme.
1555	We do not modernize *puna* (as *pugna*) because of the rhyme.
1578–79	PN7 *mayor vi tu fin que non vi tu miedo, / mayor vi tu daño que non el remiedo*; we follow editors like Kerkhof and prefer the reading in Núñez, *Las Trezientas: menor vi tu fin que non vi tu medio, / mayor vi tu daño que non el remedio.*

NOTES TO THE TEXT

1618	We do not modernize *vido* (as *vio*) because of the rhyme.
1701	We do not modernize *cedo* because of the rhyme.
1734	PN7 *con el su sobrino*; in keeping with other editors, we follow the reading in Núñez, *Las Trezientas,* of *censorino*. (See Notes to the Translation.)
1759	PN7 *turbea*; we follow the superior reading in Núñez, *Las Trezientas: trábea*.
1774	We do not modernize *onustos* because of the rhyme.
1780	PN7 *non vos*; in keeping with other editors, we follow Núñez, *Las Trezientas,* for the spelling of the object pronoun.
1789	PN7 *solo vosotros*; Núñez, *Las Trezientas, todos vosotros,* which makes more sense, since the poet speaks of people occupying humble stations, collectively.
1815	We do not modernize the phrase *maguer que* as *aunque* in this instance, since it would disrupt the pattern of stressed syllables.
1847	PN7 *pugne*; we follow the more accepted reading in Núñez, *Las Trezientas*.
1923	PN7 *Después que formada*; we follow the reading of Núñez, *Las Trezientas, de sierpe formada,* also suggested by the commentary in PN7.
1927	PN7 *e de aquella*; Núñez, *Las Trezientas, y aquella*.
1928	We do not modernize *fornece* because of the rhyme.
1967	PN7 *otros*, an adjective; Núñez, *Las Trezientas,* is more correct in writing the distributive conjunction *oras* (line 1965).
1981	PN7 *vos espero*; in keeping with other editors, we follow the spelling of Núñez, *Las Trezientas,* for the object pronoun.
1998	PN7 *demuestras*; we follow the omission by Núñez, *Las Trezientas* of the prefix *de* to maintain the twelve-syllable count.
2026	We do not modernize *seta* (as *secta*) because of the rhyme.
2029	We do not modernize *asayan* (as *intentan*) because of the rhyme.
2033	PN7 *tales dignidades*; we follow the better reading in Núñez, *Las Trezientas, indignidades,* although it adds an extra syllable.
2034	We do not modernize *discordanzas (discordancias)* because of the rhyme.
2042	PN7 *ansí lo termino*; we follow the better reading in Núñez, *Las Trezientas, asy determino su hado [y] pregono*.
2067	We do not modernize *objectos* (as *objetos*) because of the rhyme.

NOTES TO THE TEXT

2085   We do not modernize by eliminating the diphthong in *derruecan* to give *derrocan* because of the rhyme.

2172   PN7 erroneously reads *Dono primero* (which could be a copy error); Núñez, *Las Trezientas,* has *uno primero*; we do not modernize *bateados* (as *bautizados*) because of the rhyme.

2177   We do not modernize *antigo* (as *antiguo*) because of the rhyme.

2181   PN7 *seran batizates*; we follow the better reading from Núñez, *Las Trezientas, Vitisauris,* which, as Núñez notes, is a lengthening of the name Vitiza for the purposes of syllable count.

2192   PN7 *de rayo dençima*; we follow Núñez, *Las Trezientas,* to maintain the rhyme.

2193   PN7 erroneously writes *Fabula,* and its corrector *Fafila*; we follow Núñez, *Las Trezientas, Favila.*

2204   PN7 *gente*; we follow Núñez, *Las Trezientas, gentío,* to complete the twelve-syllable line.

2110   PN7 *callaran*; Núñez, *Las Trezientas* omits the *n* in keeping with the subject of the verb.

2228   PN7 *e ya do*; Núñez, *Las Trezientas,* has the correct reading.

2233   We do not modernize *membranza* (as *recuerdo*) because of the rhyme.

2304   PN7 *e Alocovin*; we follow Kerkhof in identifying the placename as Locubín.

2360   We do not change *latitantes* to the modern *ocultados* because of the rhyme.

2377   The remaining stanzas that begin here, often viewed as apocryphal (see the Introduction), are present in both PN7 and other manuscripts, as well as Núñez, *Las Trezientas.*

2382   We do not modernize *governalle* (as *governarle*) because of the rhyme.

2392   PN7 *dar fin al libro, callando al presente*; we follow the reading in Núñez, *Las Trezientas,* as it seems to give a more definitive closure to the poem.

2399   PN7 *saber* at the end of this verse, a word which the corrector changes to *plazer,* in keeping with Núñez, *Las Trezientas* (maintaining the consonant rhyme).

2400   PN7 *mando,* which the corrector changes to *mundo,* in keeping with the reading in Núñez, *Las Trezientas.*

Notes to the Translation

1–8   The first stanza dedicates the poem to Juan II of Castile and immediately reveals the classical bent of the text. God is Jupiter, and the king is likened to Caesar.

5   *the new Caesar*: Mena creates the neologism *novelo* (new) for metric reasons. English "novel," unlike Spanish, stresses recency.

7   *virtue and power abide*: The two qualities were thought to be incompatible attributes that could not coexist in one person.

8   *knee bent to the ground*: Although "knee" is singular, Mena refers to his own and the genuflections of others. Hernán Núñez, *Las Trezientas* (Seville, 1499), ed. Julian Weiss and Antonio Cortijo Ocaña, *Glosa sobre las "Trezientas" del famoso poeta Juan de Mena* (Madrid, 2015), and Francisco Sánchez de las Brozas, *Anotaciones del maestro Francisco Sánchez a las obras de Juan de Mena,* ed. Eustaquio Sánchez Salor and César Chaparro Gómez, *Obras,* vol. 2, *Poesía* (Cáceres, 1985), both have *las rodillas* (knees) in their versions of this verse.

9–56   These verses establish the subject of the poem, the unjust variability of Fortune, and the fact that the poet will venture to say things that are normally not stated. They invoke Calliope (the Muse of epic poetry and eloquence), Apollo, and the rest of the Muses. They also tell us that it is necessary for heroes to have a poet to commemorate them, or else their feats are condemned to oblivion.

15   *tersely describe*: *Breve suma,* the words employed by manuscript PN7 (Paris, Bibliothèque nationale de France, Espagnol MS 229), refer to a type of work that abbreviates a narrative.

NOTES TO THE TRANSLATION

16 *so let Apollo conclude*: Apollo is the god of inspiration. Works dedicated to him often contained the words *solvat Apollo* or, as Mena phrased it, *dé fin Apolo,* meaning that his account of past and present deeds could be ended only with the continued inspiration of Apollo. The last three stanzas of the poem return to this wish, when the Muses tell Mena that it is time to finish their joint project: "the nine Muses command me to be silent" (2383).

17 *Calliope, be favorable to me*: Calliope was the Muse of eloquence and epic poetry. Her voice was both ecstatic and harmonious.

19 *and with which*: The phrase *y por que* in manuscript PN7 modifies the noun "wings" in the previous phrase: "and [the ones] with which" *(y por [las] que)*.

21 *its ineffable voice*: Its indescribable or unknowable voice.

24 *spread from person to person*: Although the singular *gente* (people) is an aggregate noun, we opt instead to use the more idiomatic "person" rather than "people."

26 *of the Cid*: Rodrigo Ruy Díaz de Vivar, otherwise known as the Cid, was Spain's greatest hero. Mena compares his deeds to those of Scipio Africanus, the Roman general who defeated Hannibal at the battle of Zama in Africa.

28 *the agenores*: The Phoenicians Agenor and his son Cadmus were kings in northern Libya, which, as Pliny, *Natural History* 5.1, explains, is the Greek name for northern Africa. Cadmus had killed a sacred dragon that guarded a spring dedicated to Mars and was told by Minerva to sow its teeth on the ground. From these "seeds" sprang ferocious warriors, who battled each other over ownership of a jewel that Cadmus had thrown among them. Only five survived. They joined Cadmus and founded the city of Thebes. This interpretation makes most sense given the importance of Cadmus to *The Labyrinth* and to the fact that the Carthaginians who battled Scipio descended from the Agenorides. However, Núñez, *Las Trezientas,* indicates in his note to this line that "Agenores" may actually be an epenthesis for *agenos,* expanded by Mena because of verse length and rhyme. In either case, Mena may have also used *agenores* to sub-

230

NOTES TO THE TRANSLATION

tly recall the later Arab kings of Africa. Note that the first part of the stanza begins with a question—why were the deeds of the Cid and the ferocity of the Christians not as well-known as those of Africanus and the Agenores?—that is immediately answered: their great deeds and the love of those who cherished them most are not remembered because not many authors wrote about them.

33 *the mother of Ninyas*: Semiramis was an Assyrian queen who ruled Babylon for decades after the death of her husband and surrounded the ancient city with high brick walls. She was the mother of Ninyas.

37 *the walls that Phoebus erected*: The god Phoebus (or "bright") Apollo had constructed the walls of Troy. Babylon and Troy were reputed to have the strongest walls in the ancient world, yet they were both destroyed.

38 *Argolic might*: The Greek forces gathered at the city of Argos.

41–42 *spill onto me your bounty*: Manuscript PN7 has *derrama en mi tu subsidio* ("spill" or "overflow onto me your bounty"). Other manuscripts read *piero subsidio,* which, as the gloss in PN7 says, comes from "Pierides," another name for the Muses, who defeated the nine daughters of King Pieros in a song contest and were transformed into birds; Ovid, *Metamorphoses* 5.294–678, trans. Frank Justus Miller (Cambridge, MA, 1916). Together with Apollo, the Muses lived by the fountains Hippocrene or Aganippe, whose waters were a metaphor for inspiration.

46 *oh daughters of Thespis*: The Muses were the daughters of Melponeme and Zeus but, according to Núñez, *Las Trezientas,* they were much honored in Thespiae, a city near Mount Helicon in Boeotia. Ovid calls the Muses "daughters of Thespiae" (*Metamorphoses* 5.294–331).

49–96 The poet asks Fortune to allow him to speak as truthfully as he can about why, while order is the rule of heaven, disorder rules the world.

57 *the order of the sky*: The celestial firmament is seen as an orderly place.

59 *look at the Trion*: The Trion, an apocope for *Septentriones,* are the

NOTES TO THE TRANSLATION

seven stars of the Big Dipper. Their irregular movements may be considered a form of inconsistency, but they repeat in a set sequence, so they are also part of the immutable laws of heaven.

61 *and the seven Pleiades that Atlas sees*: The Pleiades are the seven daughters of Atlas and the Naiad Pleione, who were transformed into stars by the gods (Ovid, *Metamorphoses* 1.668–88). Manuscript PN7 uses *otea* (see from on high) to imply that the Pleiades are so close to the Atlas Mountains that they almost touch it.

62 *hide at the coming of winter*: Mena uses the Latinate *bruma* (winter) for the sake of the rhyme.

82 *a sea without obstructions*: The Spanish is *mar sin repunta*. The *Diccionario de la Real Academia Española* (Madrid, 1726–1739), vol. 5, p. 690b, defines *repunta* as an outthrust of the earth, that is, a "cape," and uses this stanza as an example. However, a secondary meaning of the word *repunta* is "altercation" or "ire," therefore, our translation, "without obstructions."

84 *Boreas*: Boreas is the North Wind.

85 *when the Australis churns the sea*: Manuscript PN7 has *pero si el Norte conmueve al tridente,* but with *Austro* (from Auster, the South Wind) inserted above the line by one of the correctors in place of *Norte* (North). The correction accords with the text of Núñez, *Las Trezientas*. Mena's *conmueve al tridente* (shakes the trident) refers to the trident of Neptune, the god of the sea; hence the words are used metaphorically to mean the wind "churns" or "stirs" the sea.

88 *absolute repose*: Manuscript PN7 has *reposo patente* (absolute or obvious repose). Other manuscripts and Núñez, *Las Trezientas,* read *reposo paciente* (calm or patient repose), which we do not adopt.

90 *the uncertainty of your cases*: The reference links the events brought about by Fortune to the uncertainty of the currents mentioned in the previous stanza. The term is also connected to judicial "cases" of uncertain outcome.

95 *bear witness by sight*: Mena proposes himself as an eyewitness.

97–112	The goddess Bellona transports the poet to heaven in her dragon chariot and leaves him alone on a plain near a city.
99	*and Mother Bellona, full of fury*: Bellona is the Latin goddess of war. The whip and chariot are her attributes; Lucan, *The Civil War (Pharsalia)* 7.568–70, trans. J. D. Duff (Cambridge, MA, 1928).
112	*religious in appearance and secular in behavior*: Manuscript PN7: *en son religioso y modo profano*. The verse metaphorically refers to religious and profane music. According to Sebastián de Covarrubias, *Tesoro de la lengua castellana o española* [1611] (Madrid, 1979), 1268b, "el son dize cierta correspondencia a la consonancia música"; however, the gloss to this line in Núñez, *Las Trezientas,* implies that the terms *son* and *modo* (here translated "appearance" and "behavior") both refer to the avocation of the people as revealed by their dress.
113–36	Mena describes the splendid white color of the city and wonders if his sight is sufficient to describe its brilliance, comparing the vision to a reflection in a mirror that does not satisfy the beholder.
116	*that it rivaled Parian marble*: Parian is a flawless, fine-grained, semitranslucent, pure-white marble. It is quarried on the Greek island of Paros and has been famous since antiquity. The *p* of *Paros,* however, seems to be a correction of an *f,* which would render the line *mármol de Faro* (marble from Faro, in Portugal). As Maxim P. A. M. Kerkhof, "Notas de crítica textual sobre el *Laberinto de Fortuna* de Juan de Mena," *Neophilologus* 77, no. 4 (1993): 578 and 585n28, observes, there is also precedent for this reading.
118	*reflected in the diaphanous clarity of its stones*: Mena's *el viso de la criatura* (the face or sight of the thing created) slightly anthropomorphizes the walls ringing the city by comparing them to a resplendent face.
119	*could attract as many things as possible to itself*: *Objeto* commonly means "thing," but here it implies that the purity or beauty of the wall is a magnet that attracts as many people to itself as it already contains.

NOTES TO THE TRANSLATION

124   *when looking through ocular instruments*: The gloss to Mena's *cuando los medios son especulares* in Sánchez de las Brozas, *Anotaciones,* explains in his commentary on this line that the verse can refer to something seen through an intervening object like a glass window or a magnifying glass. Mena, however, wants to see the characteristics of the city more directly. The adjective he uses *(especulares)* also points to a deeper understanding of things, as in *ciencias especulativas* (speculative sciences), in opposition to opinion or faith-based "knowledge." This is one of the topics woven throughout *The Labyrinth:* Humans want to know but cannot.

129   *Like one with a mirror before him*: Medieval mirrors cast an uneven reflection. The mercury-backed mirrors that replaced them during the Renaissance were more accurate.

137–76   Stormy events presage the arrival of Divine Providence, and Mena again wonders if his vision is up to the task. However, light pierces through the storm clouds and reveals the presence of a beautiful and well-proportioned maiden, whose arrival allows the poet to see clearly once again. He then asks her name.

142   *the fate of Polyphemus*: Polyphemus was a giant Cyclops, who was fooled by Ulysses.

143   *who, after being completely blinded*: Manuscript PN7: *que desque ciego en la gruta de leno;* Maxim P. A. M. Kerkhof, *El laberinto de Fortuna* (Madrid, 1995), corrects *leno* to *Lemo* to rhyme with *Polifemo.* However, Lemo or Lemnos has nothing to do with the story of the Cyclops and Ulysses. The error may have arisen from the fact that the scribe may have failed to write a tilde over the *n* of *leño* (log). This reading makes better sense as a reference to the stake that blinded Polyphemus, but it does not agree with the rhyme of the stanza. We prefer Núñez, *Las Trezientas*'s reading: *ciego venido en extremo.*

164   *the faculty that was lost was recovered*: The verse refers back to the faculty of sight, or *visiva potencia,* in 148.

174   *I beg you to tell me why you came forth*: *Cómo* can mean either *¿de qué modo?* (how, in what way) or *¿por qué?* (why).

NOTES TO THE TRANSLATION

176 *what is the name of Your Wisdom?*: We follow María Rosa Lida de Malkiel, *Juan de Mena, poeta del prerrenacimiento español* (Mexico City, 1984), 258, in considering *cómo se llama la tu discreción* a courtly way of asking for the name of Providence, which is given at the end of the next stanza.

177–248 The maiden reveals that she is Divine Providence, and Mena asks her to be his guide into the city and the House of Fortune. Providence agrees and says that she will reveal to him all that can be grasped by the flawed human intellect. She then takes him by the hand and goes toward the gate of the city, where they happen on a press of people converging on the same entrance. However, Providence whisks him away from that congestion and takes him to the House of Fortune.

205 *You will at least know what is the type*: Manuscript PN7's reading, *sabrás a lo menos cuál es el efecto,* has a scribal insertion of a *d* (*defecto,* "flaw"), which makes better sense. However, *efecto* can also mean the "worth" or "quality" of something or someone.

218 *give me such a branch to forewarn me*: Mena asks for a golden branch like the one from Proserpina's tree of virtue that the Cumaean Sibyl gave to Aeneas to protect him during his descent into Hades. The sense of the word that Mena uses *(avises)* combines "sight" with "warning" and "protection." He thinks that the magic branch would allow him to see more clearly and avoid mishaps, but Divine Providence tells him that it is not necessary as long as he does not seek to know what he should not, or cannot, know.

219 *Anchises*: Aeneas's father.

220 *descent into Erebus*: In Greek mythology, Erebus, or Tartaros, is a place of darkness where the souls of the dead dwell; Avernus is a volcanic crater near Cumae reputed to be an entrance to hell.

235 *as much he tries to avoid it*: Manuscript PN7's *por bien qu'el ocorra* could refer to the verb *acorrer* (Lat. *accurrere*) or *ocurrir* (Lat. *occurrere*). In modern Spanish, *acorrer* can mean "to help," and *ocurrir* to "prevent" or "avoid," in this case, the pain. We have chosen the latter.

245 *To wit, from such a brutal imprisonment*: Stanzas 30 and 31 play

NOTES TO THE TRANSLATION

with the meaning of *prisa* (hurriedness) and *priessa* (tumult). Mena is in a hurry to enter and is stopped by the great press of people who want the same. He cannot move forward or backward, just like a cruel barbed arrow buried in a wound cannot be moved without causing pain, but the wise hand of Providence delivers him from his *priessa* (that is, from being held at the gate by the multitude of people) and takes him inside.

247   *as the bearer of the Penates*: Mena's *Penatigero* refers to Aeneas, the bearer of the Penates, his household gods (Ovid, *Metamorphoses* 15.450).

248   *from the Greeks he mistrusted*: Evander, the Greek king of Pallantium, nevertheless allies with the Trojan Aeneas against the Latin king, Turnus.

249–64   Description of the House of Fortune and protestation about the insufficiency of the poet's skill to describe what he sees.

250   *of that dwelling*: The text does not make clear that stanza 32 refers to the House of Fortune, which is likened to a dwelling, or more specifically, an inn *(de aquella posada)*, a standard metaphor at the time for the world. From its highest point, Mena is able to see the world at his feet.

256   *worldly machinery*: Mena's *mundana maquina (machina mundi)* is a common phrase that can be found in authors such as Lucretius (*De rerum natura* 5.96) and Lucan (*The Civil War* 1.80).

260   *if the terms adequately express*: Manuscript PN7 uses the verb *salir* in the future *(si salran los dichos)*, and Núñez, *Las Trezientas*, uses be verb *sobrar* in the present *(si sobran los dichos)*. However, they express more or less the same thought.

265–440   These verses describe the Earth as it appears from Mena's vantage point in heaven: Asia Major, Egypt, Asia Minor, Europe, Higher and Lower Germany, Greece, Thessaly, Italy, France, Spain, Africa, the Mediterranean islands. The poet is stupefied by the sight, but Providence tells him that is not what he came to see. The section is inspired by *De imago mundi* of Honorius Augustodunensis.

266   *and the five zones*: There are five climatic zones that divide the Earth, which Mena calls Austral, Brumal, Aquilonial, Equinoc-

NOTES TO THE TRANSLATION

tial, and Solstitial; the two extremes are uninhabitable. The solstice is the moment at which the center of the sun is at its northernmost or southernmost point on the ecliptic.

270 *more beasts and peoples of strange appearance*: The comparison continues to draw on cosmography, since monsters and strange beings populate the periphery of medieval maps.

273 *In the third zone, Asia Major*: The land east of Asia Minor (Anatolia).

274 *and the land of Parthia*: Parthia was in northeastern Iran.

277 *the province of Arcusia*: Manuscript PN7 reads *Acursia,* but it is Arcusia, a region in northwestern Iran. Núñez, *Las Trezientas,* substitutes *Susia,* or Susa, a city in southwestern Iran, for no reason.

279 *and the land of the Medes*: The Medes were associated with the Zoroastrian cult of fire and the Magi.

281 *I saw the Moabites*: The descendants of the eldest of Lot's daughters, who gave rise to the Moabite people through her son Moab (Genesis 19:37). Medieval chronicles distinguished between different types of Arabs: Ishmaelites, Saracens, Moabites, and Agarenes. But *Moabitas* designates North African Moors, especially the Almoravids.

283 *Arabia and Chaldea, where astronomy*: Chaldea was a marshy region in the far southeastern corner of Mesopotamia; with Arabians, the Chaldeans were known for their knowledge of astronomy.

290 *Palestine and Phoenicia the beautiful*: Palestine and Phoenicia are Semitic areas in the eastern Mediterranean that roughly coincide with present-day Israel and Lebanon. In the Middle Ages, Phoenicia was a province of Syria, often called Syria Phoenicia.

292 *or perhaps because of Phoenix, brother to Cadmus*: Cadmus, king of Thebes, was the brother of Europa, Phoenix, and Cilix.

295–96 *and I saw Commagene . . . and the Nabataeans*: Commagene was a Greco-Iranian kingdom ruled by a branch of the Armenian Orontid dynasty. Samosata was a city on the west bank of the Euphrates River that had been the capital of the Hellenistic kingdom of Commagene before the Roman period. Nabataea was an area along the Red Sea coast, reaching as far north as Damascus, which it controlled for a short period (85–71 BCE).

297 *In the Austral region*: The wind Auster emanates from the southern region.

298 *so called because of Aegistus*: Aegisthus was the son of Thyestes and his sister Pelopia. In another version, he was the sole surviving son of Thyestes after Atreus killed his brother Thyestes's other children and served them to him in a meal. However, the note to this line in Núñez, *Las Trezientas*, attributes the immediate reference to Anselm, saying: "The province of Egypt was first called Euxia, which means abundance; after King Egyptus, it was called Egypt.... This Egyptus had a son named Lynceus, husband of Hypermnestra."

301 *the clear sky is never overcast*: It was a common belief that it never rained in Egypt, because its sky was always cloudless. For that reason, the Egyptians were the first to notice the firmament, the planets, and their configuration in the zodiac.

303 *where I saw Mauricio*: *Mauricia*, as the text gives it, is a mistake on the part of Mena. According to the note to this line by Núñez, *Las Trezientas*, Saint Anselm states that Thebes was ruled by a prince called Mauricio. It was actually the place where a legionnaire named Mauritius was in command of a troop of Roman soldiers who had converted to Christianity. Their refusal to worship the emperor led to their death and his canonization of Saint Mauritius.

305 *in the direction from which Notus blows*: As Kerkhof, *El laberinto*, says, the winds are Euros (East Wind), Zephyrus (West Wind), Boreas (North Wind), and Notus (South Wind). Manuscript PN7 and others read *Notus;* the early editions, including Núñez, read *Euro*. We have opted to remain faithful to PN7, because Notus represents a southeast wind.

310–12 *the Amazon people ... Hyrcanians*: The Amazons were female warriors who matched men in physical agility and strength, and, in order to shoot arrows better, cut off or burned their right breasts. Amazons killed their male children. The Sarmatians, Colchians, Massagetes, and Hyrcanians were peoples who settled the area of the Black and Caspian Seas up to the Caucasus.

NOTES TO THE TRANSLATION

313–17 *Then I saw the Hyperborean ... Amorreans*: The Hyperborean (or Riphaean) mountains limit the territory of a people identified by the same name. According to myth, they lived in the far northern part of the world. Armenia was a landlocked kingdom in the Caucasus area; Scythia was a kingdom in Eurasia bordered by the Vistula and encompassing the Black and Caspian Seas; and Albania was bordered by the Adriatic and Ionian Seas, and strongly resisted the Ottoman expansion in the fifteenth century. The Jews lived in Palestine, Cappadocia was in central Anatolia, and the Amorreans, or Amorites, were a Semitic people that ranged from Canaan to Syria.

318 *and of Nicaea, where gathered*: A council of Christian bishops gathered in the city of Nicaea by order of the Roman emperor Constantine in 325 CE to settle the dispute over the divine nature of Christ. It promulgated the Nicene Creed and condemned the Arian heresy.

320 *worse than the Manichaeans*: An indirect allusion to the Arian heresy.

322–24 *and saw that Galatia ... assistance*: Galatia was the name of an area in the highlands of central Anatolia (Turkey) that was bordered by the kingdoms of Bithynia and Paphlagonia to the north, Pontus and Cappadocia to the east, Cilicia and Lycaonia to the south, and Phrygia to the west. The Galatian Gauls were hired as mercenaries by Nikomedes I of Bithynia, who employed twenty thousand of them to fight his brother. When hostilities ceased, they cast off his control and began raiding Greek cities in Asia Minor. Mena's reference may therefore be somewhat ironic.

325 *the Phrygian fields mourned with such fervor*: The "Phrygian fields" were the battlefields of Troy that witnessed the death of so many combatants.

326–27 *Caria and Cilicia ... Pontus*: Caria, Cilicia, Lycia, Pamphylia, and Pontus are areas in Asia Minor. Caria was a region in western Anatolia along the coast from mid-Ionia south to Lycia and east to Phrygia. Pamphylia was a region in the south of Asia Minor, between Lycia and Cilicia. Because the greater part of this kingdom lay within the region of Cappadocia, it

NOTES TO THE TRANSLATION

was at first called "Cappadocia by Pontus," but afterward simply "Pontus," the name Cappadocia then referring to just the southern half of the region. Meanwhile, verses 326 and 327 may be transposed in PN7. Our text and translation follow the order of verses in Núñez, *Las Trezientas*. This makes more sense, because the stanza then names Pontus as the place "where Naso and Clement were banished," rather than Cilicia, as in PN7. Ovid was exiled to Pontus, and Clement to an island with a similar name.

329 *I also saw the one they called Europa*: Europa was a Phoenician princess, the mother of King Minos of Crete, who was abducted by Jupiter in the shape of a bull. Her father, King Agenor, sent his three sons (Phoenix, Cadmus, and Cilix) to her rescue, with the condition that they were not to return without her. They never found her or returned.

334 *the Riphaean Mountains and the Meotian lakes*: The Riphaean Mountains were a mythic range located in the furthest northern part of the known world. The region was the source of Boreas (the North Wind) and home to the Hyperboreans. The Maeotian lakes, swamp, or marshes were the names given to the lowlands between the mouth of the Don in southern Russia and the Sea of Azov. They were the traditional boundary that separated Europe from Asia.

336 *because they neighbored the Gothic lands*: Mena probably refers to the territory held by the Crimean Goths.

341 *destined to devastate the world*: Mena uses *vastasse* (to devastate or destroy) in the sense of "to conquer or rule."

345 *Tanais*: Mena is talking about an area between the Tanais River and the Danube, which he considers part of the *Australis regio* (Austral region).

346 *Scythia*: The Greeks gave the name Scythia to a land in the northeast of Europe that stretched to the northern coast of the Black Sea over Parthia.

348 *the Dacian people*: The Dacians, or Getae, were a people who settled a region extending southeast of the Danube to the Black Sea.

350 *Germany and upper Rhaetia*: Rhaetia is a region that consisted of

NOTES TO THE TRANSLATION

what today are Switzerland, Tyrol, and the Alpine areas of Italy and Germany.

351 *Messia, Pannonia*: Ancient Messia is now part of Bulgaria. Pannonia was a province of the Roman Empire in territories now occupied by Hungary and parts of Austria, Croatia, Serbia, Slovenia, and Bosnia Herzegovina. It was bounded on the north and east by the Danube.

355–56 *Chaeonia, Molossia . . . fountain*: Chaeonia and Molossia are the same land clustered around Epirus, according to authors quoted by Núñez, *Las Trezientas*, in his commentary on this passage. *Eladia* could be Helos, a region east of the Eurotas River in Greece. Núñez, *Las Trezientas*, writes *Calidonia* for *Eladia*. Boeotia is an area in central Greece. Epirus was home to the Chaonians, Molossians, and Thesprotians. It had a wondrous fountain of very cold water that could light torches or extinguish them.

361 *Great Thessaly was shown to us*: Thessaly, or Aeolia, is in northern Greece.

362 *the Olympian mountain*: Mount Olympus is the highest mountain in Greece and the home of the gods. It is also the name of a mountain range that stretches between Thessaly and Macedonia.

364 *embracing Corinthian Arcadia*: Arcadia is a region in the central Peloponnese.

366 *great Ocean*: The Mediterranean Sea (see Núñez, *Las Trezientas*, on this line).

368 *Saturnia*: Saturnia is a name that is used occasionally for Italy.

370 *Lugdunum and Aquitania, and . . . Narbonne*: Lugdunum was a Roman province in northern Gaul known as *Gallia Lugdunensis;* Aquitania was in southwest Gaul and was known as *Gallia Aquitania;* and Narbonne was in southern Gaul and known as *Gallia Narbonensis*.

371 *which the first Frank*: The Franks were a Germanic tribe that conquered the Roman Gallic provinces and gave the name France to the region.

374 *at Mount Jovis*: There are several places with this name, but since it probably has to do with the southern border of France, the

NOTES TO THE TRANSLATION

most likely candidates are Montjuich near Barcelona (according to the note on this line by Núñez, *Las Trezientas*) or the Jura Mountains.

378 *Tarragona and ... Celtiberia*: Tarragona was a Roman province in southern Spain known as *Gallia Tarraconensis*, and Celtiberia was part of the province known as *Hispania citerior*.

379 *lesser Carthage*: Modern Cartagena in Spain, or *Cartago Nova*, as the Romans called it.

381 *Vandalia the beautiful*: Roman Baetica is a region in southern Spain that was part of the kingdom of the Vandals and is roughly Andalucia.

382 *the land of Lusitania*: Lusitania was a Roman province in southern Spain known as *Hispania Lusitana*. Today Portugal occupies part of the area.

383 *Galicia with the Tingitania*: Galicia is the Roman province of *Gallaecia*, an area that extended from northern Portugal to Asturias and included a large section of Castile and León. *Mauretania Tingitana* was a Roman province largely coinciding with present day Morocco. Its capital was Tingis, modern-day Tangier.

387 *Syrtes of Amon, where the tripods are*: The temple of Amon in Egypt (Africa; Lucan, *The Civil War* 4.673) was famous for its oracles. They were given by a seer entranced by vapors rising from a tripod. Although this seer gave prophecies, or *suertes*, the reference could be more general. The *Syrtes major* on the coast of Libya and *Syrtes minor* on the coast of Tunisia are two bodies of water off the African north coast known to sailors for their dangerous sandbanks and for their sandstorms; see Sallust, *War with Jugurtha* 79, ed. and trans. John T. Ramsey and J. C. Rolfe (Cambridge, MA, 2013), and Lucan, *The Civil War* 9.294–96. In this case, Amon could really be a reference to north Africa (see the note to this line in Kerkhof, *El laberinto*). It appears as such in Virgil, *Aeneid* 1.146, ed. and trans. H. Rushton Fairclough (Cambridge, MA, 1918), and in Lucan's description of the attempt of Cato's men to fight against the north African winds (*The Civil War* 9.319–47).

NOTES TO THE TRANSLATION

388   *bounded by the land of Leptis*: Manuscript PN7 carries *Lopia* instead of the prominent Libyan city of *Leptis magna,* or *Leptia.* The gloss of Núñez, *Las Trezientas,* explains that Mena uses poetic license to get his rhyme.

389   *All Marmarica*: The Libyan north coast. The territory stretched to the far south as the Siwa oasis, known for its sanctuary to the god Amon.

390   *Troglodyte people*: The Troglodytes were cave dwellers believed to live by the Red Sea.

391   *the Africans*: Mena's *áforas* is calqued on the Latin cognomen, *Afri,* that refers to the African people.

393   *The Caucasus Mountain*: Núñez, *Las Trezientas,* corrects *Caucaso monte* to *Catabathmon,* a mountain range and valley in southern Libya, but Mena follows a common tradition in locating the *Caucaso monte* in Ethiopia (see the note to this verse in Kerkhof, *El laberinto*). He has already mentioned the Caucasus Mountain in line 306.

394   *Cyrenaica*: Cyrenaica (after the city of Cyrene), also known as Libyan Pentapolis, was to the west of Marmarica. Manuscript PN7 reads *Serranesca,* which Núñez, *Las Trezientas,* corrects to *Sarracénica* and others to *Sereneica.*

395   *the land of the Numidians*: The Numidians were the Berber population that inhabited present-day Algeria and part of Tunisia.

396   *there where Jugurtha*: Jugurtha (ca. 160–104 BCE) was king of the Numidians and fought against Rome.

398–99   *Gethulia, Bisante . . . the Garamantes*: The Gethulians and Garamantes were peoples of Libya. Mena is referring to Bisante in Tunisia but confuses the name with Byzantium.

400   *from the time that King Juba*: Juba I of Numidia (ca. 85–46 BCE) was an ally of Pompey and an enemy of Caesar, who defeated him.

403   *its living and dead waters*: The "live" waters are those of the Ocean Sea and the "dead" are of the Mediterranean.

405   *I saw the Stechades*: The Stechades are nine islands off the coast of France.

406   *Crete of the hundred cities*: Crete was also known as Centipolis.

NOTES TO THE TRANSLATION

407 *the Cyclades*: The Cyclades are a large island group in the Aegean that contains Delos.

408 *six less to order to see sixty*: An amplification of a number to fill a line of verse that was popular in Latin poems. The Cyclades are fifty-four islands.

409 *Naxos the round*: Naxos is the largest of the Greek Cyclades islands.

410 *Colchis, Ortygia called Delos*: Colchis was a kingdom bordering on the northeast of the Black Sea, where Medea was born and where the *Argonautica* takes place. Ortygia is a small island where Leto had Artemis before going on to Delos and giving birth to Apollo.

413 *we saw the Aeolian Islands*: The Aeolians are a group of seven volcanic islands north of Sicily named after Aeolus, god of the wind. They are sometimes called the Lipari Islands.

414 *Icaria*: Icaria is an island in the Aegean near the waters into which Icarus plunged during his ill-fated flight.

417 *Samos and the Balearic Islands*: Samos is a Greek island in the eastern Aegean. The Balearics are a Spanish archipelago in the western Mediterranean.

418 *Corsica, Ebosus, and the Vulcaneas*: Corsica is a French island north of Sardinia in the central Mediterranean, and Ebosus is Ibiza. The Vulcaneas (or Volcanics) are seven volcanic islands next to Sicily. Núñez, *Las Trezientas,* has *Sardinia* for *Bosis.*

419 *the Gorgons, islands of Medusa*: The Gorgon islands are off the coast of Africa.

421–22 *Trinacria . . . Pelorus, Pachinus, and . . . Lilybaeus*: Trinacria is the island of Sicily, and the three altars are its main mountains: Pelorus, Pachinus, and Etna (or Lilybaeus). Kerkhof, *El laberinto,* explains in his note on this line that the reading *Lelibeo* of PN7 is a correction for *Edneo* by one of the copyists. Núñez, *Las Trezientas,* has *lilybeo,* coinciding with the correction of PN7, so we keep it, because Núñez's text was the version that was most often read. The description was probably inspired by Ovid, *Metamorphoses* 5.346–408.

423 *where Typhoeus*: Typhoeus is a winged giant, also named Encela-

NOTES TO THE TRANSLATION

dus, that lay buried under Etna and whose breath was supposed to cast stones and lava from the volcano.

428 *his friends speak ill*: The Latin form is actually *retractare*, which in Spanish is *retratan* or *retraen* (to form a new judgment).

441–96 Mena continues his description of the House of Fortune. Providence explains the nature of its three wheels: they are dedicated to the past, present, and future, respectively, but only the center one moves, and the third one is veiled. Each wheel is composed of seven circles associated with one of the seven planets and one of the seven virtues. On each circle hang exemplars influenced by those planets and who do or do not live up to the mandates of the virtues. Mena's deficient intellect permits him to see only the wheels of the past and the present.

450 *the mottoes*: The word used by PN7 is *mote* (in line 452 of the text), and the reference is to a motto or cartouche with the names of those hung on the wheels of Fortune or, later, depicted on the throne of Juan II.

467 *secular and sacred*: Another way of saying religious and profane or Christian and pagan.

474 *the lowly arts given . . . by Minerva*: Minerva is the Roman goddess of wisdom and the equivalent of the Greek Athena.

476 *reserved by him*: That is, by Jupiter or Zeus, who is the god of lightning.

495 *that Lethe would not be able*: The Lethe was the river of forgetfulness, passed by the souls on their way to the underworld.

497–649 Mena describes first wheel (the order of the Moon, Diana, and chastity). Providence explains the composition of each wheel, the influence of the planets, and their relation to the virtues. Once those facts are known, the poet will be able to perceive the true nature of people. The exemplars are Hippolytus, Hypermnestra, Lucretia, Artemisia, Penelope, Argia and Hercules, Queen Mary of Castile, Queen Mary of Aragon, and Maria Coronel.

500 *slew the Minotaur at the end*: Hippolytus was the son of Theseus, the man who conquered the Labyrinth and killed the Minotaur.

NOTES TO THE TRANSLATION

501 *Good Hypermnestra*: Danaus gave his fifty daughters in marriage to the sons of his twin brother Aegyptus but told them to carry a knife with which to kill their husbands on their wedding night. All obeyed except Hypermnestra, whose husband, Lynceus, killed Danaus.

503 *the chaste Lucretia*: Lucretia (d. ca. 510 BCE) was a Roman lady who committed suicide when she was raped by Sextus Tarquinius, the son of the last king of Rome, before the Republic was established.

507 *moistening the marital ashes*: Artemisia II (d. ca. 350 BCE), sister-wife of Mausolus of Halicarnassus, mourned her husband by drinking his ashes and building the Mausoleum in memory of him.

508 *that it is sinful*: The word that the manuscript uses is *vicio* (sin), which has as a secondary meaning "a desire to do something to an extreme."

510 *you, Penelope*: Penelope was the wife of Ulysses, "the cunning one," who was denied the wind that would take him back to Ithaca and wandered for ten years. Penelope put off her suitors by stipulating that she would remarry only after completing the tapestry on which she was working. However, she undid at night what she had woven during the day.

512 *to him by Aeolus*: Aeolus is the god of the wind.

513 *raised on the wheel*: Manuscript PN7 has *sublevada*, but Mena probably meant *solevada* (raised above others), with which Núñez, *Las Trezientas*, seems to agree, because he writes *sublimada* (lifted up).

514 *Argia*: Argia was a daughter of King Adrastus of Argos and married to Polynices, who with his brother Eteocles shared the rule of Thebes on alternate years. When Eteocles chose not to relinquish the throne, the war of the "Seven against Thebes" began. Argia disobeyed the decree of King Eteocles not to bury those who warred against him and is full of merit because she recovered her husband's body and cremated it. The reading in Núñez, *Las Trezientas*, of *llena de muertos* (full of the dead) is

NOTES TO THE TRANSLATION

another possibility for *llena de meritos* (full of many merits), because Argia combed through the dead to find the body of her husband.

516 *occupied by Alcides*: Alcides and Alcaeus were other names for Heracles, or Hercules.

519 *the Calydonians*: Artemis sent a huge wild boar to devastate Calydonia, because its king, Oeneus, had not sacrificed to her. Mena confuses this story with Hercules's fourth labor, the tale of the Erymanthian boar of Arcadia, which the hero kills.

520 *from being defiled*: Mena associates the story of the vanquishing of the Harpies with Hercules, although the tale is most often attributed to Phineus, king of Salmydessus, a seer who was blinded by the gods for revealing the future and condemned to have his table defiled by half-woman, half-bird Harpies until either Zetes and Calais or Hercules killed or scared them away.

537 *Therefore, the Moon*: The Moon is the closest "planet" to the Earth, therefore it is the first circle.

544 *of the matter of each sphere*: This is the *sphera de astrologia* (sphere of astrology) found in Antonio de Nebrija, *Vocabulario de romance en latín* (Sevilla, 1516), defined there as *globus* (globe).

555 *direct your doubts to us*: The reading in PN7, *a nos* (to us), is the royal "we."

562–64 *Clotho the first . . . Atropos the third*: The names of the three Moirai, or Parcae (Fates), are Clotho, Lachesis, and Atropos.

566 *circle of Diana*: The Moon is related to Artemis, or Diana, the goddess of chastity and of the hunt.

569–608 Mena dedicates stanzas 72 to 76 to Queen Mary, the first wife of Juan II and the sister of the Infantes of Aragon.

574 *a branch of a palm*: The palm branch is a symbol of victory and of chastity.

575 *gift that Diana cherishes most*: One of Diana's attributes is the palm.

580 *not displeased by such lower standing*: Juan II, to whom the poem is dedicated, is "not displeased" because women are more chaste than men.

NOTES TO THE TRANSLATION

596   *Lady Mary*: Mary of Aragon (1396–1445), the sister of the Infantes of Aragon, became queen of Castile with her marriage to Juan II in 1420.

599   *enjoys fame for her great wealth in brothers*: Manuscript PN7's verse *goza de fama tan rica de hermanos* becomes *goza de cama tan rica de hermanos* in Núñez, *Las Trezientas*. The reading makes sense only if *cama* is an apocope of *camada*, meaning "a litter" of brothers, in which case it would not be a flattering image but may be more fitting with the reputation of the Infantes of Aragon at the time. They are King Alfonso of Aragon, King Juan of Navarre, and Pedro, Enrique, and Sancho (who died early). They intervened many times in the internal affairs of Castile.

600   *other Caesars*: Calling the Infantes of Aragon "other Caesars" is an ambivalent form of praise, because there were not supposed to be any other rulers in the kingdom of Castile than Juan II.

605   *If her human form*: Mena, in saying *trocada su humanidad*, is talking about her gender.

606   *Caeneus*: Caenis, a daughter of the king of the Laphites, yielded to Neptune and was converted into a man called Caeneus as a reward (Ovid, *Metamorphoses* 12.146–209).

610   *queen of the Aragonese*: Maria of Castile (1401–1458) acted as regent for her husband, Alfonso V of Aragon, between 1420 and 1423, and again between 1432 and 1458, when he was away on campaigns in Sicily. When Alfonso was captured in 1435 during the naval battle of Ponza, she raised money for his ransom and negotiated several peace treaties with Castile. She had been princess of Asturias before the birth of Juan II.

611   *while her king pursues the call of war*: Literally, *mientras sigue su rey los arneses* (while her king pursues the accouterments of war).

621   *luckily there was another*: The reference is to Maria, who can be considered a new Penelope, the symbol of marital fidelity and loyalty.

627   *worthy crown of the Coronels*: Doña María Coronel resisted sexual temptation by burning her sexual organs with a torch during the absence of her husband. Her hands were cruel because

NOTES TO THE TRANSLATION

they held the torch that protected her chastity, just like Penelope's hands wove and unwove her tapestry.

629 *Oh, Roman citizens*: The reading in PN7, *O quirita Roma*, refers to one of the seven hills of Rome, the Quirinalis, where the king of the Sabines lived. Mena is therefore calling upon the Roman citizens to listen.

632 *what Vestal temple*: The *Aedes Vestae* was a Roman temple consecrated to the goddess Vesta. It represented Rome's greatness. The rites of the temple were carried out by the Vestal Virgins.

636 *base blood at birth*: The subject was notable at the time because it points to an unease that involved something more than rank. Just five years after the poem was written, the first municipal laws issued against Jews were based on the language of lineage (*sangre*). Mena was aware of the tensions that led to the promulgation of these laws, but here he is clearly referring to commoners.

639 *can surpass flawless and saintly tonsures*: The text reads *roban las claras y santas coronas*—that is, the ivy crowns of the martyrs—but likely applied to priests, who were called *coronados* (crowned) because of their tonsures.

641–64 Mena turns to the king to explain that his duty is to maintain peace and punish transgressions, so that the people can live in peace. In particular, he should punish those great lords who are unchaste and flaunt justice.

663 *If they long to be spotless*: The line in PN7, *si lindos codician*, can also be translated as "if they long to be legitimate" or "good."

665–72 *Abstinence from foul union ... virtues*: Mena concludes the order of the Moon with a definition of chastity as a transformative virtue that extends beyond sex.

666 *is the nature of Chastity*: Chastity, or abstinence, is one of the seven virtues. They are grouped together as cardinal (prudence, justice, chastity or temperance, courage) and theological (faith, hope, charity).

671–72 *sheds all vices ... dons a new vestment*: This is an allusion to Romans 13:14, where Saint Paul says, "clothe yourselves with the

NOTES TO THE TRANSLATION

Lord Jesus Christ, and do not think about how to gratify the desires of the flesh."

673–792   Mena describes the second wheel (the order of Mercury and avarice). It is dedicated to those who are and are not prudent or give good and bad counsel. Exemplars are Nestor, Latinus, Capis, Laocoon, Pandarus, Polynestor, Anthenor, Eriphyle, Oppas, and Julian. After several stanzas that rail against these people and the circumstances that force us to turn a blind eye to their misdeeds, Mena alludes to the earthquake of Caesarea, which destroyed the city but left its church and clergy unharmed. Mena associates the punishment wrought by the earthquake with the present, except that now it is temples and clergy who would suffer God's wrath, and not the people. Therefore, he reminds the king of his duty to uphold the law and fight against greed, and goes on to define avarice. Just as there are seven virtues, there are seven deadly sins (pride, avarice, wrath, envy, lust, gluttony, sloth).

681   *Ancient Nestor*: Nestor, an Argonaut and a king of Pylos, was an old and wise, but boastful, counselor. He appears in both the *Iliad* and the *Odyssey*.

682   *the orators*: Mena uses the same word found in Virgil, *Aeneid* 7.153–55, *oratores (los oradores)*, to describe the ambassadors whom Aeneas sends to convince King Latinus.

683   *by the son of Faunus*: Latinus was a son of Faunus and king of the Latins who hosted the exiled Trojans when they were searching for a new home.

684   *purchased his already-dead son*: The Trojan king Priam entered the Greek camp to ransom the body of his son Hector.

685   *Capis*: Capis was a Trojan prince who feared that the Greek theft of the Palladium, a wooden image of Pallas Athena that protected Troy, would be followed by disaster. He counseled the destruction of the Trojan Horse (Virgil, *Aeneid* 2.21–27), advice that was disregarded.

687   *the sacred seer Laocoon*: Laocoon was a Trojan priest who was attacked, together with his two sons, by two giant sea serpents

NOTES TO THE TRANSLATION

sent by Minerva/Athena because of his insistence that the Trojan horse be burned.

697 *Pandarus*: Pandarus violated a truce when he killed Menelaus during the Trojan War. He fled with Aeneas to Italy. The allusion is to a passage in the *Aeneid* that tells of a competition between Eurytion (a brother of Pandarus), Hipocoon, Mnestheus, and Acestes over who could kill a dove tied high on the mast of Aeneas's ship: "Then quickly Eurytion ... called upon his brother to hear his vow, marked the dove, now exulting in the free sky, and pierced her as she flapped her wings ... and, falling, brought down the arrow that pierced her" (Virgil, *Aeneid* 5.513–18, trans. Fairclough, 507).

701 *the sinews of the strap*: The cord or strap *(amiento)* that is used to throw an arrow or lance with greater force.

702 *against the Doric people*: That is, against the Greeks. Pandarus's arrow wounded Menelaus.

705–6 *Polynestor ... Polydorus*: Polynestor was a king of Thrace who killed his nephew, the young prince Polydorus, son of Priam, because he coveted the treasure that accompanied him when he was sent to Thrace for safekeeping during the war at Troy. In Ovid, *Metamorphoses* 13.429–38, he is thrown from a cliff into the sea. The verb used by PN7 is *trayste,* with the meaning of *traicionaste* (betrayed). The verb used by Núñez, *Las Trezientas,* and Kerkhof, *El laberinto,* is *trucidar,* which means "tear to pieces" or "kill with cruelty" (modern *trocear*). But while *trucidar* makes perfect sense, so does *trayste*.

709 *vile Anthenor*: Anthenor, a counselor of King Priam, was the eponymous founder of Padua. He is a vile traitor, because he opened the gates of Troy to the Greeks in Dares's and Dictys's narratives.

711 *you were shown greeting him*: Mena considers Anthenor's deeds comparable to those of Aeneas.

712 *Virgil honors you better*: Mena is still talking about Aeneas when he refers to Anthenor, who is not treated badly in Virgil's *Aeneid*.

NOTES TO THE TRANSLATION

713 *Eriphyle, you were there*: Eriphyle was the wife of the seer Amphiaraus. She betrayed him to Polynices in exchange for the magical necklace of Harmonia, which bestowed eternal youth as well as a curse on its wearer. Amphiaraus had not wanted to take part in the war against Thebes, because he foresaw his own death. Kerkhof, *El laberinto*, argues at this line that this is a correction for Hypsipyle, which his edition renders as *Isífile*. However, PN7 and Núñez, *Las Trezientas*, coincide in reading *Erifile/Eriphyle*.

721 *cursed Oppas, and you, Julian*: Oppas and Julian allowed the Moors into Spain and were believed to be the cause of its loss.

730 *the second Cyllenic circle*: That is, the circle of Mercury, who was born in a cave on Mount Cyllene in Arcadia.

738 *pretend that great worries are pleasures*: PN7's verse, *grandes plazeres fingir por pesares*, is problematic. Read as is, it translates as "to portray pleasures as worries," but given Mena's penchant for hyperbata, it could also be understood as "to portray worries as pleasures," which makes better sense. In either case, however, Mena speaks about the problem of discerning truth.

740 *transform ... Entellus into a Dares*: In Virgil, *Aeneid* 5.387–484, an old man named Entellus fights a boxing match with Dares aboard Aeneas's ship and defeats the nimble young man.

761 *Caesarea, one reads*: According to the gloss to this line in Núñez, *Las Trezientas*, there are many cities named Caesarea that had earthquakes. Núñez's gloss identifies this one as an episcopal see on the Black Sea in the Roman province of Pontus Polemoniacus that was destroyed by an earthquake in 344 CE, and points to Saint Jerome as his source. However, Mena could also have relied on Gregory of Nyssa, *The Life of Gregory the Wonderworker*, trans. Michael Slusser, *St. Gregory Thaumaturgus: Life and Works*, The Fathers of the Church 98 (Washington, DC, 1998), 62: "For when there was a very severe earthquake in the city in our own times, and almost everything was completely destroyed, all public and private buildings ruined, that temple alone remained unshattered and unshaken, so that through even this it is manifest with what sort of power that Great One

NOTES TO THE TRANSLATION

undertook his affairs." As important is the fact that in 1431 there were two earthquakes near Granada during the battle of Higueruela, which affected the city and destroyed part of its curtain wall. Mena's stanzas 96 and 97 must therefore recall that event through the example of Caesarea, but as a warning to Christians of God's punishments.

784 *by their wisdom*: Manuscript PN7's *su sagacidad* refers back to *las leyes* (laws).

789 *she serves bullion*: Manuscript PN7's *metales* refers to silver and gold, that is, money or coinage.

793–920 Mena describes the third wheel (the order of Venus and bad and good love), which is dedicated to adulterers and fornicators, and its exemplars, namely Clytemnestra and Aegisthus, Myrrha and Cyniras, Philomela and Tereus, Canace and Macareus, Ixion and Nephele, Pasiphae and the bull, Scylla and Minos, and Macias. Mena then asks Providence to explain why these people, who sometimes appear to be wise, have given in to love. Providence explains the trickery of false love, and Mena ends with advice to the king on how to deal with criminals who give in to passion, and how to distinguish between good and bad love.

804 *and receive vile salaries for it*: The reference is to those who aid their masters in committing sins.

805 *in similar affections*: The manuscript reads *en efectos así voluntarios* (in similar effects), but we opt for the text in Núñez, *Las Trezientas*: *en afectos así voluntarios*.

810–12 *the companion ... Aegisthus*: The reference is to Clytemnestra, the wife of Agamemnon, who is the son or grandson of Atreus, king of Mycenae, and brother to Menelaus. Agamemnon was the chief (*duque*) of the Greek forces. Clytemnestra had a tryst with Aegysthus, and together they sought Agamemnon's death.

813 *we saw Myrrha among the fallen*: Myrrha had sex with her father, King Cinyras of Cyprus, and begat Adonis (Ovid, *Metamorphoses* 10.298–502).

816 *degrees*: Mena omits *de consanguinidad* (of consanguinity).

820 *who was deflowered ... in two ways*: Philomela was violated by her

brother-in-law, Tereus, king of Thrace, who was married to her sister Procne. He also severed Philomela's tongue so that she would not tell anyone. Procne found out and, in revenge, killed her son Itys and fed him to Tereus, his father.

822 *sorrowful Canace lie with Macareus*: Canace committed incest with her brother Macareus and had a child. Their father, Aeolus, compelled her to commit suicide by stabbing herself with a sword and exposed the newborn to death. Her story is told in a letter in Ovid, *Heroides* 11, trans. Grant Showerman (Cambridge, MA, 1914). Mena plays with the meaning of the last line by saying that although the child was born of incest and was an injury to humankind, since he was exposed to the elements at birth, he only injured his own life.

828 *fulfill his desires fraudulently*: The giant Ixion, who lusted after Jupiter's wife, Juno, was deceived by them when they fashioned a cloud named Nephele in her shape. The Centaurs were born from their union.

830 *Pasiphae*: Pasiphae and Minos were king and queen of Crete, where a labyrinth hid the half-human, half-beast Minotaur, which Pasiphae conceived by lying with a bull.

832 *Scylla*: Scylla was a daughter of King Nisus of Megara, who had a purple lock of hair that granted him invincibility. When King Minos of Crete invaded Megara, she fell in love with him and betrayed her father by cutting the lock.

834 *we came upon our Macias*: Late fourteenth-century Galician poet, about whom a number of legends were formed that identified him as a martyr of love. According to the gloss to this line in Núñez, *Las Trezientas,* Macias was in love with a lady in the court of the Maestre of Calatrava, who instead married her to one of his men. However, Macias would not cease wooing her. The Maestre, at the urging of the lady's husband, imprisoned Macias. The husband then murdered him with a lance threaded through a hole in the ceiling of his cell.

872 *announcing the punishment*: This completes the sense of *bullada debieran tener en la frente* (871). The noun *bullo* or *bula* refers to the seal that authenticates a document issued by a pope (a pa-

pal bull) or by a bishop granting a dispensation, a right, or confirming a position (*bullar,* "to seal"; compare Lat. *sigillare*). By extension, it stands for anything that is certified, hence *bulados* or *bullados* means "authorized" or "confirmed." The sense of the verses is that the lustful should carry a certificate similar to a *bula* on their foreheads. It is a reference to a penalty common in the law that imposed a mark on the face; see, for example, García de Santa María, *Crónica de Aragón,* quoted in Frank A. Domínguez, *Carajicomedia: Parody and Satire in Early Modern Spain* (Woodbridge, UK, 2015), 325n523, where this question is examined in greater depth.

874 *the membranes of a colt*: Mares lick the birth sac of their foals, which were then called *el benifiçio de amor* (the benefit of love). Witches use these sacs to make people fall in love or to foretell with whom one will fall in love. Mena treats the *tela del potrico* again in the *Tratado de amor,* ed. Juan Miguel Valero, "¿Juan de Mena? *Tratado de amor,*" in *Tratados de amor en el entorno de "Celestina" (siglos XV–XVI),* ed. Pedro Cátedra (Madrid, 2001), 31–49.

912 *the virtuous pure Catholic love*: The reference is to the sacrament of matrimony.

920 *To the less meritorious, greater rewards*: This rather cryptic statement refers to the abject position taken by the lover vis-à-vis the lady; as in the legend of the prodigal son, the lover's reward is proportional to his humility.

921–1064 Mena describes the fourth wheel (the order of Phoebus). This section mentions positively the theologians Saint Jerome, Saint Gregory, Saint Augustine, and Saint Thomas Aquinas; the philosophers Cratylus, Polemon, Empedocles, Zeno, Aristotle, Plato, Socrates, and Pythagoras; the rhetoricians Demosthenes, Gabinianus, Cicero, Domitius, Plotinus, Apollodorus, and Quintilian; the musicians Tubal, Orpheus, Phillyrides, and Achilles; the Sibyls (the Persian, Dimeta, the Babylonian, Erythrea, the Phrygian Albunea, the Delphic, Phemonoe, Libisa, Vetona, and the Cumaean); and the poets Homer, Virgil, Ennius, and those of Cordoba. It then mourns the passing of Enrique de Villena and the burning of his library, before reviewing

NOTES TO THE TRANSLATION

those who have fallen off the wheel: Tiresias, Erictho, Medea, Licinia, and Publicia.

926 *here citharists*: The cither is an ancient Greek instrument resembling the harp.

928 *here scholars*: Mena uses the term *quadruvista* (students of the quadrivium: arithmetic, geometry, astronomy, and music) to refer to "scholars" dedicated to these sciences.

931 *Jerome was raising*: Saint Jerome (ca. 342–420) made the Latin translation of the Bible that is known as the Vulgate, which Sánchez de las Brozas, *Anotaciones,* regards in his note as music because of its effects on people.

932 *Gregory, Augustine*: Two Gregories are possible: Saint Gregory, bishop of Nyssa, a fourth-century Cappadocean Father famed for his oratory skills, and Pope Gregory I (ca. 540–604), bishop of Rome and also a saint. The latter is the one singled out by the extensive gloss on this line devoted to him in Núñez, *Las Trezientas*. Saint Augustine (354–430), bishop of Hippo, was famous for his *City of God, On Christian Doctrine,* and *Confessions,* but he was the author of many other works as well. He also has an extensive gloss in Núñez, *Las Trezientas,* that lists his many works. For Sánchez de las Brozas, *Anotaciones,* in his note on this verse, these are prophets of the faith always waiting for the word of God to manifest itself to them.

933–34 *the saintly doctor . . . Caesar always celebrates*: Since Juan II was born on the feast day of Saint Thomas Aquinas, the saint to whom the verse refers. In Mena's verse, *jamás solemniza* actually means "always celebrates."

937 *Cratylus and Polemon*: Cratylus was a mid- to late fifth-century Athenian philosopher known through his portrayal in Plato's *Cratylus.* Polemon was the third philosopher who succeeded Plato as director of the Academy.

938 *Empedocles and knowledgeable Zeno*: Empedocles was a pre-Socratic philosopher whose cosmogony first referred to the four elements. Zeno was the founder of the philosophy known as Stoicism. He taught in Athens from about 300 BCE.

939 *Aristotle near to Father Plato*: Aristotle was a Greek philosopher

NOTES TO THE TRANSLATION

who studied under Plato. He founded the Lyceum and established the Aristotelian branch of philosophy. Plato was a student of Socrates and the teacher of Aristotle. He founded the Academy and became one of the most influential figures in philosophy.

941 *I also saw Socrates*: Socrates is considered the founder of Western philosophy. All philosophers thereafter followed his lead. He wrote no books but taught Plato the Socratic, or dialogic, method.

943 *I saw Pythagoras*: Pythagoras was a sixth-century BCE Ionian philosopher who developed the theory of metempsychosis (transmigration of souls) and the idea that the planets' movements can be described according to mathematical equations. He thought that the planets emit a tone as they move and together create a harmonious music. It is claimed that he was vegetarian and forbade meat to his followers.

945 *I saw Demosthenes and Gabinianus*: Demosthenes was a fourth-century BCE Athenian orator. Gabinianus was a celebrated rhetorician who taught in Gaul during the time of Emperor Vespasian.

946 *I saw Tully*: Tully refers to first-century BCE figure Marcus Tullius Cicero, Rome's greatest orator and one of its finest writers.

947 *Cassius Severus*: Titus Cassius Severus was a Roman rhetorician at the start of the empire, whose mordant satire condemned him to exile, first in Crete and then in the much smaller island of Seriphos.

949 *Domitius*: Gnaeus Domitius Afer was a Roman orator who lived in the early empire. He was proconsul in Africa.

950 *Plotinus with Apollodorus*: Plotinus and Apollodorus were third-century BCE Hellenistic philosophers who lived in Roman Egypt.

952 *our rhetorician Quintilian*: Marcus Fabius Quintilianus was a first-century Roman teacher and rhetorician. He was Spanish, and therefore Mena refers to him as "our" rhetorician.

953 *Jubal*: The reading in PN7 is *Tubal*, which Núñez, *Las Trezientas*, corrects to Jubal, the inventor of the vihuela and of music.

257

NOTES TO THE TRANSLATION

954   *consonant voices*: That is, polyphony.

955   *the harp that Orpheus strummed*: Orpheus played the harp when he descended to hell in search of his wife, Euridice.

957   *displayed was Phillyrides*: The reference is not to Orpheus—who, as the son of the nymph Phillyra, could be associated with the epithet Phillyrides and lent his harp to Achilles—but to another of her sons, Chiron, who "defeated" the great Achilles with the sound of his cither. See Ovid, *Ars amatoria* 1.11, trans. J. H. Mozley, *The Art of Love and Other Poems,* rev. G. P. Goold, 2nd ed. (Cambridge, MA, 1979).

959–60   *could strike and tame*: The word *herir* usually means "to wound," but here it refers instead to the act of striking notes very well when hitting the strings of the cither (*herir la cuerda;* Covarrubias, *Tesoro,* 933). Chiron played so well that he could tame the passions of Achilles, who was himself a great player of the instrument and a conqueror of others.

963   *the Sibyls*: The Sibyls were ten female prophets associated with different regions of Greece, the Middle East, Italy, and Africa.

965   *the Persian ... with Dimeta*: The Persian Sibyl is reputed to have been the first of her kind. She is from Asia Major. Núñez, *Las Trezientas,* does not identify Dimeta in his gloss about the Sibyls at line 961. Sánchez de las Brozas, *Anotaciones,* however, says here that there is a Sibyl called "Demo," which Mena may have deformed as *Dimeta* to fit the rhyme.

966   *the Babylonian; great Erythrea*: The Babylonian (or Judaean) Sibyl was credited with writing the *Sibylline Oracles.* The Erythraean Sibyl was the prophetess who presided over an oracle at the city of Erythrae in Ionia.

967   *the Phrygian called Albunea*: According to Lactantius, *Divine Institutes* 1.6, trans. Anthony Bowen and Peter Garnsey (Liverpool, 2004), the Tiburtine Sibyl is called Albunea.

968   *the Delphic*: Manuscript PN7 reads *delphyguieta* with the scribal correction *phrygineta* just above, a correction Núñez, *Las Trezientas,* accepts, although it is incorrect because the Phrygian Sibyl was located in Asia Minor and is identified with Cassandra, the daughter of Priam. Mena forces the name of the

NOTES TO THE TRANSLATION

Delphic Sibyl to fit his rhyme scheme (Kerkhof, "Notas de crítica textual," 582).

969 *Phemonoe*: Phemonoe was the Libyan Sibyl who presided over the oracle of Zeus-Ammon at Siwa Oasis in the Libyan Desert.

972 *from whom Appius*: Appius Claudius Pulcher went to Delphi (Lucan, *The Civil War* 5.67–236) to consult the Sibyl Phemonoe, because he feared the coming war. Her answer was that he would find peace before then, but only because his life would end.

973 *we saw Libisa*: The Sibyls on occasion appear with a personal name. Mena seems to refer to the Libyan, or African, Sibyl with the name Libisa.

974 *Vetona ... with the Amalthean*: The Sibyl Vetona is unidentified, but could be Ataecina, a goddess of the Vetones, a Celtic people that inhabited the region of western Spain between the Duero and Tajo, who created the *verracos,* stone sculptures of pigs abundant in the area. Amalthea was a Sibyl who presided over the oracle at Cumae, a Greek colony found near Naples.

975 *the tenth was that Cumaean*: The Cumaean Sibyl presided over the temple of Apollo in the city of Cumae, which is near Naples, Italy. She appears in Virgil's *Aeneid* and is also mentioned in *The Labyrinth* 219.

980 *Ennius*: Quintus Ennius (ca. 239–ca. 169 BCE) was considered the father of Roman poetry. He wrote the *Annales,* an epic poem of which about six hundred lines survive.

986 *Mother Cordoba*: The praise of his native Cordoba is a recurrent theme in Mena's work. He exchanged poetry with the likes of Antón de Montoro and Juan Agraz, but he really refers here to Quintilian (Marcus Fabius Quintilianus), whom he calls "our rhetorician" (line 952), and Lucan, both from Cordoba. Stanza 37 of Mena's *Coronación* and its glosses, which were written by the author himself, expand the number of sons of Cordoba to include Averroes (Ibn Rušd), Avicenna (Ibn Sina), Seneca (Lucius Annaeus Seneca), Aristotle (Aristoteles), and Trogo Pompeo (Gnaeus Pompeius Trogus).

990 *who were a marvelous reflection*: Not only do the sons of Cordoba

reflect her qualities like a mirror *(espejo)*, but they are examples for all to see.

993 *at the circle of our contemporaries*: The first two lines of stanza 125 refer to the Cordobans that Mena has just mentioned.

1010 *on the Castalian mountain*: Castalia is a spring at the foot of Mount Parnassos that is consecrated to the Muses. Therefore, the reference is to Parnassos, the abode of the worthy and the famous.

1011 *Don Enrique, Lord of Villena*: Enrique, marquess of Villena, was a prominent nobleman, writer, and scholar, whose library was burned after he was accused of witchcraft.

1013 *most erudite of writers*: *Ciente* means "aware, conscious, knowledgeable."

1018 *as in exequy*: As if they were part of the funeral rites.

1022 *of Protagoras*: In the manuscript tradition, there seems to be some confusion between Protagoras of Abdera and Pythagoras of Samos, a philosopher and precursor of Plato and Aristotle. Manuscript PN7 reads *Pitagoras*. Núñez, *Las Trezientas,* notes the error in the gloss to lines 1021–22 and identifies him correctly as Protagoras.

1034 *the magician Tiresias*: Manuscript PN7 reads *magno Tereo,* but Núñez, *Las Trezientas,* reads *mago Tyrrheo.* Núñez notes that the reference is actually to Tiresias, a blind seer who appears among the magicians and soothsayers in Dante, *Inferno* 20, ed. and trans. Charles S. Singleton (Princeton, 1980). An alternative proposed by Sánchez de las Brozas, *Anotaciones,* is Appollonius of Tiana (second to third century), a miracle worker about whom Philostratus wrote *De vita Appolloni.* We follow the text of *Las Trezientas.*

1035–36 *Erictho . . . Sextus Pompeus*: Erictho is a legendary Thessalian witch consulted by Sextus Pompeus, the son of Pompey the Great, who sought to know the outcome of the imminent battle of Pharsalus (Lucan, *The Civil War* 6.413–506).

1038 *Medea*: Medea is a witch and the main character in the *Argonautica* of Apollonius of Rhodes. For the love of Jason, she reveals the secret of how to slay the dragon that guards the Golden

NOTES TO THE TRANSLATION

Fleece and, in so doing, betrays her father, Aeëtes. Ten years later, she murders her two sons when Jason is unfaithful.

1039 *a goddess's deadly arrow*: The goddess Aphrodite causes Eros to wound Medea with the arrow of love.

1041 *The women Licinia and Publicia*: Licinia was a Roman woman killed by her relatives in 153 BCE for allegedly murdering her husband, Claudius Asellus; Publicia was the wife of Lucius Postumius Albinus (consul 154 BCE) and was similarly accused.

1051 *never let your right hand know*: This recalls a passage in Matthew 6:3: "Let not thy left hand know what thy right hand doth."

1065–96 Mena again interrupts his narrative to address Juan II, asking that compassion not be the further cause of evil and that the laws and social fabric of Castile be maintained. It ends with a stanza dedicated to the definition of the virtue of prudence.

1076 *that murder people with little reason*: According to Covarrubias, *Tesoro*, 1345a, *vianda* is "el sustento de comida que nos dà fuerça para caminar" (the sustenance from food which gives us the strength to walk). The reference is to killing those who are weak, and the verse refers to murderers who kill poor people or to those who do not need a reason to kill.

1079 *new Medeas and new Publicias*: See the notes to lines 1038 and 1041 above.

1085 *the peaceful years of your great life*: The reading in PN7, *los años quinientos de vuestra grand vida,* makes no sense. We prefer the reading of Núñez, *Las Trezientas, años quietos,* which Mena might have regarded as a forced diphthong break *(qui-ë-tos)* to fill the length of the hemistich.

1097–1360 Mena describes the fifth wheel (the order of Mars) and those who engaged in just and unjust wars. He begins by citing as heroes the members of the Metellus and Camilus families, then Petreius, Afranius, Crassus, and Mucius. He turns to Juan II, whom he sees portrayed in that circle, sitting on a throne on which are carved the people and deeds of the heroes of Spain—the Alfonsos, the Fernandos, and the battles of Navas de Tolosa and Algeciras—before once again addressing the king, who is responsible for the battles of the Vega de Granada, Real

NOTES TO THE TRANSLATION

de Ariza, and Medina del Campo. Following are long sections dedicated to the Castilian dead.

1097 *the circle of Mars*: Mars is the fifth from the Earth in the Ptolemaic order of planets. He is the god of war.

1104 The rubric of stanza 139 in PN7 reads *Alega conentigos*, a misspelling of *Alega con antiguos*. In Núñez, *Las Trezientas*, the rubric is simply *Passados* (Past).

1105 *The hardy Metelluses*: Lucius Caecilius Metellus Calvus (ca. 200–ca. 136 BCE) was a consul and governor of Hispania in 142 BCE, where he fought against Viriathus without success. His son, Quintus Caecilius Metellus Numidicus (ca. 160–91 BCE) commanded the Roman forces in Africa during the Jugurthine War.

1108 *of those Camilluses*: Marcus Furius Camillus (ca. 446–365 BCE) was a Roman soldier, hero, and dictator of the Republic, who was credited with the final defeat of the Goths following the sack of Rome in 390 BCE. The plural may refer to his adopted son, Lucius Arruntius Camillus Scribonianus, who was a Roman senator and consul during the reign of Tiberius and revolted against the emperor Claudius.

1110 *Petreius and Afranius*: Petreius and Afranius were Roman generals who led part of Pompey's army in Spain. They took part in the Battle of Ilerda against the army of Caesar. However, they lost the campaign.

1113 *We saw Crassus*: Marcus Licinius Crassus (ca. 115–53 BCE) was a politician who in the last years of the Roman Republic was a member of the First Triumvirate with Julius Caesar and Pompey, and governor of Syria in 54 BCE, when he embarked on an invasion of Parthia that resulted in his death, and which precipitated the civil war between Caesar and Pompey.

1117 *the burned hand of Mucius*: Gaius Mucius Scaevola was a legendary figure who was captured sometime between 506 and 503 BCE after trying to assassinate the Etruscan king Porsenna. To show his contempt for torture, Mucius thrust his right hand into a fire and told the king three hundred more people had sworn to kill him. The king then pardoned him and abandoned the siege of Rome. Mena says that Mucius was more unhappy over his failure to kill Porsenna than he was happy over the reprieve. The gloss of Núñez, *Las Trezientas,* identifies *el fuerte guerrero* (the strong warrior) as Porsenna.

1121 *Belligerent Mars*: Mars is the god of War.

1125 *You, Pallas*: Athena was called Pallas Athena. There were many attempts in ancient times to explain why. One is that she is so named because of the Palladium, a wooden statue, either of herself or of a friend named Pallas, held in the Acropolis. The Palladium is one of her attributes.

1136 *Daedalus*: Daedalus was the architect of the Cretan labyrinth, which housed the Minotaur.

1139 *at all the titles*: That is, at all the lands that belonged to them.

1145 *the shield made by Vulcan*: Vulcan is the smith of the gods. His forge was under Mount Etna, and he was the creator of the famous shield of Achilles, among others, whose description marks an important ekphrastic passage in the *Iliad*. The *fornaces* (modern *forjas,* or "forges") of the Spanish text is a neologism used for the sake of rhyme.

1154 *of the Alfonsos*: There were eleven kings named Alfonso, who accomplished great feats of arms. Mena, however, treats few of them individually when describing battles. See Joaquín Gimeno Casalduero, "Sobre las numeraciones de los reyes de Castilla," *Nueva Revista de Filología Hispánica* 14, no. 3/4 (1960): 271–94, on the numbering of the kings of Castile.

1155 *kings named Fernando*: There were four kings named Fernando who expanded Castile: Fernando I (1016–1065), Fernando II (1137–1188), Fernando III (ca. 1199–1252), and Fernando IV (1285–1312).

1158 *of our Enriques*: There were four kings named Enrique: Enrique I (1204–1217), Enrique II (1334–1379), Enrique III (1379–1406), and the future Enrique IV (1425–1474), who was the son of Juan II.

1161 *Las Navas de Tolosa*: Las Navas de Tolosa is the name of a battle that took place in 1212 against the Almohads and represents an important turning point in the Reconquest. The Christian forces were led by Alfonso VIII.

1162 *a triumph of great divine mystery*: Only a few men were lost in the

NOTES TO THE TRANSLATION

1212 battle of Las Navas de Tolosa, as opposed to the heavy losses inflicted on Caliph Miramamolín (Muhammad al-Nasir).

1166–68 *the two Algeciras... Abu al-Hasan*: There were two battles of Algeciras. The first took place in 1278 under Alfonso X, when the Christian naval forces of Castile confronted those of the Emirate of Granada and the Marinid Sultan of Morocco. The second is Alfonso XI's siege of Algeciras in 1344, which resulted in a Christian victory against Abu al-Hasan Ali ibn Othman *(Albohacen)*, a Moorish king of the Marinid dynasty.

1169 *the new-won titles*: "Titles" means "lands" or "kingdoms."

1176 *toga and olive wreath and not weapons with small shields*: The reference is to things worn in times of peace or war.

1177–1208 These lines are about the Battle of the Vega de Granada, waged by Juan II in 1431. According to the note to this line in Núñez, *Las Trezientas,* ten thousand Moors lost their life. Although a great victory for the Christians, it was ultimately inconclusive, since the Christians had to abandon the siege.

1193 *Like Typhoeus*: When the Etna volcano rumbles or spouts lava, we are witnessing the protests of the giant Typhoeus, who was punished for challenging the power of Jupiter by being tied under the volcano and was condemned to support Sicily forever: his feet were under Cape Lilibeo; his right arm, under Cape Faro or Pelorus; his left arm, on Cape Passero; and his head, under Mount Etna.

1194 *the forges of the Milanese*: The comparison is with the hammering noise of the forges of Milan, famous for its ironwork, particularly in armor.

1196 *Lyaeus's temple*: Lyaeus is another name for Bacchus (Ovid, *Metamorphoses* 4.11). The reference is to the Bacchantes, or Maenads, women who worshiped the Greek god Dionysus (the Roman Bacchus) and performed a wine-induced, maniacal dance during the Bacchanalia to the sound of loud music and crashing cymbals.

1197 *the back-and-forth*: Mena's *la vuelta* probably means *la revuelta*, shortened for the sake of the meter.

1200 *the son of good Zebediah*: The biblical Zebediah is mentioned in all

NOTES TO THE TRANSLATION

the gospels. He had two sons, but the stanza refers to one of them, the apostle James, significant because he is the patron saint of Spain and his name figures in its battle cry: *Santiago y cierra España!* (Saint James and close for Spain!).

1201 *the shadow of that fig tree*: The Battle of the Vega de Granada was also called the Battle of the Fig Tree, or *de la Higueruela*, according to the note to this line in Núñez, *Las Trezientas*, but Mena refers to the carvings on the throne of Juan II, which are themselves shadows of reality.

1205 *where one expects to find mummies*: According to the gloss in Núñez, *Las Trezientas*, the winds in the Sahara cause sudden and violent sandstorms that raise hills of sand and mummify the people buried in them. See Juan Casas-Rigall, *Juan de Mena y el Laberinto comentado: Tempranas glosas manuscritas* (ca. 1444–1479) (Salamanca, 2016), 36, for an exhaustive treatment of *carne de momia* (mummy flesh) and *arena de momia* (mummy dust) as apothecary ingredients.

1209 *Oh virtuous, magnificent war*: Mena refers to the Reconquest.

1227 *deleted and rubbed out*: Manuscript PN7 reads *unos de estados otros raídos*, other manuscripts, like Núñez in his early edition, *Las Trezientas*, have *testados* (deleted or erased) instead of *estados*. We opt for Núñez's reading. The carvings on the throne are erased and expunged or tarnished because these are civil wars of which Mena disapproves and is not willing to give them immortal fame by naming them.

1231 *Real de Ariza, and Velamazán*: The battles of Real de Ariza and Velamazán took place in 1429 and 1430 between the forces of Juan II of Castile and Alfonso of Aragon. Both were inconclusive.

1233 *the civil fury of Medina*: Stanzas 155–57 treat the 1441 siege of Medina del Campo, which was the result of a civil war and not the sort of just and holy war of which Mena approved. It ended with reconciliation of the Castilian and Aragonese parties.

1243–48 *Whom do you seek?... to him*: A comparison is made between the meeting of Juan II and his opponents in Medina, and a passage in the gospel of Saint John, in which Jesus is shown praying in a garden with his disciples when the Romans and the Jews come to get him: When he asks, "Whom do you seek?" they answer, "Jesus the Nazarene," and he responds, "I am." In both instances the question elicits an answer.

1244 *those he freed from the desert*: The reference is to the Jews.

1249 *in an arena*: The *palestra* (arena) was the place where Greek boxing and wrestling matches took place and came to signify either type of match.

1265–1360 These lines are dedicated to the death of the Count of Niebla. During the seventh siege of Gibraltar in 1436, Enrique Pérez de Guzmán (the second Count of Niebla) unsuccessfully attempted to capture the city from the sea and instead drowned during high tide.

1266 *sublimated on Mars's throne*: Manuscript PN7's *trono mavorcio* means "the throne of Mars," one of whose names is Mavors.

1278–79 *Count . . . of Niebla*: The person mentioned is Enrique Pérez de Guzmán, second Count of Niebla, who drowned during a sea assault on the castle of Gibraltar with eight of his men.

1280 *on that fated day*: The word *fadado* is now an archaism, meaning "fated."

1283 *the labels attached to all of their names*: It was common to identify the names of individuals and events portrayed in medieval paintings, carvings, and sculptures with *tituli*, or explanatory labels of varying length. In this case, the persons carved on the throne are identified by name, but this stanza names only the principal person: the Count of Niebla.

1288 *lose their uniqueness*: Manuscript PN7's *nombre* plays on the fact that the word is also an apocope for *renombre* (luster or fame).

1307 *with extended manes*: Comets were thought to portend death and carnage. We keep to PN7's *crines extendidas* (manes extended) rather than the more idiomatic "extended tails."

1311 *nocturnal . . . birds*: The nocturnal "birds" are owls and bats. Núñez, *Las Trezientas,* calls them birds of evil augury. Interestingly, the owl was an attribute of Minerva that was associated with dreams.

NOTES TO THE TRANSLATION

1322   *the Birsean wall*: The walls that circled Carthage and its castle, Birsus.

1323   *good Palinurus*: Palinurus was the Aeneas's pilot before he died. Aeneas sees him among the souls not ferried across the Acheron by Charon, because he was left unburied (Virgil, *Aeneid* 6.337–71). Aeneas, who is characterized as "the very human king" in verse 1325 of *The Labyrinth*, sees Palinurus and wants to touch his hand.

1326   *the Acheron*: The Acheron is one of the rivers of hell, known in Greek mythology as the "river of woe."

1328   *in Avernus*: Avernus is the entrance to the underworld (Hades).

1330   *the words of a sage*: The term *saje* means "wise" or "sage"; "words of the sage or wise one" therefore refers to what is known only to the wise and gives weight to the quartermaster's interpretation of the signs.

1336   *twice on the blood of kings*: Alfonso XI died from the plague during one of the sieges of Gibraltar. The master of the fleet warns the count not to let a similar fate take the life of someone who shares the blood of Alfonso.

1349   *his Delian cradle*: Apollo, and, according to some sources, also Artemis, was considered to have been born on the island of Delos.

1354   *of our forests*: The word used by Mena is *montaña*, probably because of the rhyme. The term is interchangeable with *monte*, and both can mean "forest."

1358   *nor cormorants fly*: The word used by Mena is *marinos*, a type of "sea crow" that is usually translated as "gull" or "cormorant."

1359   *nor swans*: Mena calls swans *caistros* because the birds lived on the banks of the Caytrus River in Ionia.

1361   *halcyons*: The term alludes to a fable concerning a seabird commonly known in English as the kingfisher. The verses evoke the "halcyon days," as the commentary in PN7 explains, because the bird was said to nest in the dead of winter in close proximity to the sea, but if it noticed a storm was coming, it would fly over the water, crying out mournfully in the hope

NOTES TO THE TRANSLATION

that the sea would calm down and its hatchlings would survive the rising tide. The birds' two-week nesting period before and after the winter solstice was referred to as halcyon days.

1369–74 *the crow... the heron... the coot*: As Kerkhof points out in his edition, Mena derives these avian premonitions from Virgil, *Georgics* 1.389, as well as Lucan, *The Civil War* 5.555–56.

1390–91 *the count... fortified town*: We have had to change the order in which these verses appear to clarify their meaning.

1394 *his son*: Juan de Guzmán, the first Duke of Medina-Sidonia (province of Cadiz). After writing *The Labyrinth*, Mena wrote *Tratado sobre el título de duque* (1445), a treatise about the noble rank of duke that was dedicated to this figure.

1406–7 *the shield wall... the sails*: We have translated *pavesada* as "shield wall," in keeping with nautical war terminology. The *empavesada* refers to either the shields that the men carry, which are put up to guard against arrows shot at them while disembarking, or to a kind of netting used to shield ships from projectiles. The metaphor "wings" *(alas)* likely indicates that *pavesada* refers to the first. The *troceos* are the poles wrapped in leather that were used with the stays, or rigging ropes, to furl and unfurl the sails.

1425 *cannons*: The Spanish *truenos* literally means "thunderclaps" and evokes the detonation of cannons.

1443 *at that moment*: We have chosen this translation for *donde estaba* because it encompasses the timing (and not just the place) of the attempted rescue.

1458 *even though we should not*: The count's men speak to the peril of being under the ramparts.

1476 *they craved more*: The verb used in the Spanish, *anhelar*, conveys the idea of the desire for air of someone who is gasping, as well as a more general sense of yearning for something.

1499 *Juan de Mayorga*: Juan Pimentel, count of Mayorga (province of Valladolid), was the son of the count of Benavente. According to the note by Sánchez de las Brozas, *Anotaciones*, he was well known for his military feats and died of a head wound while ax throwing.

NOTES TO THE TRANSLATION

1501 *oars*: We have opted for a direct translation here. The image echoes the metaphor of the wings *(alae)* of Fortune, which itself echoes a figure found in Virgil, *Aeneid* 1.301, and Ovid, *Metamorphoses* 5.588, as Kerkhof, *El laberinto,* notes at this line.

1511 *such a brother*: The brother alluded to is Alonso Pimentel, a count who served both Juan II and Enrique IV.

1513 *pierced by an arrow*: This refers to the death of Diego de Rivera, an Andalusian nobleman. According to Núñez's commentary in *Las Trezientas,* a Moorish crossbowman shot him in the head as soon as he removed his faceplate to speak with the mayor of Alora (Granada). Manuscript PN7 places stanzas 193–96 here, and then goes back to stanza 190 (as enumerated in *Las Trezientas*).

1517 *not little celebrated in song*: Mena alludes to a frontier ballad, or *romance,* known as *Alora, la bien cercada* (Alora, well under siege), recounting how Diego de Rivera is tricked into exposing himself in an effort to negotiate the surrender of Alora's castle.

1518–19 *adelantado . . . your border*: During the late Middle Ages, *adelantados* were appointed to serve as military commanders, in keeping with our translation, but after the conquest of frontier regions, they could exert legal authority and rule more as governors: for this reason we have not translated the title. The possessive pronoun refers to the contemporaneous king, Juan II.

1521–28 *Emathia*: A part of Macedonia between the Grecian rivers Axius and Haliacmon that in Lucan includes Thessaly and is where he locates the civil war between Caesar and Pompey the Great. As noted in the commentary by Sánchez de las Brozas, Scaeva was a centurion who fought bravely for Caesar, was terribly wounded, and lost one eye to a barrage of arrows and lances that pierced his shield. See also Lucan, *The Civil War* 6.214–50.

1524 *Gortinian*: From an important city in ancient Crete under the Romans (Lucan, *The Civil War* 2.214–15) that was associated with the production of bows and arrows. There is some disagreement among editors regarding whether Mena is using *cortino* as an adjective to describe the arrow or as a personification of the person that gave or inflicted the wound. *Las Trezientas*

NOTES TO THE TRANSLATION

entertains both possibilities. We have tried to maintain the sense of this term as a place-name, in keeping with Lucan (and the Sánchez de las Brozas commentary).

1526–27 *where that sad Aulus . . . him of manly virtue*: In Lucan, *The Civil War* 6.228–39, the wounded Scaeva asks to be brought to Pompey's camp, and then stealthily draws his sword and decapitates his captor, Aulus. The personal pronoun "him" refers to Scaeva.

1529–36 *You advanced . . . adelantado*: In Spanish, the verb *(adelantar)* may function here as a play on words with the title of *adelantado* of Diego de Rivera.

1537–44 *He who appears . . . call him victorious*: The reference is to the death of Rodrigo de Perea, Lord of Cazorla (province of Jaén). According to the commentary of Núñez in *Las Trezientas,* this powerful knight was surrounded by an army of Moors from Granada, wounded and held captive, then killed by the enemy when they dressed his wounds with a poultice made from poisonous plants.

1545–50 *Curio . . . Juba*: The reference is to the Gaius Scribonius Curio the Younger, who commanded an army for Caesar that was tasked with conquering Africa. He was defeated by Juba I of Numidia in an ambush and died in the course of the battle (Lucan, *The Civil War* 4.581–798).

1561 *The other young man*: The person alluded to is Pedro de Narváez, son of the magistrate of Antequera (province of Málaga), who in honor of his father, refused to flee when outnumbered by Moors in combat, preferring instead to die.

1571 *Evander . . . Pallas*: Mena refers to a story in Virgil, *Aeneid* 8.514, 10.365–487, concerning the young Pallas, son of Evander (king of Pallantium), who fights courageously with Aeneas. When Pallas dies in battle, Aeneas avenges the youth's death as if his own son had been killed. In keeping with the rubric, in verse 1571 Rodrigo is being compared to Evander, and Pedro to Pallas.

1577 *Juan de Merlo*: Merlo was head of the royal guard and died in the service of his king not long before *The Labyrinth* was com-

NOTES TO THE TRANSLATION

posed. His exploits are recounted in the *Crónica del señor rey don Juan, segundo de este nombre,* ed. and expanded by Lorenzo Galíndez de Carvajal (Valencia, 1779), p. 338 (entry for the year 1433, chapter 4).

1587 *Enrique of Ramstein*: A German knight who was defeated in combat by Juan de Merlo in the city of Basel.

1590 *Lord of Charny*: A French knight named Pierre de Brecemonte, who was also defeated in combat by Juan de Merlo in the city of Arras.

1601 *He whom*: The reference is to Lorenzo Dávalos, chamberlain of Prince Enrique (oldest son of Juan II). He died of a head wound near the town of Escalona, during a battle against partisans loyal to the constable Álvaro de Luna; see *Crónica del señor rey don Juan,* pp. 425–26 (entry for the year 1441, chapter 13).

1609 *beloved by the lord prince*: This refers to Enrique, the aforementioned son of Juan II, since Lorenzo was his chamberlain.

1611 *mourned by his sad mother*: As Lida de Malkiel, *Juan de Mena,* 75–77, has shown, the figure of the mourning mother of Lorenzo is based on similar passages in Virgil, *Aeneid* 9, 11, and 14, describing the sorrows of family members weeping over the bodies of their lifeless loved ones.

1650 *you saw*: The personal pronoun in this verse refers to the narrator.

1652 *the lioness*: As Núñez explains in his commentary to *Las Trezientas,* the reference is to a belief, found also in Isidore, that lion cubs sleep for three days after birth, whereupon their mothers awaken them by standing over them and roaring.

1658 *holy keeper of the keys*: This title alludes to Fernando de Padilla. He held the position of *clavero* of the Order of Calatrava (third in Rank after the *maestre* and the *comendador mayor*) and was in charge of the keys of the convent of Calatrava la Nueva. He was also elected master of the chivalric Order of Calatrava. When the convent was under siege by Prince Enrique, he was accidentally killed by a stone fired from his own squire's slingshot.

1671 *I curse you, Mallorcans*: As Núñez, *Las Trezientas,* points out at

NOTES TO THE TRANSLATION

this line, Mena follows ancient authorities in attributing the invention of slingshots to inhabitants of the Balearic Islands, since according to Isidore, *Etymologies* 14.6.44, the name of the islands comes from the Greek word meaning "throw"—and the largest of the islands is Mallorca.

1675 *Milo*: This figure is identified by the gloss that accompanies this stanza in PN7 as Milo of Croton, a giant wrestler famed in Greek myth for being able to carry a bull on his shoulders for sacrifice. He is cited here as an example of brute strength, as opposed to the virtue of fortitude.

1705–1848 Mena describes the sixth wheel (the order of Jupiter). Stanzas 215–19 then identify positive and negative past rulers: Octavian, Codrus, the Deciuses, Torquatus, the Brutuses, the Catos, Fabricius, and the Dionysiuses of Syracuse. The section compares them to Juan II (stanzas 220–22), bemoaning the sins of greed and envy as opposed to true justice.

1708 *public matters*: Here the poet's word choice could be a calque of Cicero's *De re publica*.

1713 *Octavian*: Refers to the emperor Augustus, whose rule ushered in a golden age known as the *Pax Romana,* following a period of civil wars. Mena will compare Juan II to Octavian as the "new Augustus," before starting his treatment of the seventh wheel of Saturn (verse 1834).

1715 *untroubled*: While some editors read the word as the verb, *pacificó*, we translated it as an adjective, which scans better.

1716 *gates of Janus*: Ceremonially closing the gates of Janus (god of temporal and spatial transitions and passages) occurred under the reign of Augustus and symbolized Rome being at peace.

1717–18 *the brave Roman ... Tarpeian tower*: Reference to Marcus Manlius, a celebrated Roman consul, who bravely defended the Capitoline when a Gallic tribe besieged the Eternal City in the fourth century BCE, as told in Pliny, *Natural History* 4.29, trans. H. Rackham, 10 vols. (Cambridge, MA, 1938–1962).

1721–22 *Codrus ... Deciuses*: The king of Athens, Codrus was said to have scarified himself in order to fulfill the oracle of Apollo's prophesy that war with the Dorians would end only if this ruler died

NOTES TO THE TRANSLATION

by enemy hands. "Deciuses" is a reference to the illustrious Roman family of plebeian origins that included Publius Decius Mus, who, also following an oracle, sacrificed himself in battle for the benefit of his people. See, respectively, Valerius Maximus, *Memorable Doings and Sayings* 5.1 and 1.5, ed. and trans. D. R. Shackleton Bailey (Cambridge, MA, 2000).

1725 *Torquatus*: Mena refers to Titus Manlius Torquatus, an austere Roman leader who served with Publius Decius Mus. As the Sánchez de las Brozas commentary notes, he was known for having his own son executed for disobeying lawful orders, by leaving his post to engage in combat with the enemy.

1730 *Brutuses*: The Sánchez de las Brozas commentary identifies these figures as, first, Lucius Junius Brutus, a Roman founder who expelled the Roman king Tarquinius after Lucretius's suicide, and Marcus Junius Brutus, who sought to liberate the Roman Republic from tyranny by killing Julius Caesar.

1733–36 *Catos, the good Uticensis and the Censor*: As Kerkhof notes in his edition, this reference alludes to Marcus Porcius Cato, a morally upright political and military leader who was elected censor in the second century BCE, and his great-grandson of the same name, who committed suicide in Utica (hence the epithet "Uticensis") rather than receive honors from the tyrant Julius Caesar. Mena seems to conflate them under the theme of self-sacrifice, although, as the Sánchez de las Brozas commentary points out, only Cato the Younger killed himself. However, Cato the Elder can be said to have figuratively "martyred" himself, insofar as he exposed himself to the continual attacks of his enemies by insisting on austere, anti-Hellenic policies during his censorship.

1737–44 *Fabricius*: This figure is Gaius Fabricius Luscinus Moncularis, who was a statesman serving as consul and censor in the third century BCE. He turned down a lucrative bribe when negotiating peace on behalf of Rome, and was known for his integrity and virtuous frugality—as can be seen in his appearance in Dante, *Purgatorio* 20, and the description in the Sánchez de las Brozas commentary to *The Labyrinth*.

NOTES TO THE TRANSLATION

1765   *purple state clothes*: We have translated *múrice ropa* in this way, in order to convey the color described in the stanza's gloss in PN7: clothing dyed with a tint of purple that could be worn only by emperors and kings.

1770–72   *town encircled by flame*: The gloss in PN7 identifies the place as Madrid, and Núñez, *Las Trezientas,* notes that the ambassadors bearing gifts were from France according to some, and from Germany according to others.

1814   *Amyclas*: Refers to a humble fisherman in Lucan, *The Civil War* 5.540, who, in the dark of night, takes Caesar in his sailboat across the Adriatic Sea.

1822   *Dionysiuses of Syracuse*: History records only two tyrannical rulers of Syracuse named Dionysius, father and son, who reigned during the fifth and the fourth centuries BCE and whose ruthless legacy is mentioned in Dante, *Inferno* 12.107. As Kerkhof, *El laberinto,* suggests at this line—following John G. Cummins, ed., *El Laberinto de Fortuna* (Madrid, 1968)—it is possible that Mena describes three figures based on mentions of kings named Dionysius in Latin histories: the king of Sicily, another king persevering in tyranny, and a king who was the son of an elder Dionysius.

1825   *Ionos*: Mena refers to the story told in Lucan, *The Civil War* 6.402–5, that a Thessalian prince by this name was the first to mint coins.

1849–2136   Mena describes the seventh wheel (the order of Saturn). This section continues the theme of justice, giving negative examples of powerful rulers who would let crimes go unpunished, and portrays the present hero, Álvaro de Luna, constable of Juan II, who dominates Fortune and is blessed by Providence. The future is gleaned through a scene of necromancy, in which nobles attempt to discover the outcome of contemporaneous civil conflicts in Spain.

1859   *Tydeus*: Son of Oenius, one of the "Seven against Thebes," whom, according to the gloss here in Núñez, *Las Trezientas,* Mena associates with Álvaro de Luna on the basis of his small stature, yet great strength.

NOTES TO THE TRANSLATION

1860 *Nestor*: The epitome of a wise counselor from the time of the Trojan War, who was depicted in Homeric epic, as Kerkhof points out in the note to this line in his edition.

1880 *Álvaro de Luna*: The constable and favorite of Juan II is exalted by Mena as a hero who overcomes his enemies, exemplifies noble virtues, and tames Fortune, reconciling her with Providence (see the Introduction).

1887–88 *his firm beliefs . . . always victorious*: These verses can be read as hyperbaton, since the last two lines belong to the sequence of qualities assigned to Luna.

1902 *a woman shown*: This refers to the witch of Valladolid, whose characterization as a necromancer, magically causing the cadaver of a condemned man to reveal the future, is based primarily on the figure of the sorceress Erictho in Lucan, *The Civil War* 6.

1921 *lung of lynx*: According to the commentary of Núñez, *Las Trezientas,* the magical ingredients are drawn from classical poetry and used in a necromantic spell cast by the witch of Valladolid during the conflict between Álvaro de Luna and the Infantes of Aragon and their followers. In the poem, enemies of Alvaro sought to discern the fortunes of the powerful constable through the witch. Expecting his downfall, they would abandon or turn against him.

1923 *of a serpent*: According to Núñez, *Las Trezientas,* the reference is to a story in Pliny, *Natural History* 12, concerning a serpent that is born from the body of a dead man, specifically in marrow of the spine. As Kerkhof, *El laberinto,* suggests, Mena (or his source), as well as a commentator in PN7, seems to have thought that the "hyena" alluded to in the previous verse was a snake, as opposed to the four-legged African scavenger.

1927–28 *that stone*: This appears to be a reference to the eaglestone, or aetite, which was purportedly used by eagles to cool down the eggs in their nests. It was also employed as an amulet during childbirth to prevent miscarriages and premature births.

1929 *lot of remora*: Mena adopts the name for the fish from Lucan, *The Civil War* 4.675, and adapts it his Spanish end rhyme. As

NOTES TO THE TRANSLATION

Núñez, *Las Trezientas*, notes, he draws on Pliny, *Natural History* 9, in reference to how the remora (also known in English as the suckerfish) was said to attach itself to boats.

1937   *dogs that fear water*: Lucan, *The Civil War* 6.671, indicates that Ericho employed in her magic foaming drool from the mouths of dogs fearing water—that is, they are rabid dogs, since rabies was treated as a disease of hydrophobia in antiquity and throughout the Middle Ages.

1938–39   *the Libyan serpent cerastes, ash of the Phoenix*: The name of this north African snake comes from a Greek word for horned and was also used by the sorceress in Lucan, *The Civil War* 6.679 — as are the ashes of the mythic bird, the phoenix (6.680).

1940   *bones of the wings*: The commentary in PN7 notes that in another manuscript this verse starts with the image of "eyes" *(ojos)* being located on the wings of dragons, as in Lucan, *The Civil War* 6.675, instead of "bones" *(huesos)*. However, that variation does not occur in PN7, *Las Trezientas*—or, as Kerkhof, *El laberinto* notes, any other extant version of the poem.

1953   *the sorceress searches*: In both PN7 and *Las Trezientes*, stanzas 245 and 246 appear out of order; however, Núñez, *Las Trezientas*, makes a note of the error, and editors have consistently restored the correct order, as we have done.

1959   *conjures up Orcus*: The Spanish text reads [*h*]*uerco*, which can also evoke the infernal dwelling where the demonic Orcus (also mentioned in Lucan, *The Civil War* 6.715) lives—so in this sense the invocation could be understood as metonymic.

1970   *Pluto . . . Proserpina*: The god who rules Hades, and his queen, daughter of the fertility goddess Ceres in Roman myth.

1977   *Cerberus*: This three-headed mythological creature is said to guard the entrance to Hades and is sometimes depicted feeding on the dead with its mouths.

1980   *vile boatman*: This is a reference to Charon, who takes payment to ferry the dead across the river Styx into Hades.

1984   *the one who first brought you*: The reference is to Hercules, who is said to have taken Cerberus from Hades as one of his Twelve Labors.

NOTES TO THE TRANSLATION

1987   *with a live snake*: The necromantic scene in Lucan, *The Civil War* 6.726–27, also calls for a live snake to be used like a whip to strike the body.

1995   *Hecate*: Greek goddess of the underworld who became closely associated with magic and witchcraft. Again, Mena draws on Lucan, *The Civil War* 6.736–38, in which Erictho calls on her as a wretched and cadaverous figure, needing to mask her face before the upper gods.

2006   *Demogorgon*: In his commentary, Núñez, *Las Trezientas*, identifies Demogorgon as the father of pagan gods, who resides in the depths of Hell, and as a fearful divinity of the earth. While an unnamed, evil being who looks upon the gorgon's (that is, Medusa's) head is invoked by Erictho (Lucan, *The Civil War* 6.744), Mena could also be familiar with the meaning of Demogorgon as the father of the Fates in the work of Giovanni Boccaccio, *Genealogie deorum gentilium libri* 1.5, ed. Vincenzo Romano, 2 vols. (Bari, 1951).

2008   *the Stygian waters*: This reference is to the rippling waters of the river Styx in Hades, where the giant Demogorgon could be found.

2021   *they do them great harm*: As the Sánchez de las Brozas commentary explains, the "infernal ones," or demons, suffer this harm because, by keeping the peace with Muslims, Christians deprive them of infidel souls to torture in hell. The demons avenge themselves by sowing discord among the Christians so that they will sinfully make war on their coreligionists.

2037   *you who command*: The king, Juan II, should be advised to turn internal strife exhibited by his Christian subjects on Muslim enemies.

2066   *to the chameleon*: As Núñez, *Las Trezientas*, notes, according to Pliny, *Natural History* 8.51, the chameleon always holds its head up and keeps its mouth open, since the creature relies solely on air for its sustenance.

2074   *Labienus*: An officer in the army of Julius Caesar during Rome's conquest of Gaul. He later took the side of Pompey during the civil war and was killed in Hispania.

NOTES TO THE TRANSLATION

2087–88   *so it happens . . . with many masters*: We have had to transpose parts of these verses in order to clarify their meaning.

2097–98   *the matter . . . adversaries*: The "matter" that has "concluded" refers to a time when Álvaro de Luna had to flee, before making his way back into the king's good graces, as Núñez, *Las Trezientas,* explains. The "adversaries" are enemies of Álvaro de Luna, who turned against him during his time as constable and royal favorite (see the Introduction).

2104   *the great misfortunes*: As it turns out, the predicted events are unfortunate for the enemies of the constable, but, as we will see, fortunate for him (and for this reason they prefer to disbelieve the true meaning revealed by the witch, as Núñez, *Las Trezientas,* notes).

2116   *turned back to copper*: As Núñez, *Las Trezientas,* explains in his commentary, this stanza refers to a gilded copper statue that was commissioned by Álvaro de Luna to be placed in his tomb at the cathedral of Toledo. The constable's enemies, led by Prince Enrique, had the statue destroyed.

2123   *frozen carrion*: As Núñez makes clear in his commentary, the sense of the image is that lions prefer fresh meat, instead of leftovers from an earlier kill that, if not so famished, they would normally leave to scavengers.

2131–32   *satisfied by the bronze simulacrum . . . she is favorable*: The prophesy of the constable's downfall in verse 2110 is made to signify solely the destruction of this statue. In fact, in the years after the composition of *The Labyrinth,* Álvaro de Luna's fortunes took a turn for the worse, and he was executed in Valladolid in 1462.

2137–38   *Phoebus . . . Phaethon*: According to Ovidian myth, when Phaethon was granted a wish, he asked his father, Phoebus, to allow him to drive the sun god's chariot. Phaethon, however, lost control of the chariot, and part of the earth was scorched (*Metamorphoses* 2.1–325).

2147–50   *while sleeping . . . my guide*: As Núñez, *Las Trezientas,* makes clear, the poet wonders whether the vision was only a dream, since

NOTES TO THE TRANSLATION

just now he sees the morning light. Having appeared during the night, the figures seen in the vision might have been phantasms (suggested by the Spanish *fantaseado*). But Providence can resolve his doubts, since she accompanied him through the House of Fortune as a guide.

2161 *king of kings*: An encomium describing Juan II as overshadowing previous kings starts here and continues to the end of stanza 291. Mena catalogs Visigothic rulers of Hispania, followed by kings who reigned after the Muslim conquest, seen as predecessors to the Castilian monarchy, the Trastámara royal family, and Juan II.

2169 *Geryon*: This refers to a giant who lived on a western island of Erytheia in Hesperides, identified during Mena's time as Spain, as in Enrique de Villena, *Los doce trabajos de Hércules* 10, ed. Pedro M. Cátedra (Santander, 2007). More specifically, the island was sometimes associated with Cadiz, a southwestern port city on a narrow peninsula (evoked above in verse 82). One of Hercules's labors was to capture the giant's cattle, which he accomplished after shooting Geryon with poisoned arrows.

2170–71 *Chinda . . . Goths*: This refers to the Visigothic king of Hispania, Chindasuinth (r. 642–653). We have shortened his name, in keeping with the poetic version used by Mena. "Cindus" is the name found in the *Poema de Fernán González*, stanzas 26–27, which gives a similar sequence of early rulers up to the time of the Castilian judges (see the note to verse 2222, below), drawing on a Latin chronicle dating to around 1200 known as the *Chronicón Villarense* or *Liber regum*.

2174 *Wamba . . . consuetude*: This king (r. 672–680) was spuriously attributed with the "Division of Wamba," delineating the accepted constitution of dioceses in the Visigothic kingdom prior to the Muslim conquest of the peninsula. We have translated *nuevo uso* (literally, "new usage") as "consuetude" to reflect the idea of a custom given legal bearing. Wamba's nephew, Egica, succeeded him to the throne.

2179 *acts of Egica*: This Visigothic king (r. 687–702) presided over the

NOTES TO THE TRANSLATION

Seventeenth Council of Toledo, which introduced church reforms relating to liturgical practices and notoriously decreed severe persecution of Iberian Jews.

2180–81 *Erwig ... Witiza*: Egica was in fact the son-in-law (or *hijo yerno*) of Erwig, as Louise Vasvari Fainberg points out in the note to this line in her edition, *Laberinto de Fortuna* (Madrid, 1976). As PN7 and Núñez, *Las Trezientas,* both identify him as the son of Erwig (r. 608–687), we have translated the verse as such. Witiza was the son of Egica and succeeded him to the throne (in 694 or 695).

2183–84 *deeds of ... Rodrigo*: We have given the Anglicized version of Visigothic names prior to the Muslim conquest, which occurred during the reign of Rodrigo (Roderic), the last Visigothic king of Hispania (710–711). Mena gives a neo-Gothicist account of kingship, passing from Visigothic Hispania to Asturias following the conquest.

2185 *this one, poor Pelayo's deeds*: The point of comparison with "this one" is here and elsewhere the current king, Juan II, surpassing rulers of old. Pelayo, the semilegendary eighth-century figure, was said to be related to the Visigothic royal family. He was celebrated as having made a successful last stand in the mountains of Asturias, where his small band of followers was outnumbered by Muslim invaders.

2192 *flame comes from after lightning*: As Núñez, *Las Trezientas,* notes, the comparison echoes a simile found in Lucan comparing war waged by Julius Cesar to thunder and lightning (*The Civil War* 1.151–57).

2193–94 *Favila ... acts of Alfonso the First*: Favila was the son of Pelayo; his brief reign (737–739) preceded that of his brother-in-law Alfonso I, who established the kingdom of Asturias, and took control of many surrounding areas.

2202 *Orense*: We have normalized the spelling of this city and province in northwestern Spain (Galician *Ourense*), on the border with Portugal, that is given in PN7. Other manuscripts have different readings, as Kerkhof, *El laberinto,* notes. In Núñez,

NOTES TO THE TRANSLATION

    Las Trezientas, instead of Orense, the place identified at the start of this verse is the Portuguese city of Avis.

2208–9 *forgotten... Fruela... his errors*: In this section the then-current king Juan II *(este)* is being compared to past rulers, as also in verses 2224, 2228, 2231, and 2315. The oldest son of Alfonso I was Fruela I of Asturias (known as "the Cruel"), who murdered his brother Vimara out of envy, and then was himself assassinated in 768.

2217–20 *Alfonso the Second... a temple*: This king was celebrated during his reign (791–842) for making Oviedo the capital of his kingdom and sponsoring building projects in the city, including a Romanesque basilica dedicated to Christ the Savior with altars for each of the apostles.

2222 *Calvo Laín... Nuño Rasura*: Two legendary judges said to have administered the border region of old Castile after the reign of Alfonso II of Asturias. "Calvo" and "Rasura" are nicknames meaning "bald" and "shaven" but are not usually translated since they became cognomina for these semimythic figures. They were traditionally identified as ancestors of the epic heroes Rodrigo Díaz de Vivar (El Cid) and Fernán González.

2224 *this one*: Once again, the point of comparison is the current king, Juan II.

2225–28 *Fernando... Sancho... Alfonso the third... this one*: At this point, Mena skips a number of kings in the line of succession, to commemorate Fernando I of Castile and León (r. 1035–1065), known as "the Great," and his sons Sancho II of Castile (r. 1065–1072) and Alfonso VI of Castile and León (r. 1072–1109). As Vasvari Fainberg, *Laberinto,* 211–12, explains, Mena calls the latter king "the third" Alfonso because he omits rulers of León who share the name. He counts Asturian kings up to the time of the Castilian judges, followed by Castilian monarchs (in keeping with his earlier-mentioned neo-Gothicist ideology). After citing the deeds of Alfonso VI, he again refers to those of Juan II (identified as "this one").

2230 *the fourth Alfonso*: This refers to Alfonso VII of Castile and León

NOTES TO THE TRANSLATION

(r. 1126–1157), who took on the title of *imperator totius Hispaniae*, or "emperor of all Spain," as he was able to claim lordship over other Peninsular rulers, such as the king of Navarre and the Count of Barcelona, among others.

2232 *the second Sancho*: The oldest son of Alfonso VII, Sancho III of Castile (r. 1157–1158).

2233 *the fifth Alfonso*: The only son of Sancho III, Alfonso VIII of Castile (r. 1158–1214), celebrated for his great victory in 1212, when he routed the Almohads in the battle of Las Navas de Tolosa. Earlier in his long reign he had suffered a demoralizing defeat to the Almohads at Alarcos (1195).

2238–39 *the first Enrique . . . killed in Palencia*: This refers to Enrique I of Castile (r. 1214–1217), who suffered an untimely death. According to chronicles, the teenaged king was playing with other noble boys of his age in Palencia, when one of them threw a roofing tile from the top of a tower, which accidentally—and fatally—struck Enrique in the head.

2241 *Don Fernando*: This refers to Fernando III of Castile and León (r. 1217–1252, assuming the throne of León in 1230). Known for his piety and martial zeal, he conquered much of the territory of Andalusia that had been ruled over by Muslims since the eighth century. He was canonized as a saint in 1671.

2267 *Gazules*: This refers to Alcalá de Gazules (province of Cadiz), whose Muslim residents began paying tribute to Fernando III as their sovereign following the conquest of Seville (1248), like other towns mentioned in this section.

2278–79 *Alfonso . . . empire*: This refers to Alfonso X of Castile and León (r. 1252–1284), son of Fernando III, and known as the "wise king" for his dedication to legal, scientific, and esoteric learning, including Jewish and Muslim sources of knowledge. He sought to become Holy Roman Emperor due to his mother's lineage as granddaughter of Frederick I.

2285–89 *ransom . . . in silence*: This story was recorded in the *Crónica de Alfonso X* (chapter 17) and is also mentioned in the Sánchez de las Brozas commentary. It recounts how Alfonso X generously provided funds for Marie de Brienne to ransom her husband, the Latin emperor of Constantinople, Baldwin II, from the Turks. The last verse of the stanza seems to refer to literary works also being attributed to this "wise king."

2292 *deeds of the third Fernando*: This is Fernando IV of Castile and León (r. 1295–1312), who was best known for recovering Gibraltar from the Muslim kingdom of Granada (1309), and Alcaudete, in the year of his death.

2294–96 *he died summoned . . . singing*: These verses refer to a story told in late medieval chronicles about the death of Fernando IV. The king was said to have ordered the execution of two brothers for the assassination of one of his favorite knights. Before he had them thrown from a cliff overlooking the town of Martos (province of Cordoba), the brothers warned that this was unjust and that consequently Fernando would soon be summoned by God. Some weeks later, the young king died in his bed, supposedly fulfilling the prediction. In the last verse of the stanza, Mena refers to a ballad commemorating this legend, known as the *Romance de los hermanos Carvajales*.

2297–2302 *the seventh Alfonso . . . Marinid kings*: This refers to Alfonso XI of Castile and León, who was the second great-grandfather of Juan II. During his reign (1312–1350), the Marinid rulers of Morocco captured Gibraltar and defeated the Castilian naval blockade at the port town of Algeciras (1340). But, before his death, he achieved a victory against the Marinids at Río Salado and recovered Algeciras, in addition to towns mentioned in this stanza.

2311 *Benzaide*: This refers to what is now the city of Alcalá la Real (province of Jaén). Alfonso XI conferred its new "royal" place-name after conquering the stronghold in 1341.

2314–18 *Don Pedro . . . Don Enrique . . . great-grandfather*: This stanza first contrasts Juan II with Pedro I of Castile and León (r. 1350–1369), known as "the Cruel," who succeeded Alfonso XI as his legitimate son. His marriage was arranged with the French noblewoman Blanche de Bourbon, whom he abandoned for his Spanish mistress. This ended an alliance between France and Castile and resulted in conflict with Aragon, as well as a civil

NOTES TO THE TRANSLATION

war in which the English backed Pedro's cause against his illegitimate brother, Enrique de Trastámara. This half brother assassinated and succeeded him as Enrique II of Castile and León (1369–1379), the great-grandfather of Juan II.

2319 *grandfather*: This reference is to Juan I of Castile and León (r. 1379–1390), the oldest son of Enrique II.

2321–22 *Don Enrique . . . peacemaker*: Juan II's father, Enrique III of Castile (r. 1390–1406), was able to restore peaceful relations with the English through his marriage to Catherine of Lancaster (1388), and also signed a treaty with Portugal near the end of his reign (1402).

2328 *exalted Don Juan*: The encomium of Juan II that began with stanza 271 now comes to an end. The poet is able to see that his king will be victorious in keeping the peace and will hopefully triumph over the Moors but discerns no further details as the vision of Providence leaves him, ascending into the heavens.

2354 *particles*: According to Núñez, *Last Trezientas,* the particles *(átomos)* comparison refers to an optical effect produced when the sun's rays pass through an aperture (such as a window or a hole in a wall) and illuminate otherwise invisible particles floating in the air.

2371–72 *she who . . . by divine order*: We have had to transpose parts of these verses in order to clarify their meaning.

2377 *my thoughts*: The final three stanzas, 298–300, are usually considered to be apocryphal, but form the accepted conclusion to the poem in both PN7 and *Las Trezientas*. As Núñez notes in his commentary, another tradition attributed to Juan II himself expands the poem to a number of stanzas equaling the number of days in a year. As Kerkhof, *El laberinto,* observes in his note to this verse, twenty-four additional stanzas do appear in a 1509 Zaragoza edition, but they are generally rejected as not only spurious but also in conflict with the laudatory rhetoric of Mena's poem (something the Sánchez de las Brozas commentary also makes clear). These twenty-four stanzas were also printed as an independent work in the late fifteenth-century *Cancionero de Llavia* and *Cancionero general* (in the former they appear together with the last three from *Las Trezientas*). See Linde M. Brocato, "Publishing Juan de Mena: An Overview of the Editorial Traditions," *Revista de cancioneros impresos y manuscritos* 1 (2012): 1–40.

2400 *succor*: We have translated *favor* in the final verse as "succor," in keeping with the commentary of Núñez, *Las Trezientas,* explaining how everyone has the capacity to appreciate and be favored by the dignity and majesty of Divine Providence.

Bibliography

Editions and Translations

Azáceta, José María, ed. *Laberinto de Fortuna*. In *Cancionero de Fernández de Ixar,* vol. 1, pp. 229–412. Madrid, 1956.
Blecua, José Manuel, ed. *Laberinto de Fortuna*. Madrid, 1943.
Cummins, John G. *Laberinto de Fortuna*. Salamanca, 1968.
Gómez Moreno, Ángel, and Teresa Jiménez Calvente, eds. *Obras completas de Juan de Mena*. Madrid, 1994.
Kerkhof, Maxim P. A. M., ed. *El laberinto de Fortuna*. Madrid, 1995.
——, ed. *Laberinto de Fortuna*. Clásicos Castalia 223. Madrid, 1997.
Lope-Rivière, Monique de, and France Autesserre, eds. *Labyrinthe de Fortune*. Paris, 2019. http://books.openedition.org/esb/1168.
Nigris, Carla de, ed. *Laberinto de Fortuna*. Barcelona, 1994.
Pérez Priego, Miguel Ángel, ed. *Laberinto de Fortuna*. Madrid, 1976.
Vasvari Fainberg, Louise, ed. *Laberinto de Fortuna*. Madrid, 1976.
Weiss, Julian, and Antonio Cortijo Ocaña, eds. *Glosa sobre las "Trezientas" del famoso poeta Juan de Mena*. Madrid, 2015. Abridged online edition, https://www.ehumanista.ucsb.edu/publications/trescientas.

Further Reading

Bermejo Cabrero, José Luis. "Ideales políticos de Juan de Mena." *Revista de estudios políticos* 188 (1973): 153–76.
Brocato, Linde M. "El famosíssimo poeta Juan de Mena: Producción y lectura de sus obras impresas." In *Juan de Mena: De letrado a poeta,* edited by Cristina Moya García, 187–203. London, 2014.
——. "Publishing Juan de Mena: An Overview of the Editorial Traditions." *Revista de cancioneros impresos y manuscritos* 1 (2012): 1–40.

BIBLIOGRAPHY

Burke, James F. "The Interior Journey and the Structure of Juan de Mena's *Laberinto de Fortuna.*" *Revista de estudios hispánicos* 22 (1988): 27–45.

Castillo Cáceres, Fernando. "El trono de Juan II en el *Laberinto de Fortuna.*" *Cuadernos de historia de España* 74 (1997): 67–100. Also in *Estudios sobre cultura, guerra, y política en la corona de Castilla (siglos XIV–XVII)*, 183–218. Madrid, 2007.

Deyermond, Alan. "Estructura y estilo como instrumentos de propaganda en *Laberinto de Fortuna.*" In *Poesía de Cancionero del siglo XV*, 207–9. Valencia, 2007.

Domínguez, Frank A. "Laberintos, *mappae mundi*, y geografías en *El Laberinto de Fortuna* de Juan de Mena y *Las Trezientas* de Hernán Núñez." *La corónica: A Journal of Medieval Spanish Language and Literature* 40, no. 1 (2011): 149–82.

Foulché-Delbosc, R. "Étude sur le *Laberinto* de Juan de Mena." *Revue Hispanique* 9 (1902): 75–138. Translated into Spanish by A. Bonilla and San Martín. *Juan de Mena y el arte mayor.* Madrid, 1903.

Gericke, Philip O. "Mena's *Laberinto de Fortuna*: Apocalypse Now?" *La corónica* 17 (1989): 1–17.

———. "The Narrative Structure of the *Laberinto de Fortuna.*" *Romance Philology* 21, no. 4 (1968): 512–22.

Lapesa, Rafael. "El elemento moral en el *Laberinto de Mena*: Su influjo en la disposición de la obra." *Hispanic Review* 27 (1959): 257–66.

Lida de Malkiel, María Rosa. *La idea de la fama en la edad media castellana.* Mexico City, 1952.

———. *Juan de Mena, poeta del prerrenacimiento español.* Mexico City, 1984.

Medina Ávila, Blas. "Juan de Mena, propagandista del poderío real absoluto (reflejo literario de una idea político-jurídica)." *Anuario jurídico y económico escurialense* 41 (2008): 803–30.

Mendoza Negrillo, Juan de Dios. *Fortuna y Providencia en la literatura castellana del siglo XV.* Madrid, 1973.

Yorba-Gray, Galen B. "The Future as Eschatological Presence in Juan de Mena's *Laberinto de Fortuna.*" *Journal of Christianity and Foreign Languages* 5 (2004): 23–39.

Index

Abu al-Hasan, 1168
Acheron, 1326
Achilles, 958, 960, 1147
Adonis, 815
Aegisthus, 299, 812
Aeneas, 219–20, 247–48, 711–12, 1325–28
Aeolian Islands (Lipari), 413
Aeolus, 512
Afranius, 1109–12
Africa, 385–92, 949, 1163, stanza title 49
Africanus, Scipio, 26
Agamemnon, 810–12
Agenores (Agenor and Cadmus), 28. *See also* Cadmus
Albania, 314
Albendín, 2266
Alcaudete, 2293
Alcides. *See* Hercules
Alfonso I (of Asturias), 1154, 2194–2208
Alfonso II (of Asturias), 1154, 2217–20
Alfonso VI, 1154, 2226–28
Alfonso VII, 1154, 2230–31
Alfonso VIII, 1154, 2236

Alfonso X, 1154, 2278–88
Alfonso XI, 1154, 1336, 2297–99
Algeciras, 1166, 2310
Almodóvar, 2265
Alora, 1517, stanza title 190
Alps, 349, 365
Álvaro de Luna (Constable of Castile), 1858–61, 1873–96, 1906–8, 2041–55, 2097–98, 2106–20, 2129–36, stanza title 233
Amalthea. *See* Cumaean sibyl
Amaya, 2199
Amazons, 310
Ammonites, 284
Amorreans, 317
Amphiaraus, 714
Amyclas, 1814
Anchises (father of Aeneas), 219
Andalusia (Baetica), 381
Andujar, 2249
Anthenor, 709–12
Aphrodite. *See* Venus
Apollo (Phoebus, Delius), 16, 37, 42–43, 253, 411, 1349–50, 2137–38, stanza titles 116, 138
Apollodorus, 950
Appius Claudius Pulcher, 972

289

INDEX

Aquilonial (zone), 267
Aquinas. *See* Thomas Aquinas, Saint
Aquitania, 370
Arabia, 283
Aragon, 610, 1230, stanza title 77; Infantes of, 599–600
Arcadia, 364
Arcos, 2270
Arcusia, 277
Argia (daughter of Adrastus of Argos), 514, stanza title 65
Argos, 38
Arian (heresy), 320
Aristotle, 939–40
Arlanza, 1289
Armenia, 314, stanza title 64
Arras, 1590, stanza title 199
Artemis. *See* Diana
Artemisia II, 505–9, stanza title 64 stanza titleAsia Major, 273–96, stanza title 35
Asia Minor, 321–28, stanza title 41
Assyria, 278
Astorga, 2198
Asturias, 2203
Ataecina. *See* Vetona
Athena (Minerva, Pallas), 474, 688, 1125–26, stanza title 196
Athens, 1021
Atlantic Ocean, 403
Atlas, 61
Atropos. *See* Fates
Augustine, 932
Augustuses (emperors), 1775. *See also* Caesar(s); Octavian

Aulus, 1526–28
Auster. *See* South Wind
Austral (zone), 266, 297
Avernus, 1328

Babylon, 33
Babylonian sibyl, 966
Bacchus (Dionysus, Lyaeus), 1196
Badajoz, 2284
Baena, 2257
Baeza, 2250
Baldwin II (of Constantinople), 2286
Balearic Islands, 417
Baños (province), 2250
Basel, 1587, stanza title 199
Basques, 2205
Bellona (goddess), 99–103
Benamejí, 2312
Benzaide (Alcalá la Real), 2311
Bisante, 398
Bithynia, king of. *See* Nikomedes I
Boeotia, 355
Boreas. *See* North Wind
Braganza, 2196
Brecemonte, Pierre de (lord of Charny), 1590
Britons, 376
Brumal (zone), 267
Brutuses (Lucius Junius and Marcus Junius), 1729–33

Cadiz, 82
Cadmus, 292. *See also* Agenores
Caeneus, 606

INDEX

Caesar(s), 5, 600, 934, 1111–12, 1815–16, 2074. *See also* Augustuses; Octavian
Caesarea, 761
Calatrava la Nueva, convent of, stanza title 208
Calliope, 17. *See also* Muses
Calvo Laín, 2222–24s
Calydonians, 519
Camilluses (family), 1108
Canace, 822–23
Cañete, 2305
Capis, 685
Capitoline, 1718
Cappadocians, 317
Carcabuey, 2305
Caria, 326
Carrion, 1289
Cartagena, 379
Carthage, 379, 1106, 1322, 1547, stanza title 194
Cassius Severus, 947–48
Castalia (Parnassos), 1010
Castile, 598, 1015, 1122, 1175, 1763, 2175, 2284, stanza titles 72, 75
Castile, Constable of. *See* Álvaro de Luna
Castro, 2257
Castrotorafe, 2253
Catos (Marcus Porcius Cato Uticensis and Cato the Elder), 1733–36
Caucasus (African mountain), 306, 393
Celtiberia, 378
Centaurs, 825
Cerastes, 1938
Cerberus, 1977–78
Chaeonia, 355
Chaldea, 283
Charny, lord of. *See* Brecemonte, Pierre de
Charon, 1980–84
Chinchilla, 2281
Chindasuinth, 2170–72, 2180
Chiron. *See* Philerides
Christ, 1241–45
Cicero, Marcus Tullius. *See* Tully
Cid (Rodrigo Díaz de Vivar), 26
Cilicia, 326
Cinyras, 815
Clement, Saint, 328
Clotho. *See* Fates
Clytemnestra, 810–12
Codrus, 1721–22
Colchis, 311, 410
Commagene, 295
Constantinople, 2286
Cordoba, 985–91, 2258, stanza title 124
Corinthia, 364
Coronel, María, 627–28, stanza title 79
Corsica, 418
Crassus, Marcus Licinius, 1113–16
Cratylus, 937
Crete, 406
Cuenca, 282
Cuevas, 2303
Cumaean sibyl (Amalthea), 974–76
Curio, Gaius Scribonius, 1545–54, stanza titles 193, 194

INDEX

Cyclades (Aegean Islands), 407
Cyllenic (circle), 730
Cyrenaica (Pentapolis), 394

Dacians, 348
Daedalus, 1136
Danube, 346
Dares (*Aeneid* character), 739–40
Dávalos, Lorenzo (royal chamberlain), 1601–12, 1619–20, 1627–28, 1634, 1642–43, 1650–51, stanza titles 201, 203
Deciuses (family), 1722–24
Delius. *See* Apollo
Delos, 410, 1349
Delphic sibyl, 968
Demogorgon, 2006–8
Demosthenes, 945
Diana (Artemis), 566, 575, stanza title 63
Dimeta (sibyl), 965
Dionysus (god). *See* Bacchus
Dionysiuses of Syracuse (family), 1822
Domitius Afer, Gnaeus, 949
Don River. *See* Tanais
Duero, 1291

Ebosus (the island Ibiza), 418
Ecija, 2258
Egica, 2179–80
Egypt, 298–302, stanza title 38
Emathia, 1521
Empedocles, 938
Ennius, Quintus, 980
Enrique I, 1158, 2238–39

Enrique II, 1158, 2318
Enrique III, 1158, 2321–28
Enrique IV, 1158, 1609
Entellus, 739–40
Epirus, 356–60
Equinoctial (zone), 267
Erebus, 220
Erictho, 1035–36
Eriphyle, 713–20
Erwig, 2180
Erythrea (sibyl), 966
Espejo, 2261
Estepa, 2258
Ethiopia, 385
Etna, 1146. *See also* Lilybaeus
Euphrates, 281, 289
Europa, 329
Europe, 83, 308, stanza title 42
Eurytion, 698–700
Evander (king of Pallantium), 248, 1571, stanza title 196

Fabricius Luscinus Moncularis, Gaius, 1737–44, 1747
Fates (Atropos, Clotho, Lachesis), 562–64, 1582–84, 1807, stanza title 71. *See also* Fortune
Faunus, 683
Favila, 2193
Fernando I, 1155, 2225
Fernando III, 1155, 2241–72
Fernando IV, 1155, 2292–96
Fortune, 6, 9, 49, 65, 89, 199, 250, 1129, 1348, 1389, 1469, 1501, 1554, 1563, 1613, 1670, 1801, 1873, 1888, 2053, 2117, 2130, 2239, stanza

INDEX

titles 2, 7, 9, 10, 15, 31, 56. *See also* Fates
France, 369–76, 1108, stanza title 47
Franks, 371
Fruela I (of Asturias), 2209–12

Gabinianus, 945
Galatia, 322
Galicia, 383, 2203
Garamantes (people), 399
Gazules, Alcalá de los, 2267
Germany, 337–50, 2279, stanza title 43
Geryon, 2169
Gethulia, 398
Gibraltar, 1294, 1335, 1391, 1394–1403
Golden Age, 368
Gorgons (African islands), 419
Gortinia, 1524
Gothia, 338
Goths, 341, 2163, 2170–86
Granada, 1177–92, 1520, stanza title 148
Greece, 248, 353–60, 502, 617, 702, 811, stanza title 45
Gregory the Great, 932
Guzmán, Juan de (duke of Medina-Sidonia), 1394–95

Harpies, 520
heaven(s), 4, 67, 1573, 1621, 1841, 1999, 2159, 2240, 2300, 2325
Hebrews, 316. *See also* Jews
Hecate, 1995–2000
Hector, 684

Hellín, 2281
Helos, 355
Henry of Ramstein, 1583
Hercules (Alcides), 516–20, 1984, stanza title 65
Hesione, 621
Hesperia, 379
Hippolytus, 497–500
Homer, 977–78
Hornachuelos, 2262
Hungary, 352
Hyperborean mountains, 313
Hypermnestra, 501–2
Hyrcanians, 312

Ibiza. *See* Ebosus
Icaria, 414
Icarus, 415
Idumaeans, 285
Iliad, 978
Indus, 275
Ionos, 1825–27
Iria Flavia, 2196
Italy, 366, 368, stanza title 46
Ixion, 825–28

James, Saint, 1200
Janus, 1716
Jerez, 2269
Jerome, 931
Jews, 1244–45. *See also* Hebrews
Jordan (river), 293
Jovis (mountain bordering France), 374
Juan I, 2319–20
Juan II, 1, 578–80, 614, 777–84,

INDEX

Juan II *(continued)*
  905–12, 934, 1065–88, 1130–44, 1169–78, 1237–48, 1519, 1761–75, 1834–40, 2037, 2161–2336, 2367–68, 2373–76, stanza titles 81, 98, 114, 134, 142, 147, 212, 230
Juba I (king of Numidia), 400, 1548
Jubal, 953
Jugurtha (king of Numidia), 396
Julian (count of Ceuta), 722–28
Juno, 827
Jupiter, 2–4, 339–40, 475–76, stanza titles 214, 232

Labienus, 2074–76
Labyrinth, 499–500
Lachesis. *See* Fates
Laocoon, 687
Las Navas de Tolosa, 1161, 2234
Latinus, 683
Lebanon (mountain), 293
Lebrija, 2270
Ledesma, 2196
Leptis, 388
Lerida, 1112
Lethe (mythic river), 495
Leucaspis (companion of Aeneas), 1327
Libisa (sibyl), 973
Libya, 83, 1938
Licinia, 1041–44
Lilybaeus (Mount Etna), 422. *See also* Etna
Locubín, 2303
Lucretia, 503–4

Lugdunum, 370
Luque, 2262
Lusitania, 382
Lyaeus. *See* Bacchus
Lycia, 327
Lynceus, 299

Macareus, 822–23
Macías, 834–64, stanza titles 105, 106
Madrid, 1770–72
Mages, 1029
Mallorcans, 1671
Manichaeans, 320
Manlius, Marcus, 1717–18
Marchena, 2261
Marinid(s) (royal family), 2302
Marmarica (Libyan coast), 389
Mars, 1097, 1121, 1266, 1498, 1678, stanza titles 138, 214
Martos, 2253, 2295
Mary, Saint, 294, 756
Mary of Aragon (queen of Castile), 569–608, stanza titles 72, 75, 77, 78
Mary of Castile (queen of Aragon), 609–24
Massageteans, 311
Mauretania. *See* Tingitania
Mauricio (ruler of Thebes), 303
Mausolus, 505, stanza title 64
Mayorga, Juan de (count), 1499–1512, stanza title 188
Medea, 1038–40, 1079
Medeas, 1079

INDEX

Medellín, 2249
Medes, 279
Medianites, 285
Medina del Campo, 1233–54, stanza title 155
Mediterranean Sea, 289, 353, 366, 403
Medusa, 419
Meotia (border of Europe and Asia), 334
Mercury, 730, stanza title 85
Mérida, 2283
Merlo, Juan de, 1577–92, stanza title 198
Mesopotamia, 282
Messia, 351
Metelluses (family), 1105–6
Milan, 1194
Milo of Croton, 1675–76
Minerva. *See* Athena
Minos, 831
Minotaur, 500
Mnestheus, 699
Moabites, 281
Molossia, 355
Montánchez, 2283
Montiel, 2249
Montoro, 2262
moon, 537, 546, 1345
Moors, 467, 1163, 1185, 1409, 1429, 2038, 2200, 2251, 2310, 2374, stanza title 152
Moratilla, 2265
Mucius Scaevola, Gaius, 1117–20
Murcia, 2246

Muses, 17–24, 41–48, 1010, 2380
Myrrha, 813–15

Nabataeans, 296
Narbáez, Pedro de, 1561–76, stanza title 196
Narbáez, Rodrigo de, 1564, 1571, stanza title 196
Narbonne, 370
Naso, Publius Ovidius (Ovid) 328
Naxos, 409
Nephele, 887–28
Neptune, 85
Nestor, 681, 1860
Nicaea, 318
Niebla, 2284
Nikomedes I (of Bithynia), 323
Nile, 300
Ninyas, 33
North Star, 58
North Wind (Boreas), 84
Notus. *See* South Wind
Numidia, 395
Nuño Rasura, 2222–24

Octavian (Emperor Augustus), 1713–20, 1834. *See also* Augustuses; Caesar(s)
Odyssey, 978
Olympus, 362–64
Oppas, 721–22
Orcus, 1959
Orense, 2202
Orontes (companion of Aeneas), 1327

INDEX

Orpheus, 955–56
Ortygia, 410
Ovid. *See* Naso, Publius Ovidius
Oviedo, 2219

Pachinus (mountain on Sicily), 422
Padilla, Fernando de (master of Calatrava), 1657–70, stanza title 208
Paduans, 710
Palencia, 2239
Palestine, 290
Palestrae, 1250
Palinurus, 1323
Palladium, 686
Pallas (Athena). *See* Athena
Pallas (son of Evander), 1571–72, stanza title 196
Palma, 2258
Pamphylia, 327
Pandarus, 697–98, 701–4
Pannonia (region), 351
Paros, 116
Parthia, 274
Pasiphae, 830–31
Paul, Saint, 671–72
Pedro I, 2314
Pelayo, 2185–2186
Pelorus (mountain on Sicily), 422
Peñas, 2282
Penates, 247–48
Penelope, 510–12, 622, stanza title 64
Pentapolis, 397
Perea, Rodrigo de (lord of Cazorla), 1537–60, stanza title 193

Pérez de Guzmán, Enrique (count of Niebla), 1265–1488, stanza titles 159, 182, 184, 186, 187
Persia, 278, 965
Persian sibyl, 965
Petreius, 1109–12
Pimentel, Alonso (count of Benavente and Mayorga), 1511–12
Pimentel, Juan (count of Mayorga), 1499, 1505–12, stanza title 188
Phaethon, 2138–44
Phemonoe (sibyl), 969–72
Philerides (Chiron), 957–60
Philomena, 817–20
Phoebus. *See* Apollo
Phoenicia, 290
Phoenix, 291–92, 1939
Phrygia, 325
Phrygian sibyl (Albunea), 967
Pisuerga, 1289
Plato, 939
Pleiades, 61
Plotinus, 950
Pluto, 1970–71, 2001
Polemon, 937
Polydorus, 706
Polynestor, 705–8
Polyphemus, 142–44
Pompeus, Sextus, 1035–36
Pompey, 2076
Pontus, 327
Portugal, 2202
Priam, 684
Priego, 2305
Prime Mover, 1006
Proserpine, 1970–71

296

INDEX

Protagoras, 1021–24
Publicia, 1041–44, 1079
Pythagoras, 943–44

Quintilian, 952

Ramstein. *See* Henry of Ramstein
Real de Ariza, 1231, stanza title 154
Red Sea, 298
Rhaetia, 350
Rhodes, 406
Rivera, Diego de, 1513–36, stanza titles 190, 191
Riphaean Mountains, 334
Rodrigo (Visigothic king), 2184
Romans, 367, 629, 698, 936, 948, 976, 980, 1115, 1717, 1742
Rute, 2305

Salamanca, 2197
Saldaña, 2198
Salvatierra, 2254
Samos, 417
Sancho II, 2226
Sancho III, 2232
Sancho IV, 2289–90
Sarmatians, 311
Saturn, stanza title 232
Scaeva, 1521–28, stanza title 191
Scipio Africanus. *See* Africanus, Scipio
Scylla, 832
Scythia, 346
Segovia, 2195
Semiramis (Assyrian queen), 33
Sepúlveda, 2201

Severus, Cassius, 947
Seville, 2268
Sicily (Trinacria), 421, 1193
Simancas, 2198
Socrates, 941–42
Solstitial (zone), 268
South Wind (Notus, Auster), 85, 305
Spain, 5, 343, 377–84, 595, 616, 727, 1012, 1111, 1131, 1758, 1835, 2020, stanza title 48
Statius, 304
Stechades (French islands), 405
Styx, 2008
Synod, 319
Syracuse, 1822
Syria, 295, 314
Syrtes (of Amon), 357

Tanais (Don River), 345
Tarifa, 2290
Tarragona, 378
Teba, 2305
Tereus, 817–20
Thebes, 303
Thespiae, 46
Thessaly (Aeolia), 361–64, stanza title 46
Thomas Aquinas, Saint, 933
Tiber, 247
Tigris, 275
Tingitania (Mauretania), 383
Tiresias, 1034
Toledo, 2111, 2227
Torquatus, Titus Manlius, 1725–28
Trinacria. *See* Sicily

INDEX

Trion (Septentriones), 59, 333
Troglodytes, 390
Trojans, 1321
Troy, 37, 325, 620, 1148
Trujillo, 2261
Tully (Marcus Tullius Cicero), 946
Turks, 2287
Tydeus, 1859
Typhoeus (Enceladus), 423, 1193

Ubeda, 2249
Ulysses, 144, stanza title 64
Uticensis. *See* Catos

Valladolid, witch of, 1902–2048, 2097–2120
Vejer, 2270
Velamazán, 1231

Venus (Aphrodite), 670, 793, 910, 1039, stanza titles 100, 116
Vestal temple, 632
Vetona (sibyl), 974
Vilches, 2250
Villena, Enrique de, 1011–20
Virgil, 712, 979
Viseo, 2199
Vulcan, 1145
Vulcaneas (Sicilian islands), 418

Wamba, 2174–76
Witiza, 2181–82

Zamora, 2196
Zebediah, 1200
Zeno, 938
Zueros, 2266